AF782952

Dirk Lanzerath, Aurélie Halsband (eds.)
The Rediscovery of Bioethics

**Bioethics / Medical Ethics** | 8

**Dirk Lanzerath** is a professor of philosophy at Universität Bonn, where he leads the German Reference Centre for Ethics in the Life Sciences (DRZE). He also serves as a secretary general of the European Network of Research Ethics Committees (EUREC). As an expert in medical ethics, he is deputy chairman of the Central Ethics Committee at the German Medical Association (ZEKO). His research projects address new ethical issues in artificial intelligence, modern brain research, bioeconomics, and biodiversity.
**Aurélie Halsband** is head of the Scientific Department of the German Reference Centre for Ethics in the Life Sciences (DRZE) at Universität Bonn. Her research addresses ethical implications of emerging biotechnologies and artificial intelligence, as well as the normative foundations of intergenerational justice and sustainability.

Dirk Lanzerath, Aurélie Halsband (eds.)

# The Rediscovery of Bioethics

Lessons Learned and Future Directions

[transcript]

This publication is funded by the North Rhine-Westphalian Academy of Sciences, Humanities and the Arts as project of the Academy Program of the Federal Republic of Germany and the state of North Rhine-Westphalia.

**Bibliographic information published by the Deutsche Nationalbibliothek**
The Deutsche Nationalbibliothek lists this publication in the Deutsche Nationalbibliografie; detailed bibliographic data are available online at https://dnb.dnb.de


Hermannstraße 26 | D-33602 Bielefeld | live@transcript-verlag.de



Cover concept: Maria Arndt
Cover illustration: Rolf Hecken / Unsplash
Printing: Elanders Waiblingen GmbH, Waiblingen
https://doi.org/10.14361/9783839428214
Print-ISBN: 978-3-8376-7892-5 | PDF-ISBN: 978-3-8394-2821-4
ISSN of series: 2702-8267 | eISSN of series: 2702-8275

Printed on permanent acid-free text paper.

# Contents

## Impactful Bioethics



## Inclusive Bioethics

## Appendix

# Preface
## The Rediscovery of Bioethics – Lessons Learned and Future Directions

*Dirk Lanzerath, Aurélie Halsband*

Today, bioethics is discussed in terms that diverge strikingly from its early roots in the medical ethics of the 1960s. It need not be reinvented altogether, yet it must be rethought, placed within new horizons, and, in this sense, *rediscovered*. The rediscovery we envisage is not a backward glance steeped in nostalgia, but a renewal – both methodological and substantive – that refines and reorients the field for the present.

Anniversaries offer a distinctive occasion to reflect upon the history of a discipline and to contemplate its future. More than a quarter of a century ago, the founding of the German Reference Centre for Ethics in the Life Sciences (DRZE) in 1999 represented a significant milestone in the development of bioethical research in Germany. To celebrate its twenty-fifth anniversary, the DRZE convened an international scientific symposium in 2024. The present volume gathers the insights and reflections emerging from that event, bringing together philosophical as well as interdisciplinary perspectives on the challenges and opportunities that shape bioethics today.

Bioethics belongs in a present in which clinical practice, technological innovation, ecological crises, and social tensions are inseparably interwoven. The classical questions of autonomy, well-being, non-maleficence, and justice remain fundamental, yet the contexts in which they must be answered have shifted profoundly. Research today is less a self-contained domain than a social practice that shapes expectations, distributes risks, negotiates responsibilities, and generates – or at times undermines – trust. The notion of a rediscovery therefore entails understanding bioethics anew as an ethics of life understanding: a reflective practice that makes explicit, and evaluates, the complex relations among human beings, other living beings, environments, institutions, and infrastructures of knowledge.

One of the first lessons to be drawn from the past decades is that *implementation and institutionalisation* are indispensable for sound bioethical judgement. For discourse to be sustainable, there must be spaces in which information is consolidated, methods clarified, controversies moderated, and learning processes enabled. Ethics committees, reference centres, curated repositories of knowledge, programmes of teaching and training, and forums for public debate among diverse stakeholders together constitute the infrastructure upon which deliberative and responsible decision-making can rest. Yet institutionalisation alone does not suffice to realise the reflective support that ethics can provide, unless institutions themselves remain capable of learning. When procedures solidify into mere checklists, when ethical guidance is fragmented and reduced to bureaucratic routines, ethics risks degenerating into an administrative impediment. To rediscover bioethics therefore also means turning inward: calling upon institutions to remain flexible, to acknowledge uncertainty, to cultivate a tolerance for error, and to engage in the translational work that mediates between technical languages, legal domains, and *Lebenswelten*. At the same time, it requires bioethics to remain attentive to the full scope of normative questions raised by the remarkable advances of the life sciences and the proliferating possibilities of human intervention into life. A significant lesson has thus been the emergence of a broader conception of bioethics – one that includes, but is by no means confined to, medical ethics. Bioethical reflection, accordingly, is no longer restricted to individual human health, but directed towards the wider notion of human flourishing amidst profound scientific, technological, ecological, and political transformations.

Against this backdrop, bioethics has learned to distinguish between measurable outputs and broader societal *impact*. The pathways through which knowledge and technology enter society are increasingly circular: health apps, AI-based systems, and biotechnological products are often introduced in a form of public trial, where user feedback becomes an integral part of their further development. In this way, society – intentionally or not – functions as a co-laboratory. This evolving dynamic shifts the normative focus. Complementing the often-criticised individualism of traditional bioethics, community-oriented considerations – addressing the common good, equitable distribution, global access, and long-term ecological consequences – have gained prominence. Those reflecting on the future of bioethics must therefore attend not only to protection against unevenly distributed burdens but also to conditions for fair participation, such as access to research benefits. What is at stake is an ethics of impact – one that does more than retrospectively evaluate benefits, risks, and responsibilities. It prospectively shapes them as well, moderating the remarkable, ongoing advances in the life sciences and associated technologies.

*Inclusion*, finally, embodies the recognition that bioethics without diverse perspectives remains blind. Participation is not an optional addition but a prerequisite for sound and legitimate judgement. Stakeholders – including patients, caregivers, communities, minorities, and holders of indigenous knowledge – bring insights and values that are not only morally significant but also epistemically enriching. Yet inclusion is not automatic: it demands resources, time, and pedagogical skill to translate between perspectives, to channel conflicts productively, to reflect on power dynamics, and simultaneously to safeguard academic freedom. An inclusive bioethics preserves the autonomy of research while opening it to those voices most directly affected by its outcomes.

These three guiding concepts – *Implementation, Impact, and Inclusion* – define key objectives that shape the future of bioethics. They also point to specific challenges for theory, practice, and society at large. From a theoretical perspective, rediscovering bioethics requires methodological pluralism: principle-based ethics, virtue ethics, and consequentialist approaches must be brought into dialogue, enriched, and extended by social-scientific analysis. Normative orientation must be pursued under conditions of complexity and uncertainty, where convictions are fragile and judgments inherently fallible. Accordingly, bioethical expertise can only fully develop through interdisciplinary cooperation, in a shared, multi-disciplinary effort to understand and evaluate the opportunities that lie ahead. The task is to sharpen normative categories in light of emerging phenomena: autonomy in the era of data-driven systems, justice in the face of global inequalities, responsibility within the horizon of planetary health ... Such a bioethics takes seriously the insight that norms are neither mere conventions nor directly perceivable. Rather, they arise in engagement with reality, in the contest of reasons, and through processes of public justification.

In practical terms, rediscovering bioethics requires its early and continuous integration into research, technology development, and care. In laboratories, clinics, engineering contexts and real-world environments, ethics is not merely applied retrospectively; it is co-designed from the outset. This encompasses study design, data use, risk communication, technology assessment and evaluation of downstream effects, as well as the negotiation of legitimate aims and limits. In teaching, this translates into ethics as a competence-building endeavour; ethical skills must become habitual for students, researchers, and practitioners alike. Students in medicine and nursing, but also in the sciences, agriculture, social sciences, and even the humanities require formats that connect case-based and systematic perspectives, that confront rather than smooth over dilemmas, and that cultivate collective judgment – through simulations, boundary cases, and engagement with those directly affected. Good practice flourishes in spaces of reflection where uncertainties can be openly articulated, and workable heuristics rigorously tested.

Socially and culturally, bioethics now operates within fragmented public spheres whose dynamics have diverged from classical, linear models of communication. Algorithmic attention economies, shaped by AI-driven social media, polarised debates, and geopolitical tensions, have transformed the resonance spaces in which ethical questions are negotiated. Trust in scientific expertise, including ethical guidance, is fragile and must be reinforced through transparency, openness about the limits of knowledge, and fair participation. At the same time, research requires protection against political instrumentalization and economic monopolisation. Culturally attuned bioethics recognises that ethical self-understanding is an integral part of democratic practice – and that it can only succeed when disagreement remains possible and the lived realities of those affected are heard.

From all this follow the *Lessons Learned* and *Future Directions*. We have seen that attentive implementation, responsible impact, and consistent inclusion are mutually dependent. The path ahead calls for a bioethics that keeps institutions and methodologies adaptable, anticipates consequences systematically, and treats participation as a design principle. It operates across scales – from the clinic to regional health systems to global questions of justice – integrating clinical, ecological, and social perspectives into coherent judgments. It employs clear, yet not reductionist evaluation frameworks that render qualitative arguments visible without compressing them into mere metrics. Equally, it invests in education: cultivating the ability to exchange reasons, to endure disagreement, to recognise the limits of its proper expertise, and to assume responsibility for decisions made collectively.

*The Rediscovery of Bioethics – Lessons Learned and Future Directions* invites us to view bioethics as a collective learning endeavour. To rediscover bioethics is to sharpen our understanding of what is at stake: the integrity of research, the protection of stakeholders, the credibility of institutions, the fairness of distribution, and the care for our ecological coexistence. When institutions foster trust, when impact is shaped responsibly, and when inclusion is practiced consistently, bioethics can fully unfold, providing a clarifying, connecting *practical reason* for life amidst complex conditions.

Dirk Lanzerath and Aurélie Halsband

# Implementing Bioethics

# The Rediscovery of Bioethics

## From an Ethics of Life Science to an Ethics of Life

*Dirk Lanzerath*

The roots of bioethics date back to the late 1960s and early 1970s – a period of significant technological, social and moral transformation. Rapid developments in biomedicine, such as in organ transplantation, reproductive medicine and life-prolonging interventions, pushed conventional ethical and legal concepts, methodologies and approaches to their limits. Most importantly, the deeply invasive and unprecedented nature of biomedicine made it evident that classical medical ethics – which has its origins in classical antiquity – needed to be expanded methodologically. Gaining new impetus and relevance required applied ethics to establish closer links with theoretical debates in ethics and the philosophy of science (Edel, 2020). A milestone of the respective methodological development within modern bioethics are Tom Beauchamp and James Childress' *Principles of Biomedical Ethics*, a refinement of preliminary works growing out of the "Belmont Report" (1978) (Sims, 2010). Since 1979, eight editions of the *Principles* have been published (Beauchamp & Childress, 2019). The book is internationally highly respected and well received, and has been translated into many languages, now also into German (Beauchamp & Childress, 2024).

During the late 1960s and early 1970s, academic philosophy was strongly influenced by the 'linguistic turn', which led to a focus on analytic methods in philosophy based on language, semantics, and meaning. Although this contributed to a refinement of ethical theory formation and the development of metaethics, it was hardly applicable to real-world situations. Additionally, the tension between deontological, utilitarian and virtue-based approaches was much more pronounced in ethical theory at that time than in more recent discourses of practical philosophy, which are open to establishing connections between moral theories (Höffe, 2010). In response to the practical challenges posed by medicine and technology, environmental crises, the rise of new social movements, and the emancipation of the individual subject, significantly more practice-oriented approaches in ethics emerged, along with diverse subfields, such as e. g. technology ethics within applied ethics. This in turn paved the way for a philosophical and critical reflection on the role of the life sciences and other sciences within society (May & Delston, 1994).

In the United States, bioethics was initially developed in response to moral dilemmas arising from everyday medical practice, such as the scope of patient rights, just allocations of scarce goods within the healthcare system, and end-of-life decisions. In view of these challenges, institutions such as *The Hastings Center* (founded in 1969) and the *Kennedy Institute of Ethics* (founded in 1971) in the US, as well as the *Nuffield Council on Bioethics* (founded in 1991) in the UK, helped establish the systematic reflection on medical ethics issues in relation to normative frameworks such as human rights, autonomy, and justice. The Kennedy Institute of Ethics, including its *National Reference Center for Bioethics Literature* (NRCBL), served as a model for the establishment of the German Reference Centre for Ethics in the Life Sciences (Deutsches Referenzzentrum für Ethik in den Biowissenschaften, DRZE) in 1999.

During that same period, US-American biochemist Van Rensselaer Potter developed a broader vision of bioethics inspired by ecology. In his book *Bioethics: Bridge to the Future* (1971), he defined bioethics as a new discipline that should address key aspects of human flourishing. For Potter, bioethics forms a bridge between the natural sciences and the humanities, linking biological knowledge and ethical responsibility. He believed that in the face of environmental destruction, nuclear threats, and social inequality, humanity's survival could only be ensured by combining scientific knowledge with ethical reflection. His vision aimed to foster a *global sense of responsibility* that integrated both environmental and health issues (Potter, 1999).

Although this broader concept of bioethics kept playing a role (Clements, 1985), medical ethics and environmental ethics tended to develop separately, with the term 'bioethics' often referring only to clinically oriented bioethics (Emmerich, 2015). It is only within the last three decades that these two traditions have begun to converge more closely. Bioethics has since evolved into an interdisciplinary field that considers ecological, technological, social, and political issues equally. Since at least the 1990s, bioethics has been used as an umbrella term for a wide range of ethical discourses, including medical, environmental, and research ethics, as well as animal ethics and global justice issues in connection with the life sciences.

Today, bioethics faces even more profound challenges. There is a growing awareness of the close intertwining of human and non-human nature. Climate change, biodiversity loss, and the increased occurrence of zoonotic infections – diseases transmitted from animals to humans – make these interconnections impossible to ignore. Human behaviour in social, ecological, and economic spheres are mutually dependent, making it essential to consider the perspectives of *social ethics* and *bioethics* together (Frewer, 2011). At the same time, the distinction between basic research and its application is becoming increasingly blurry in many scientific fields, particularly in translational medicine. This results in a closer *interconnection* between *bioethics and research ethics*. The relationship between society and research processes has also intensified: research is now embedded in social contexts from an earlier stage, and social practices feed back into research in turn (Lanzerath, 2023).

Furthermore, fundamental changes in political systems and profound transformations in social communication are creating additional challenges. New media, especially social networks, generate dynamics that differ significantly from traditional, linear communication models. This poses a considerable interdisciplinary challenge, as not all disciplines have an equal presence on social media regarding a given topic. Consequently, the necessary multi-perspective view of current problems is not reflected, as demonstrated by the response to the coronavirus pandemic. This inevitably changes the dynamics and locations of forums for bioethical discourse.

It is against this backdrop that bioethics has undergone significant and multiple changes over the past few decades. The medical and clinical ethics of the 1970s and 1990s have developed into a more inclusive bioethics that considers the coexistence of different life forms. Consequently, the current bioethical discourse addresses not only individual health and health systems at the societal level, but also *planetary* health. The relatively new concept of *planetary health* combines medical and ecological bioethics. According to this view, environmental problems are not merely "natural" crises but affect human flourishing as a whole. The deterioration of nature is often accompanied by social weakening in affected communities (Horton et al., 2014).

Although medical and environmental ethics diverged for a long time, the *rediscovery of bioethics* in the 21st century – under the banner of planetary health, for example – explicitly builds on Potter's idea of building bridges between knowledge and values, science and everyday life, and health and the environment. This broad bioethical approach has produced remarkable ethical symbioses and interdisciplinary synergies. This finding provides justification for the rediscovery, further development and shaping of bioethics in the context of changing global social and academic conditions.

## New Social Orders as a Challenge

Modern bioethical challenges arise not only from scientific and technological developments, such as the creation of artificial embryos from induced pluripotent stem cells (iPS cells) or the use of artificial intelligence in diagnostics and environmental research, but also from current *political and social upheavals*. For example, the organisation of research and societal modes of participation in science have fundamentally changed. Policies concerning ethical conduct are more participatory and thus require the appropriate *involvement of various stakeholders*.

Furthermore, the scientific community is calling for broader opportunities to access and collaboratively utilise health data and other forms of information that support research practices promoting the common good. This novel development, as well as the early introduction of emerging technologies into society, is turning society itself into a laboratory, giving biomedical research a collective character (Van de Poel, 2017). Side effects of drugs are being tested on a larger number of individuals, and technical devices, medical products, and health apps – many of which are AI-based – are being delivered in a semifinished state and gradually improved through a series of updates. While many of these trends are well-founded, from a research ethics perspective it must be recognised that laboratories and research institutions are protected spaces with clear rules, including ethical ones. Outside these spaces, however, these rules are watered down, and consumers become research participants with limited protection. If society itself is increasingly becoming a laboratory, a new ethical approach is needed for these procedures and scenarios.

One example of the need to rethink and redefine the ethical framework is a fair approach to the sharing of research findings. Closer interaction between research and society does not necessarily mean that all members of society have equal access to the benefits of research. The exchange of health data between healthcare providers and researchers, for example, is considered a new paradigm in the life sciences and in the healthcare systems that benefit from such collaboration [...]. Bioethics is therefore shifting from an individualised, autonomy-focused perspective to a collective perspective, oriented towards the common good (Ravitsky, 2025). Donations of personal health data for research purposes can undoubtedly have a collective benefit, for example. However, the motives of researchers' appeals to the common good must be critically questioned in practice. When it comes to the use of research results – e.g. drugs or vaccines – it is often no longer the idea of the common good that guides business, but rather market forces. This creates a significant injustice, particularly between the Global North and Global South. This is particularly true when research is conducted in the Global South, but products resulting from this research are exclusively distributed in the Global North. Against this backdrop, the concept of *access and benefit sharing*, as set out in the Nagoya Protocol on the utilisation of genetic resources from natural habitats, could guide modern bioethics towards a more equitable distribution of benefits (Lanzerath, 2025).

However, the relationship between research and society is not the only social order changing as a result of scientific processes. In parallel, forms of public communication are also changing, for example through the dominance of social media and algorithmically controlled information dissemination. These are increasingly eclipsing the influence of traditional media forms. Consequently, bioethical discourses are no longer comparable to those when bioethics first emerged.

Finally, *shifts in political power* can be observed worldwide, affecting not only social interactions in general, but also science and education. There has been a shift in moral boundaries, with traditional taboos softening and increasingly *aggressive forms of conflict* emerging when dealing with controversial bioethical issues. This has even led to a massive threat to academic freedom by autocratically acting politicians. Therefore, the challenges lie not only in new technologies, but also in new forms of social polarisation. Keywords such as 'fake news', 'wokeness', and 'cancel culture' point to a changed cultural resonance space (Rosa, 2018) for ethical debates. Such negative national influences on the work of researchers can also impact and restrict international research activities in the long term due to international cooperation in research. This raises the fundamental question: *how can ethical discourse succeed in times of crisis and new social orders under such volatile conditions?*

The coronavirus pandemic, as a social and scientific crisis, has exposed significant social deficits in various domains of health policy. Several political responses to the threat posed by the virus have exacerbated these deficits and contributed to the disruption of societies. Furthermore, the lack of interdisciplinary cooperation in the early stages of the crisis has contributed to the fact that scientific expertise – especially to manage a crisis – has been misperceived in society (Palamenghi et al., 2020; Lanzerath, 2024). The relationship between scientific expertise, political decision-making and public communication was considerably under pressure. Society's attitudes towards science ranged from critical to openly hostile, but conversely, exaggerated expectations of science were also widespread. This culminated in the slogan 'Follow the science'. However, this attitude aligns more closely with scientism, i.e. the belief that science has all the answers and can replace all existing knowledge about the world. However, science is not synonymous with truth, and the claim to truth in science only ever applies to a very narrow field illuminated by the relevant discipline. While science has undoubtedly provided invaluable insights during the pandemic, not all scientists have adhered to reflect its own limitations, with ethics sometimes being perceived as a nuisance. For example, AJOB published a letter (Stoeklé & Hervé, 2020) about research during the pandemic: "However, now really isn't the time for ethical reflections. [...] Ethics is only really useful if you have the time, and right now, time is exactly what we do not have." Ethics committees should simply approve research projects more quickly. However, ethical reflection is particularly necessary in times of crisis. The European Network of Research Ethics Committees (EUREC) therefore felt compelled to point out in a position paper that, although work processes and administrative prerequisites can be expedited in a crisis, scientific standards and ethical norms must still be upheld, even under considerable time pressure. It is therefore appropriate to approach research ethics in an interdisciplinary manner, rather than simply following it. Against this social backdrop, *horizon scanning* and *anticipatory perspectives* are crucial. Integrating ethical reflection directly into the research process (RE4GREEN; re4green.eu) is now a central pillar of *social trust* in science, and thus a key prerequisite for responsible research and sustainable innovation, especially when preparing for future crises (PREPARED; prepared-project.eu).

## Research as a Social Practice: The Complex Interactions Between Research and Society

In many countries and cultures, people recognise the profound impact that science and research have on societies and individuals. This is particularly apparent in areas such as medicine, energy production, and agriculture. Unfortunately, they can also be seen in reports on modern military operations, in which AI is playing an increasingly decisive role. Just a few decades ago, some researchers argued that the only moral dimension of science was gaining knowledge and verifying facts. Furthermore, science was seen as an activity without any "moral dimensions", while the ethical implications of research were considered to be the responsibility of politics and society. Even in the early 20th century, this attitude was widespread, particularly among physicists, who distanced themselves from ethical responsibility by invoking methodological objectivity to justify their involvement in developing rockets and bombs (von Braun, 1977) However, even then, this view was highly questionable and by no means unanimous, as the debates surrounding Niels Bohr, Werner Heisenberg, and Carl Friedrich von Weizsäcker clearly demonstrate (Gottstein, 2001).

From an ethical perspective, research and society have become so deeply interconnected that they can no longer be viewed as separate. *Science is a social practice* embedded within wider society. Therefore, research ethics and a modern ethos of science are not limited to compliance with internal rules and methodological standards. Rather, they also encompass an *external responsibility* where the social roles of scientists and citizens overlap.

This complex responsibility is succinctly summarised in the European Code of Conduct for Research Ethics, which calls on researchers to respect "colleagues, research participants, research objects, society, ecosystems, cultural heritage, and the environment" (ALLEA, 2023, p. 5). Nevertheless, this poses a major challenge for every individual researcher and is often overwhelming. In short, it demands not only adhering to the rules of good scientific practice – such as avoiding plagiarism and handling data carefully – but also requires critical reflection on scientific methods and objectives within the professional community and with regard to their social and ecological implications. This is where the requirements of research ethics and bioethics converge.

This modern scientific attitude of responsibility in no way contradicts Max Weber's thesis that science is value-free (Weber, 1917). Weber was well aware that values play a role in selecting research questions, even though he sought to separate methodologically the acquisition of knowledge and its evaluation. Integrating social responsibility into the research process is therefore a key factor in promoting social trust in science because the latter is largely publicly funded and therefore requires justification.

In bioethics, in particular, the question of how environmental ethics and sustainability can be successfully integrated into the research process is becoming more urgent and prominent. Can the means and goals of research be designed in such a way that sustainable thinking and responsible action become effective in the research process itself, and not only in its application?

This question concerns not only environmental and agricultural sciences, but also health and (the) life sciences. After all, health systems also face challenges posed by climate protection and planetary health, such as zoonoses, heat-related deaths, and unsustainable hospital architecture. Various research projects, such as RE4GREEN, are therefore working to integrate social and ecological responsibility into the scientific process. The European Commission, for example, has developed guidelines for researchers on assessing and managing environmental risks so that the research it funds meets increased environmental, ethical, and sustainability criteria (EU Commission, 2025).

In so-called 'green bioethics', the broad field of *bioeconomy* has emerged. This field is particularly dependent on a successful interaction between science, society, and the economy. The concept of bioeconomy profoundly impacts biological, social, and ecological systems, thereby raising ethical challenges that are addressed through bioethical reflection. In view of these challenges, central questions about responsibility towards nature arise: do processes of bioeconomy, such as industrial agriculture, biotechnological optimisation, or the use of synthetic organisms, exceed environmental limits, or may they cause even a new threat to biodiversity?

Questions of global justice are also coming to the fore, particularly in economic considerations. Who benefits from biotechnological innovations? How are genetic resources accessed, and are the benefits of resulting research distributed fairly? Furthermore, how can we prevent economically powerful actors in the Global North from taking advantage of local populations or indigenous communities in the Global South?

Meanwhile, technology and risk assessment are increasingly representing key areas of ethical analysis. New processes, such as genome editing using CRISPR/Cas9 and synthetic biology, raise fundamental questions about their potentially irreversible and long-term effects on the environment and society. Clarification is needed on who bears responsibility for unintended effects that may affect future generations, and on how scientific uncertainty should be dealt with. Additionally, questions arise concerning democratic legitimacy and social participation. To what extent are affected groups involved in the development and evaluation of bioeconomic innovations? To what extent are transparency, public oversight, and ethical governance necessary in this context?

Current developments in the application of CRISPR technologies in agriculture exemplify these areas of tension: efficiency gains are linked to issues of patenting and the concentration of economic power. Another example is the practice of so-called 'bioprospecting', where companies search for genetically exploitable resources in species-rich regions of the Global South, often without the local population receiving a fair share of the economic returns. The trend towards a *circular bioeconomy* – such as using waste materials from agriculture or the food industry to produce bioplastics or biofuels – also raises questions about the relationship between sustainability, efficiency, and social responsibility (Lanzerath, 2022).

Given this context, it is clear that a purely technical and economic view of the bioeconomy is insufficient. In the absence of an ethical framework innovation risks becoming trapped in recurring patterns of exploiting nature and exacerbating social inequality, albeit in a new technological guise. Bioethics must therefore bring normative principles such as *justice, responsibility, transparency, and intergenerational equity* into the debate. Bioeconomic strategies will only fulfil their promise of a *sustainable* and *just transformation* if they take these perspectives seriously.

## New Challenges Drive a Growing Demand for Advice

Discourses on research ethics and bioethics help to build trust in research processes within society.[1] Additionally, an increasing number of ethical advisory bodies are becoming involved in the research process. For example, to protect participants in clinical research, medical research has been subject to codes, guidelines and laws that explicitly define the requirements for protecting human subjects. *Independent research ethics committees* have also been established, and the conduct of medical research depends on their positive assessment. Particular attention has been paid to research involving physical intervention that poses a risk to participants.

However, it has long been recognised – and is now clearer than ever – that verbal communication can also be *dangerous or traumatic*, for example in qualitative interviews in the social sciences. Similarly, mishandling or disclosing

1 This and the following section have been developed as part of the iRECS project (improving Research Ethics Expertise and Competences to Ensure Reliability and Trust in Science) which received funding under the EU's Horizon Europe research and innovation programme (Grant Agreement number: 101058587). Views and opinions expressed are those of the author only and do not necessarily reflect those of the European Union (EU) or the European Research Executive Agency (REA). Neither the European Union nor the granting authority can be held responsible for them.

*personal data* can cause considerable harm to individuals, especially in an increasingly data-driven world where the risk of data misuse is high. For this reason, *research ethics committees* are being established not only in medicine, but also in psychology, the social sciences, economics, and environmental and technical sciences.

There is also a growing awareness that the profound impact of research on society significantly expands the scope of responsibility for researchers. Society therefore has higher expectations that individual researchers and research institutions will significantly increase their ethical reflection on the prospective social impact of their research activities, rather than waiting until these activities are implemented and applied in society (McCrea et al., 2024).

This development also influences modern *bioethics*. In view of the growing social, technological, and ecological challenges, it must increasingly address *research ethics issues in other disciplines* – such as research with and on AI, synthetic biology, climate research, the geoengineering debate, and agricultural and food research. Modern *bioethics is thus developing into an interdisciplinary field* that not only examines norms, but must also create spaces for dialogue on responsibility, risk assessment, and social negotiation processes. This also applies to questions of *justice, global access to know-how, the interests of vulnerable groups, and the protection of common goods* such as a stable climate, sufficient water supply, biodiversity conservation, and cultural heritage.

Many *research funding bodies* (e.g. the EU, the DFG and the NIH) as well as renowned scientific journals are now also taking these developments into account. They often require ethical advice or opinions before projects can be funded or results published, even outside the field of medicine. The integration of ethics and ethical advice is thus becoming an increasingly important criterion for quality and integrity across disciplines.

This creates new challenges for research ethics and bioethics. Careful consideration must be given to when and how ethics committees are involved, to ensure they do not become a mere administrative obstacle. Ethics must not be reduced to checklists and formalities; rather, it should primarily be a *communicative, reflective, and discursive process.* Therefore, when incorporating bioethics and research ethics into research institutions like universities, the emphasis should extend beyond merely expanding traditional ethics committees to include the development of intelligent *research ethics governance that promotes targeted advice, awareness-raising, and structural integration* into various disciplines. This includes continuing education and training opportunities, building platforms for interdisciplinary exchange, and creating research institutions that deal with applied ethics, such as bioethics and research ethics. This is because these are new academic questions that must be carefully examined from a normative perspective. Research ethics is not primarily a review process but rather to be seen as a collective learning process about the ethical boundaries and social prerequisites of good scientific practice.

## Science and Society: From Scandal to Discourse, From Expert Groups to Stakeholder Participation

Against this backdrop, research ethics and bioethics have undergone a remarkable transformation in recent decades. A *proactive*, dialogue-oriented culture of discourse has developed, replacing a more reactive, scandal-driven approach to ethics that formulated moral guidelines in response to undesirable developments. Nowadays, normative reflection often begins before the application of new technologies, not just after something has gone wrong. Social groups, affected parties and stakeholders are increasingly being involved in the ethical evaluation process (Slunge et al., 2017).

A key challenge lies in the fact that many citizens have little insight into the workings of science, let alone the mechanisms of research ethics or ethics committees. However, if genuine participation is to be made possible, a new *relationship between science and society* based on mutual understanding and dialogue is needed.

Researchers and scientific institutions should therefore communicate more transparently about their goals, methods, and questions, and seek targeted engagement with social groups, including patients, environmental initiatives and business and cultural representatives. This principle, known as *stakeholder involvement*, is no longer optional in many research projects; many research funding bodies, led by the European Commission, now require the structured participation of relevant groups in their programmes (Andersen et al., 2021).

Although this development is beneficial and science can learn from participation, it also creates new areas of tension. Shaping the relationship between science and society cannot be left to scientists alone. Politicians are also responsible for participation, transparency, and societal dialogue. If they shirk this responsibility and delegate stakeholder management entirely to researchers, the latter may become overwhelmed, particularly in a system already burdened by application and reporting requirements. Participation must not become an additional burden that complicates the research process unnecessarily; rather, it should improve the connection between science and society in practice-oriented research.

On the other hand, there is the question of preserving the freedom of science. While this was primarily threatened by state control in the 19th and 20th century, today it can also be endangered by the unilateral or excessive influence of certain interest groups. If research is geared primarily towards the expectations or wishes of stakeholders, critical, disquieting, or long-term research questions may be suppressed. Participation must therefore be carefully structured and evenly balanced, paying special attention to groups that are particularly affected or vulnerable, while also being mindful of science's autonomy and openness. At the same time, however, freedom of science is now under threat from government interference, particularly from autocratic regimes (Fernandez & Hutchens, 2025).

## Ethics as a Practice of Understanding Life: A Starting Point for Rediscovering Bioethics

The relationship that modern humans have with their own nature, as well as with the natural world, has led to many productive achievements in the Anthropocene. However, this has also had negative consequences for human health and the environment (Bartmann & Halsband, 2023). Thus, engaging with human and non-human nature through thoughts and actions reveals a resistance. This resistance must be examined from a new normative perspective as humans encounter nature both as a given framework imbued with motivational elements and as a second nature (Lanzerath, 2021; Christ & Honneth, 2022).) they feel compelled to understand and shape.

The resistance each human being encounters through their basic perceptions from early childhood offers first indications that something exists outside of human thought – something that happens to them and that they can confront, including themselves as persons. Whether this resistance is perceived as either positive and malleable or negative and to be overcome is induced either immediately through reflex – a sensitive or affective process – or through a later act of reflection. Since modern times, humans have gained more and more opportunities to overcome resistance when confronting nature because they are motivated to emancipate themselves from it or to outwit it as an instantiation of their own nature. This is one of the triggers of the current socio-ecological crisis (Pope Francis, 2015, pp. 10–13, 59–61). Breaking down resistance leads to ever deeper intervention in nature, which in turn gives rise to new and different forms of resistance. How we deal with our own nature and the surrounding natural world is thus becoming a crucial question of modernity.

The "life endowing" applications evoked by Francis Bacon and made possible by the natural and biological sciences and engineering due to their ability to overcome resistance require special moral consideration, as they have life-prolonging potential as well as the capacity for manipulation and self-destruction. This has led authors such as Hans Jonas and Gernot Böhme to proclaim the "end of the Baconian age" (Jonas, 1979, pp. 251–255; Böhme, 1993). Hans Jonas rightly states that 'Homo faber' is now turning 'his skill upon himself' (Jonas, 1979, p. 47). This is because these skills affect his own nature, making him capable of destroying himself and becoming the subject of biotechnological manipulation. It is the creative capacity of the second nature that makes this threat to the first nature possible in the first place. And yet, this capacity is a prerequisite for the second nature and thus has the power to shape but also to endanger it. Humans are no longer fully aware of their metabolic (Schäfer, 1993) and ethical-aesthetic embeddedness in nature.

This observation of unlimited feasibility as fiction, in both the passive and active senses, coincides with the uncertainty that compels us to constantly rethink our actions, which are increasingly freed from external and natural boundaries. As resistance through outdated norms and cultures has broken down, this has had positive aspects, such as liberation and enlightenment. However, it has also led to cracks in the normative self-image that need to be understood and mended. This resistance and fragility reveal the close connection between external and internal uncertainty, with which the subject of modernity is confronted. A normative self-image can only be developed if humans establish a relationship with the objectification of their own and other natures and find normative landmarks from which to shape their lives and flourish. The central question, then, is why we assess things and events in the world in a particular way, attaching meaning to them and wanting to change them through our actions.

In metaethical discourses on this subject, it is rarely denied that – by reflecting – we seek our own reasons for our actions. However, it is controversial whether these reasons are found unconditionally, whether they simply correspond to an unbound use of reason as in logic and mathematics, or whether generating moral propositions is more similar to producing our propositions about non-moral events and thus requires a connection to 'reality'. Moral realists argue that morality is not merely structured by the subject as arbitrary, conventional, or consensual – and thus possibly only relative – but is instead endowed with elements that correspond to the objects of our perceptual, non-moral knowledge (for more on moral realism see, for example, Sayre-McCord, 1988; Brink, 1989; Shafer-Landau, 2003). In this case, morality would not be a purely subjective or social construct but would have essential elements of / essentially be an enterprise of reconstruction and discovery. Under these conditions, moral propositions would also refer to facts or certain properties of facts, enabling us to assume an "aesthesis" of morality. The 'nature of the good' would then be an aspect of the real world. We would learn to perceive it based on a natural ability, just as we learn to see or smell. However, such abilities can only develop appropriately through the interaction of natural disposition and social education, in order to avoid pathological formations. It seems to be easier to stumble over a tree root than a norm; therefore, norms are often considered less real. However, it is precisely when our morality reaches the limit of its applicability and insight, or when we are accused of violating a norm, that we become acutely aware of the reality of norms, whatever they may be. The reality of norms is just as much a part of the obstacles we may stumble over as elements of biological nature. Understanding this stumbling is the task of ethical reflection, while avoiding falling as a result of stumbling is the goal of moral practice in life. In order to address the logocentric hubris of the Enlightenment and modernity, we must ground our relationships with ourselves and with nature in normative and interdisciplinary ways. In bioethics, this will require taking into account the metabolic and ethical-aesthetic embedding of humans and other living beings in nature.

## References

ALLEA (2023). *The European Code of Conduct for Research Integrity. Revised Edition 2023*. ALLEA | All European Academies. http://www.doi.org/10.26356/ECOC

Andersen, P. D., Hansen, M., & Selin, C. (2021). Stakeholder inclusion in scenario planning—A review of European projects. *Technological Forecasting and Social Change, 169*, 120802. https://doi.org/10.1016/j.techfore.2021.120802

Bartmann, M., & Halsband, A. (2023). Climate Justice: Ethical Aspects. In D. Lanzerath, M. Bartmann, & A. Halsband (Eds.), *Climate Justice. Ethical As-*

*pects and Policy Aspects* (pp. 13–88). Nomos. https://doi.org/10.5771/9783495993798

Beauchamp, T. L., & Childress, J. F. (2019). *Principles of Biomedical Ethics* (8th ed.). Oxford University Press.

Beauchamp, T. L., & Childress, J. F. (2024). *Prinzipien der Bioethik* (J. Pelger, Trans.; D. Lanzerath & A. Halsband, Eds.). Verlag Karl Alber. (Original work published in 2019). https://doi.org/10.5771/9783495998045

Böhme, G. (1993). *Am Ende des Baconschen Zeitalters*. Suhrkamp.

Brink, D. O. (1989). *Moral Realism and the Foundations of Ethics*. Cambridge University Press. https://doi.org/10.1017/CBO9780511624612

Christ, J., & Honneth, A. (Eds.). (2022). *Zweite Natur. Stuttgarter Hegel-Kongress 2017*. Vittorio Klostermann.

Clements, C. D. (1985). "Therefore Choose Life": Reconciling Medical and Environmental Bioethics. *Perspectives in Biology and Medicine, 28*(3), 407–425. https://doi.org/10.1353/pbm.1985.0011

Edel, A. (2020). Ethical theory and moral practice: On the terms of their relation. In J. P. DeMarco & R. M. Fox (Eds.), *New Directions in Ethics* (pp. 317–335). Routledge. https://doi.org/10.4324/9781003031475

Emmerich, N. (2015). What is Bioethics? *Medicine, Health Care and Philosophy, 18*(3), 437–441. https://doi.org/10.1007/s11019-015-9628-7

Fernandez, F., & Hutchens, N. (2025). Restrictions on US academic freedom affect science everywhere. *Nature Human Behaviour* 9, 1303–1304 (2025). https://doi.org/10.1038/s41562-025-02248-9

Frewer, A. (2011). Zur Geschichte der Bioethik im 20. Jahrhundert. In T.-L. Eissa & S. L. Sorgner (Eds.). *Geschichte der Bioethik: Eine Einführung* (pp. 415–437). Brill | mentis.

Gottstein, K. (2001). Heisenberg's Message to Bohr: Who Knows? *Physics Today, 5*(4), 14–,92. https://doi.org/10.1063/1.1372099

European Commission (2025). Guidance Note on Assessing and Managing Risks of Environmental Harm in EU-Funded Research, 2025

Höffe, O. (2010). Prospect: Aristotle Or Kant? Against A Simple Alternative. In O. Höffe (Ed.), *Aristotle's "Nicomachean Ethics"* (pp. 225–246), Brill. https://doi.org/10.1163/ej.9789004177628.i-259.86

Horton, R., Beaglehole, R., Bonita, R., Raeburn, J., McKee, M., & Wall, S. (2014). From public to planetary health: a manifesto. *The Lancet, 383*(9920), 847. https://doi.org/10.1016/s0140-6736(14)60409-8

Jonas, H. (1979). *Das Prinzip Verantwortung. Versuch einer Ethik für die technologische Zivilisation*. Insel.

Lanzerath, D. (2022, 08. June). Natur. In *Staatslexikon*. https://www.staatslexikon-online.de/Lexikon/Natur

Lanzerath, D. (2023). Research Ethics and Research Ethics Committees in Europe. In T. Zima & D. N. Weisstub (Eds.), *Medical Research Ethics: Challenges in the 21st Century* (pp. 423–439). Springer. https://doi.org/10.1007/978-3-031-12692-5_22

Lanzerath, D. (2024). Vertrauen in Wissenschaft und Forschung: Hohe Ansprüche in Krisenzeiten. In D. Lanzerath, & S. von Kielmannsegg (Eds.), *Medizinische Forschung und COVID-19. Strukturelle Herausforderungen für Deutschland* (pp. 113–130). LIT Verlag.

Lanzerath, D. (2025). Access and Benefit-Sharing: Gesundheitsdaten in der medizinischen Forschung nutzen. *Zeitschrift Für Medizinische Ethik, 71*(1), 53–69. https://doi.org/10.30965/29498570-20250108

Lanzerath, D., Schurr, U., Pinsdorf, C. & Stake, M. (Eds.). (2022). *Bioeconomy and Sustainability. Perspectives from Natural and Social Sciences, Economics and Ethics*. Springer. https://doi.org/10.1007/978-3-030-87402-5

May, L., & Delston, J. B. (Eds.). (1994). *Applied Ethics. A Multicultural Approach*. Routledge.

McCrea, R., Coates, R., Hobman, E. V., Bentley, S., & Lacey, J. (2024). Responsible innovation for disruptive science and technology: The role of public trust and social expectations. *Technology in Society, 79*, 102709. https://doi.org/10.1016/j.techsoc.2024.102709

Palamenghi, L., Barello, S., Boccia, S., & Graffigna, G. (2020). Mistrust in biomedical research and vaccine hesitancy: the forefront challenge in the battle against COVID-19 in Italy. *European Journal of Epidemiology, 35*(8), 785–788. https://doi.org/10.1007/s10654-020-00675-8

Pope Francis (2015, 24. May). *Laudato Si'. On care for our common home. Encyclical Letter* 202. Vatican Press. https://www.vatican.va/content/francesco/en/encyclicals/documents/papa-francesco_20150524_enciclica-laudato-si.html

Potter, V. R. (1971). *Bioethics: Bridge to the Future.* Prentice Hall.

Potter, V. R. (1999). Fragmented Ethics and "Bridge Bioethics". *The Hastings Center Report, 29*(1), 38–40. https://doi.org/10.2307/3528538

Ravitsky, V. (2025), in this volume. (Reprinted from "A Path Forward – and outward: repositioning bioethics to face future challenges", 2023. *Hastings Center Report, 53*(5), 7–10. https://doi.org/10.1002/hast.1510)

Rosa, Hartmut (2018). The idea of resonance as a sociological concept. *Global Dialogue*. 8(2), 41–44.

Sayre-McCord, G. (Ed.) (1988). *Essays on Moral Realism.* Cornell University Press.

Schäfer, L. (1993). Das Bacon-Projekt: Von der Erkenntnis, Nutzung und Schonung der Natur. Frankfurt a.M.

Shafer-Landau, R. (2003). *Moral Realism: A Defence.* Oxford University Press. https://doi.org/10.1093/0199259755.001.0001

Sims, J. M. (2010). A Brief Review of the Belmont report. *Dimensions of critical care nursing*, 29(4), 173–174. http://doi.org/10.1097/DCC.0b013e3181de9ec5

Slunge, D., Drakenberg, O., Ekbom, A., Göthberg, M., Knaggård, Å., & Sahlin, U. (2017). *Stakeholder Interaction in Research Processes – A Guide for Researchers and Research Groups.* University of Gothenburg. http://doi.org/10.13140/RG.2.2.12460.39047

Stoeklé, H. C., & Hervé, C. (2020). COVID-19: Act First, Think Later. *The American Journal of Bioethics*, 20(7), W1. https://doi.org/10.1080/15265161.2020.1761199

Van de Poel, I. (2017). Society as a laboratory to experiment with new technologies. In D. Bowman, E. Stokes & A. Rip (Eds.), *Embedding New Technologies Into Society: A Regulatory, Ethical and Societal Perspective* (pp. 61–87). Jenny Stanford Publishing.

von Braun, W. (1977). Responsible Scientific Investigation and Application. In A. M. Schlesinger & H. O. Hess (Eds.), *The Nature of a Humane Society: A Symposium on the Bicentennial of the United States of America* (p. 101). Fortress Press.

Weber, M. (1988). Der Sinn der »Wertfreiheit« der soziologischen und ökonomischen Wissenschaften. In J. Winckelmann (Ed.), *Gesammelte Aufsätze zur Wissenschaftslehre von Max Weber* (pp. 489–540). Mohr Siebeck.

# Reference and Discourse

## On the Foundation and Development of the DRZE

*Ludger Honnefelder*

What were the reasons for establishing the *German Reference Centre for Ethics in the Life Sciences* (DRZE) 25 years ago? The historical circumstances that led me and my colleagues in and around the Bonn *Institute for Science and Ethics* (IWE) in Bonn to create such a centre at the University of Bonn have already been told. More important for looking back after 25 years is the question of what the *challenges* were to which the foundation attempted to respond, what significance they had then and what significance they still have today.

The birth of the sheep Dolly in 1996, the first-ever successful cloning of a mammal, was only the occasion for founding the DRZE. The reason for its creation was the entirely new set of challenges that Dolly's birth represented. The then German Federal Minister of Education, Science, Research and Technology (BMBF), Jürgen Rüttgers, therefore asked the seven scientists he consulted for an expert opinion not only for their assessment of the biological circumstances, but also for their evaluation of the ethical, social, and legal aspects. The group (of which I was a member) quickly realised that the challenges raised by Dolly's cloning could only be answered by interdisciplinary exchange and normative discourse, for which adequate ways and methods had yet to be found. Among them, a reference centre appeared to be urgently needed.

## I.

Dolly's birth was a bombshell that revealed not only to the scientific world but also to the wider public the profound implications of the new life sciences, which had been evolving since the mid-20th century: that extraordinary breakthroughs in research, especially the discovery of the molecular basis of life and the analysis of the human genome, had provided the biomedical sciences with a completely new dimension of understanding as well as opportunities for intervention, which now powerfully began to open up uncharted possibilities: what had previously been predominantly *descriptive* biology had become *constructive* biology, Mendelian inheritance was expanded by molecular genetics, medicine shifted from curative to preventive practice, and traditional agriculture evolved into modern biotechnology.

What made the new possibilities for intervening in the world of living organisms so unfamiliar to the scientific community and the general public, and to the subject of a debate accompanied by both visions of the future and horror scenarios, were the associated *cognitive, normative, and social challenges*: for what kind of knowledge were the insights gained through the new genome analysis? How to understand, for example, a process such as cloning? How to assess the consequences of the previously unknown possibilities? And what was the nature of research that irreversibly interfered with its living object?

However, the scope of the new research findings and the depth of the insights and interventions were linked not only to scientific-cognitive, but also to *normative* questions, with regard to ethics, law, and society, such as the legitimacy of the goals, the acceptability of the means, and the assessment of intended and unintended consequences – questions that could only be answered through a dialogue between the life sciences and the normative disciplines of ethics, social sciences, and law – a discourse whose scope was hitherto unknown, requiring a new language and terminology, and yet seeking its institutional place.

Legally binding regulations on the pending normative issues could only be agreed upon through *political debate*, which in turn required the participation of the relevant social groups and a correspondingly broad *public debate*. It became clear, however, that this would require novel collaboration between traditionally distinct stakeholders: the scientific community and the public sector, science and practice, the natural sciences and the humanities, ethics and law.

## II.

The novelty of the debates that were to be held also brought new difficulties: for example, a new *interdisciplinarity* had to be developed within the new life sciences in order to achieve understanding and cooperation between the traditional medical disciplines and the new field of genome analysis.

Above all, a completely new kind of interdisciplinarity was needed in order to assess the new insights and their medical and biotechnological application from a *normative* perspective, which necessitated a *paradigm shift* in medical ethics. The traditional framework of a virtue based professional medical ethics had proven not to be superfluous, but too narrow for the diagnostic and therapeutic applications of new possibilities. However, the right places and ways for "bioethics" that replaced it had yet to be found.

Since biomedical research and the resulting areas of application took place in a global context, the new normative debate also had to take place through *international exchange*. However, there were two main problems: the differences in the terminology used, which made communication difficult, and above all the differences regarding normative issues, both in terms of entrenched moral convictions and the legal structures that determined the regulations required.

Not least, the cloning of Dolly made it clear that the expansion of insights and action associated with the new life sciences was not to be understood as a one-off event, but as an open-ended, accelerating *process* in which the rapid *scientific progress*, the immense *social expectations* and the *economic interests* of a growing industry began to combine into a "spiral" – as Dan Callahan, founder of the *Hastings Center Report*, who accompanied the global debate, put it in 2006 – a "spiral" whose dynamics first had to be navigated. If recipients were not to become the object of a self-perpetuating development, then, in addition to the traditional ethical principles of non-maleficence and beneficence or care and the resulting research ethics, the preservation of patient autonomy and distributional justice had to become increasingly important topics of bioethical debate.

All of this required platforms for which *new institutional paths* had to be found – for dialogue between scientific disciplines, for exchange between science, the public and politics, and for national and international legal regulations.

## III.

When the seven experts mentioned above were asked to provide a statement ("Human cloning. Biological foundations and ethical and legal evaluation"), they were not only confronted with the challenges already listed. They also realised that they could not base their assessment on either established discourse or a sufficiently detailed body of information. There was a lack of necessary information both on internal developments in science worldwide and on the public debates that were taking place in other research-intensive countries regarding the new options for action. But, most importantly, there were no suitable and sufficiently advanced models and methods for the new interdisciplinary discourse that had become necessary.

Confronted with the Minister's request, the seven experts came to the conclusion that, given these shortcomings, the scientific community had an obligation to provide everything that was necessary in a qualified manner to form an opinion on how to deal with the new options for action opened up by the new life sciences, and to clarify the associated ethical, legal and social issues.

The seven authors of the statement on cloning – including Ludwig Winnacker, Hubert Markl and Wolfgang Frühwald, leaders of the main German research institutions at the time – therefore found it necessary to add an emphatic recommendation to their statement: "An effective contribution to this discourse from the German side", they wrote at the end of their statement, "presupposes a comprehensive clarification of the matter and a profound examination of the internationally held positions and their justifications." The statement concludes: "To master this task, professional interdisciplinary ethical discourse in Germany should be further developed and promoted."

## IV.

Following proposals to implement this recommendation, the German government decided to create a twofold programme: broad funding of research projects by the *German Research Association* (DFG) aimed at establishing bioethical competence, and the establishment of a reference centre to lay the indispensable foundations for this research. As a result of the call for proposals, the *Institute for Science and Ethics* (IWE), which had been based at the University of Bonn since 1993, took on this task and set up the centre as part of the Academy Programme of the Union of the German Academies of Sciences and Humanities, more specifically as a Research Project of the North Rhine-Westphalian Academy of Sciences, Humanities and the Arts to be based at the University of Bonn.

As the development of the new field of bioethics had already shown, a reference centre was necessary for three main tasks:

For a comprehensive provision of the *information* that is indispensable for qualified bioethical judgments in the complex fields of international life sciences and their possible biomedical applications.

For the development of *communication channels and tools* that are required for professional, interdisciplinary, bioethical decision-making and for the creation of various formats to continuously document and make accessible the status of decision-making in key problem areas of bioethics.

For the development of interdisciplinary bioethical collaborative research as well as for scientific training and the promotion of young researchers, which enables the DRZE to facilitate the networking of the bioethical debate in the European Union (EU).

## V.

For all three tasks, the emerging centre in Bonn was able to draw on cooperation with existing bioethics centres as well as on the experiences gained there, particularly with two institutions that had been established early on in the US: the *Kennedy Institute of Ethics* based at Georgetown University, founded in 1971, which set the first standards for qualified bioethical discourse with its library documenting the English-language bioethical debate, the *Bioethicsline* database and its annual *Intensive Course of Bioethics*. The other one was *The Hastings Center* in New York, which had developed a key platform for new bioethical debates through its *Hastings Center Report*.

Faced with the challenges that became apparent when Dolly was born and drawing on global experience, the DRZE was able to make important steps in all three areas for the German and European bioethical debate:

- To name just a few points, it created not only a *library* and *documentation* that collects all relevant publications, holds all periodicals on the many-faceted bioethical debates, and documents the complex societal debate. In cooperation with the *Kennedy Institute* and several other centres, it has also created *BELIT*, the world's most comprehensive database of its kind, as well as a trilingual *Thesaurus* that facilitates international exchange and research.
- To form professional, interdisciplinary qualified bioethical judgments, the necessary foundations and methods have been developed, and various formats have been created to continuously document and make accessible the

current state of the art in bioethical thought in the central areas of concern in various formats.
- Operating as a platform for interdisciplinary bioethical collaborative research as well as for the further training and promotion of early career researchers, the DRZE has become an institution that enables the networking within the bioethical debate in the *European Union* (EU).

## VI.

The exchange to which the DRZE has invited participants on the occasion of a first review after 25 years will make clear that the challenges to which the founding of the DRZE sought to respond have not diminished, and that the spiral, described by Dan Callahan – of research rapidly expanding the possibilities for intervening, the resulting growth in people's expectations worldwide, and the market serving these expectations – has lost none of its momentum.

However, the exchange will also show the extent to which the scientific community has come to regard the examination of the ethical, legal and social issues surrounding this dynamic development, which was still seeking its proper place at the time of Dolly's birth, as a task specifically incumbent upon it. To ensure the continued success of this important task, and to enable interdisciplinary bioethical decision-making that does not constantly need to re-establish its foundations, but can draw on established principles and methods, a reference centre such as the DRZE will be indispensable for future development.

# Connecting Principles to Cases
## Reflections on Specification and Balancing

*James F. Childress*

### Commemoration and Dedication

This is my first academic essay related to *Principles of Biomedical Ethics* (*PBE*) since Tom L. Beauchamp (b. 1939), my co-author of that book over 8 editions, died 19 February 2025. I present this essay in memory of Tom, a dear friend and collaborator over the last half century as we co-wrote edition after edition of *Principles of Biomedical Ethics* in English. We were fortunate to see it appear in ten foreign language translations, including *Prinzipien der Bioethik*, edited by Dirk Lanzerath and Aurélie Halsband and translated by Julia Pelger (Beauchamp & Childress, 2019/2024). I dedicate this essay to Tom's memory and to our fifty years of fruitful and enjoyable collaboration.

### Moral Principles and Rules

Principles and rules are "general action guides specifying that some type of action is prohibited, required, or permitted in certain circumstances." (Solomon, 1978; see also Hare, 1989, pp. 49–65) These terms for general action guides are often used interchangeably, but principles are typically broader, more general, more abstract, less determinate, and sometimes more foundational. By contrast, rules tend to be narrower and more specific, definite, and concrete. Rules often specify or derive from one or more principles.

In moral deliberation, we frequently reach moral judgments and make ethical decisions about acts and policies without direct reference or appeals to action-guiding principles or rules. Often, such principles and rules are implicit rather than explicit in our moral deliberations and decision making. However, occasions arise that elicit or call for direct appeals to principles/rules for guiding actions. These occur particularly (1) when we are uncertain about what to do, perhaps because we face a novel situation involving, for example, a new technology, or (2) when we face internal or external conflicts about what we ought to do – perhaps even "dilemmas," or (3) when we need to justify our actions, advice, recommendations to others in ethics consultations or in committee deliberations about policies as well as in public discourse. On such occasions, we expect principles to guide our actions, judgments, decisions, etc., but questions inevitably arise about how this guidance proceeds and about how strong or weak it is.

## A Pluralistic Framework of Unranked Principles

While several frameworks in ethics and bioethics feature a variety of general principles, they often employ these principles in quite different ways. For example, *PBE* defends a pluralistic framework that features several unranked moral principles. Following British philosopher W.D. Ross, these principles are considered *prima facie* binding, that is, binding, other things being equal (Ross, 1930, esp. pp. 19–36, 88). Insofar as a principle applies to a particular situation by identifying a morally relevant feature in that situation, it is binding, but other principles may identify other morally relevant but conflicting features in that situation. These principles are all *prima face* binding, but which one(s) become *actually* binding depends on their relative weight, strength, or stringency in those circumstances. Actions that harm individuals or limit their liberties are wrong *prima facie* (i.e., a judgment of wrongness applies unless the act is justifiable because of other principles/rules that are weightier or stronger in the circumstances) or, in other language, they are wrong *pro tanto* (i.e., wrong to a certain extent or unless there is a compelling justification).[1]

The labels "four principles approach" and "principlism" have been applied to PBE's pluralistic framework of unranked moral principles. The former is a neutral or positive description provided by a friendly supporter; the latter originated as a negative label from critics, but the term is now often used neutrally.[2]

1 For a discussion of the distinction between *pro tanto* and *prima facie*, see Shelly Kagan (1989, p. 17). Kagan prefers *pro tanto*, rather than *prima facie*, but notes that Ross used *prima facie* with effectively the same meaning.

2 See, respectively, Gillon (1994), Clouser & Gert (1990). Both labels are commonly used. See also Gillon (2015).

Other types of principle-based approaches in bioethics include appeals to a single principle such as utility or to several principles that are rank-ordered in advance of a particular situation. *PBE*'s pluralistic framework of unranked principles features respect for autonomy, nonmaleficence, beneficence (which includes both providing benefits and utility), and justice – along with several derivative rules, including truthfulness, privacy, confidentiality, and fidelity.[3]

## Orders of Presentation, Consideration, and Priority

Some readers have supposed that by presenting respect for autonomy first we are in fact endorsing its normative priority. That is a mistaken supposition. It is important to distinguish (1) order of *presentation* of principles from both (2) their order of *practical consideration* and (3) their order of *normative priority*. Even though we present respect for autonomy first, all *PBE's* principles are unranked; they are all *prima facie* binding in advance of particular situations. Yet, in the order of practical consideration, some principles should be considered before others are brought to bear in particular situations. For instance, it is important to determine whether a protocol for research involving human participants offers a probable balance of benefits over harms (for possible participants and the society) before seeking prospective participants' informed consent. In such a situation, a prospective participant's refusal to consent to be enrolled in the research trumps or triumphs so that this research cannot go forward with that individual as a participant.

## Bridging or Closing the Gap between Principles and Particular Situations

General principles are supposed to guide actions in particular circumstances. A major concern is how to bridge or close the gap between general principles and specific situations to better guide concrete actions. This involves two questions. First, how can we bridge or close the gap between abstractly formulated principles and rules, on the one hand, and concrete judgments, on the other, since those principles are not only broad but also indeterminate? Second, how can we resolve contingent conflicts of principles in particular circumstances, where they provide different and contradictory directives? The first gap arises in any appeal to principles, for instance, in the need to connect the principle

3 For an effort to reconcile various lists of principles in bioethical frameworks, see Robert M. Veatch (2020).

of justice to concrete situations of scarce medical resources. The second gap arises only when multiple principles, such as beneficence and respect for autonomy, come into conflict. As a character in Tom Stoppard's play *Professional Foul* puts it, "There would be no moral dilemmas if moral principles worked in straight lines and never crossed each other." (Stoppard, 1978, p. 99)

Throughout, the interpretation of principles will be important in bridging or closing the gap, for instance, by clarifying and sharpening concepts, such as harm and autonomy. Even if rational deduction from principles or a subsumption of cases under principles may sometimes be sufficient, conflicts of principles in many cases – the "interesting" cases! – necessitate other strategies. *PBE* has adopted two strategies beyond interpretation and application. These involve specifying principles and balancing principles. Specification renders principles more specific, concrete, determinate, and definite for a particular situation and may in the process dissolve or resolve conflicts. Balancing operates to determine which principle(s) outweigh or override the other(s) when they conflict in a particular circumstance. At the risk of oversimplification, we can say that these processes of specification and balancing focus on two distinguishable but related dimensions of principles and rules. One dimension is their range or scope, the other dimension is their weight, strength, or stringency. In *PBE*, the former requires specification, while the latter requires balancing *prima facie* principles and rules.

## Specification and Balancing

Interpreters often have divergent and sometimes even contradictory views of the processes of specification and balancing in *PBE*. Prior to the publication of the $4^{th}$ edition in 1994, only the process of balancing was explicitly presented in the text. The $4^{th}$ edition included for the first time a section in Chapter 1 on "Specifying and Balancing Principles" (Beauchamp & Childress, 1994, pp. 28–37). Subsequent editions included sections on "Specifying Principles and Rules" and "Balancing Principles and Rules" or "Weighing and Balancing" under the broader heading of "Conflicting Moral Norms." In these editions, the influence of Henry Richardson's formative work on specification, over against deductive application and balancing, is evident (Richardson, 1990). However, as David DeGrazia argues, specification was already present, at least implicitly, in earlier versions of *PBE*. Even though we did not adequately explain what we were doing, we were, according to DeGrazia (1992), "already using the methods of specification throughout [the] text."[4] Certainly some elements of specification appeared, at least implicitly, before we formally adopted the term and practice of specification, but to that point we had focused explicitly only on balancing.

Following our explicit incorporation of specification alongside balancing, interpreters of *PBE* have disagreed about which, if either, of these is primary. Henry Richardson complains that *PBE* fails to sufficiently purge balancing from its approach and continues to draw on it too much (Richardson, 2005; and Richardson, 2000 for an earlier version). Oliver Rauprich (2011) claims that we "endorse specification too defensively and cautiously" and argues that we need to use it more thoroughly and less defensively.[5] Timothy Furlan views *PBE* as making a "switch" from balancing to specification, "while still relying on balancing principles in specific cases when conflict is unavoidable." (Furlan, 2024, p. 4) And John Arras holds that *PBE* has "relegated this sort of move from principles to cases [i.e., balancing] to a marginal corner in the toolbox of principlism," while still drawing on it as a last resort (Arras, 2017, pp. 14–17).

Which of these portrayals most closely fits recent editions of *PBE*? In fact, in later editions we continue to feature both specification and balancing as ways of addressing conflicts, view them as co-equals, and employ each in analysing and resolving different cases. From the 4th edition on, theoretically, methodologically, and practically, we explicitly employ both specification and balancing to connect principles to concrete cases, including dilemmatic cases. Since the 4th edition, both processes have been identified as co-equals, without any indicated priority, either in terms of temporal use or overall superiority. We sometimes suggest that balancing is well suited for reaching judgments in particular cases in the clinical setting (as in a featured case of disclosure to a patient of her positive HIV test), while specification "is especially useful for developing more *specific policies* from already accepted general norms." (Beauchamp & Childress, 2019, p. 20) However, we do not press or further develop this ten-

4 DeGrazia agrees with Richardson that some of the best work in bioethics was already using specification implicitly even though not explicitly identified as such. See Richardson (1990, p. 280).

5 See also the fuller discussion of applications of the "four principle approach" in Gordon, Rauprich & Vollmann (2011), with a response in the same issue by Tom L. Beauchamp (2011, pp. 301–303).

tative proposal, and at most it only indicates a tendency, not a hard and fast division of labour in *PBE* or elsewhere.

## Varieties of Specification

Much of the recent use of and appeal to the process of specification in bioethics dates to Henry Richardson's influential 1990 article, which, as previously noted, shaped the evolution of *PBE*. However, Timothy Furlan mistakenly claims that specification was "first named and detailed by Richardson and expanded and specifically applied to medical ethics by David DeGrazia." (Furlan, 2024; see also DeGrazia, 1992; Strong, 2000) The mistake lies in the claim that Richardson's important version of specification defines and exhausts specification as a method in bioethics. In fact, the history of specification is more extensive and diverse than that.[6] As philosopher R.M. Hare contends, "any attempt to give content to a principle involves specifying the cases that are to fall under it.... Any principle, then, which has content goes some way down the path of specificity." (Hare, 1989, p. 54)

### Specification in Selected Religious Traditions

There is a long tradition of specification in Roman Catholic moral theology, for instance (see, for example, Pilsner, 2006). Even when not identified by name, the process of specification is employed in the encyclical *Evangelium Vitae* (1995) by Pope John Paul II (1995; see also Childress, 1997). This encyclical notes that in the Hebrew Bible/Old Testament, the precept "You shall not kill" is recognized as a divine commandment in the Decalogue and was already part of the original divine-human covenant, expressing human life's "sacred and inviolable character" and functioning as a basis for social life. This negative precept also encouraged a "positive attitude of respect for life."

> As time passed, the Church's Tradition has always consistently taught the absolute and unchanging value of the commandment 'You shall not kill'.... Yet from the beginning, faced with the many and often tragic cases which occur

6 For similar debates about specifying and balancing moral rights, see Aariel Zylberman (2021); Phillip Montague, (2015); Hallie Liberto (2014); William L. Parent and William J. Prior (1996).

> in the life of individuals and society, Christian reflection has sought a fuller and deeper understanding of what God's commandment prohibits and prescribes. There are in fact situations in which values proposed by God's Law seem to involve a genuine paradox.

These "tragic," even paradoxical, situations include justified killing in self-defence or in protecting the life of another or the common good of the family or the state. Representing the tradition's specification of "You shall not kill," Pope John Paul II holds "that the direct and voluntary killing of an innocent human being is always gravely immoral." This specifies, qualifies, and narrows the range or scope of the precept "You shall not kill." The specified precept becomes, in effect, "You shall not voluntarily and directly take the life of an innocent human being." This specification presupposes a distinction between direct and indirect (thus creating space for the rule of double effect, widely used in Roman Catholic moral theology in assessing actions that bring about death), as well as distinctions between voluntary and non-voluntary, between human and non-human, and between guilty and innocent. The latter two sets of distinctions concern moral status.[7] Who counts as a human being? And who qualifies as innocent?

Paul Ramsey, a Protestant theologian and ethicist who was an important pioneer in modern bioethics through many works, including his seminal *The Patient as Person* (2002; see also Ramsey, 1980), directly employed the language and method of specification, describing the process of specification as one of deepening our understanding of the *meaning* of moral principles and rules, an approach consistent with *Evangelium Vitae*.[8]

## Richardson's Model of Specification

Still, among the several varieties of specification, the work of philosopher Henry Richardson provided the main impetus for its incorporation into bioethics as a process to close the gap between general principles and concrete situations, especially in cases of conflict. Richardson focuses on qualifying principles and narrowing their range and scope by clauses spelling out "what,

7 See the role of specification in addressing moral status in Beauchamp & Childress (2019, chapter 3, esp. pp. 84–88).

8 Paul Ramsey (1968, esp. pp. 76–93; 1967). For Ramsey, specification involves exemption making but not exception making; on this general point, see the recent presentation by Katja Stoppenbrink (2022).

where, when, why, how, by what means, by whom, or to whom" the action is to be done or not done (Richardson, 1990, p. 295). These qualifiers, which involve an extensional narrowing of the principle involved, are drawn from questions raised by casuists.[9] *PBE* features Richardson's approach but does not always strictly follow it.

The broad principle of respect for autonomy can be specified in rules of voluntary informed consent and refusal that are widely endorsed in clinical medicine and research involving human participants. It can also be specified to cover a situation in which a previously competent individual is now decisionally incapacitated: clinicians should respect the autonomous choices of a patient who, while decisionally capable, provides an advance directive regarding the use of certain life-sustaining medical procedures under certain circumstances if and when the patient becomes incapacitated.[10]

While Richardson's approach to specification is very valuable, his overall aspirational vision of "progressive specification" is problematic in various ways. "Progressive specification" in bioethics seems to promise a code or ethical rule book – the vision of some specifiers. This, in my view, is unrealistic and, even if it could be achieved, it would be unwieldly, even with the help of artificial intelligence (AI). Moreover, it would distort bioethics, not only because of the misplaced promise of codification, but also because the process of specification and the product of specified rules may ignore, neglect, or downplay critical issues in conflict situations.[11] The process and product direct attention away from the rougher edges of moral conflict to the smoother dissolution or resolution of conflict, paying inadequate attention along the way to the conflicting values that are sacrificed or lost in the specification even though those values, at least partially, motivate the specification.

---

9 Richardson (1990, p. 295); see further the circumstances laid out by Albert R. Jonsen and Stephen Toulmin (1988, p. 253).

10 This is a more fully developed version of an earlier example in *PBE*; it seeks to address some of Richardson's reservations presented in "Specifying, Balancing, and Interpreting Bioethical Principles," (2005, p. 210).

11 Points similar to the ones made in this paragraph are well made by Joseph P. DeMarco and Paul J. Ford (2006).

## Varieties of Balancing

### Different Conceptions of the Weight or Strength of Principles

We now turn from the range and scope of principles and rules to their weight and strength. Two positions at the opposite ends of the spectrum of weight or strength view principles either as mere maxims or as absolute guides.

*Principles as maxims*. Principles as maxims provide rules of thumb, suggestions, or advice without the characteristic of *prescriptivity*, as philosopher R.M. Hare (1989, pp. 49–50) calls it. Even though these maxims lack bindingness, they can still be useful heuristically in decision making, but I will not discuss them further in this essay.

*Principles as absolute*. A principle could be considered to be absolute, that is, unconditionally binding. While this could be plausible for a single-principle framework, such as utilitarianism, it is implausible for a pluralistic framework because multiple and competing absolute principles would produce contradictory and incoherent directives, ultimately destroying the framework. However, we should not rule out the possibility of a few absolute specifications in the form of definite rules.

*PBE's* principles and rules, as *prima facie* binding, are non-absolute; they do not bind absolutely and unconditionally. Nevertheless, some specified or derivative principles/rules may in fact qualify as absolute.[12] The specifying and qualifying clauses may be so narrowly and tightly drawn around one or more principles that an absolute rule emerges – one that needs and permits no further specification or balancing. Examples include the prohibitions of murder and cruelty (the unnecessary infliction of pain and suffering). These specify several principles, as does the prohibition of rape. These absolute specifications obviously set major ethical boundaries and limits on human conduct, but they do not extend far into the bioethics terrain. Another kind of example seeks absolute status by attempting to build in all possible exceptions. It might say "Do X except in A, B, and C circumstances," but this is highly unlikely to encompass all the possible exceptions (Beauchamp & Childress, 2019, p. 19).

*Principles as ranked or lexically ordered*. A third conception of the relative weight and strength of different principles figures more broadly in bioethical

---

12 In *PBE*, we refer both to specified rules and to derivative rules; for Richardson's more precise usage, see his "Specifying, Balancing, and Interpreting Bioethical Principles," (2005, p. 208).

theory and practice: a rank or lexical ordering of principles, in advance of concrete situations. For example, Robert Veatch lexically ranks non-consequentialist principles over consequence-maximizing ones (Veatch & Guidry-Grimes, 2020, chapter 4; Veatch, 2005).[13] A lexical order is a hierarchical arrangement of principles, in which one principle or set of principles must be satisfied before one turns to another principle or set of principles. Veatch allows – and indeed requires – balancing *within* consequentialist and *within* non-consequentialist categories, the latter encompassing (a) respect for persons/humans, including autonomy, veracity, fidelity, etc., and (b) justice. But he does not permit weighing and balancing *across* consequentialist and non-consequentialist classes of principles, only *within* each of them.

In my view, any ethical theory that, in advance or a priori, assigns absolute priority to some principle or set of principles over against one or more or all other principles, such as non-consequentialist over consequentialist principles in Veatch's framework, encounters decisive counterexamples. It creates an implausible absolutist requirement through rank or lexical ordering.

*Principles as prima facie – the need for balancing*. A fourth view considers principles and rules as *prima facie* binding in advance of concrete situations and then determines their relative weight or strength by balancing them in those situations. All the principles and rules in *PBE* – except for a few absolute specified rules – are equally *prima facie* binding, their actual bindingness to be determined in the concrete situation, all things considered. For *prima facie* principles and rules, in contrast to a rank or lexical order or absolute specifications, the process of weighing and balancing is required. Few if any objections surround balancing *within* principles, such as beneficence as applied in a risk-cost-benefit analysis. What is controversial is balancing *across* principles, weighing and balancing one principle against another or others, to guide actions – what we propose in *PBE*.[14]

---

13 For a response to Veatch's lexical order, see Beauchamp & Childress (2020, esp. pp. 566–567). W.D. Ross assigned greater stringency to nonmaleficence than to beneficence and also suggested that certain duties have "a great deal of stringency." Still, he stressed "no general rules can…be laid down" and, drawing from Aristotle, "the decision rests with perception." (Ross, 1930, pp. 22, 41–42).

14 Matthew Shea (2020) argues that *PBE's* balancing needs a hierarchical account of human well-being as well as more attention to the virtues. For a response, see Tom L. Beauchamp and James F. Childress (2020, esp. pp. 567–68). We agree that several virtues are indispensable to successful balancing (and specification), but we "reject the model of a hierarchical theory [of value] that provides an a priori ranking that dictates

In my view, such balancing is appropriate on its own, as a co-equal method with specification in connecting general principles to concrete situations, but it can also function if and when specification fails. However, I do not hold that balancing should be employed only as a last resort, only after efforts at specification fail, as some interpreters of *PBE* suppose. The main criticism of balancing focuses on the role of intuition in this process. This is a legitimate criticism, but there are ways to reduce intuition's role and to limit or counterbalance its impact in intersubjective public discourse and deliberation, where various intuitions, including those for which reasons can be given, are presented, supported, and challenged. The goal is to achieve coherence in a reflective and perceptive equilibrium in an intersubjective public, deliberative, justificatory context, not simply as one individual's reflective or perceptive equilibrium.[15]

## Constrained Balancing

Other appropriate constraints can be brought to bear on balancing. In later editions of *PBE*, the language shifted from "balancing" to "constrained balancing," with constraints added to reduce the play of intuition. Many of the conditions of constrained balancing are non-controversial and even obvious. Nevertheless, it is important to spell out these conditions because they are frequently overlooked in practice (see also Childress, 2020).

Following is a list of several conditions of constrained balancing in public deliberation and justification:

- Reasons can be given for holding that principle X is *weightier or stronger* than conflicting principle Y in a particular situation.
- Infringing Y will *probably protect* X.
- Infringing Y is *necessary* to protect X in the sense that no morally preferable alternative action is available.

---

outcomes," and instead we seek "to enable principlism to work better within a loose, thin, rough consensus about various harms and benefits."

15 In addition to the widely familiar Rawlsian *reflective* equilibrium, what Martha Nussbaum calls a *perceptive* equilibrium is also important. See Martha C. Nussbaum (1990, p. ix): "The essays argue for a conception of ethical understanding that involves emotional as well as intellectual activity and gives a certain type of priority to the perception of particular people and situations, rather than to abstract rules." See esp. chap 6 for her discussion of perceptive equilibrium.

- The specific infringement of Y is the *least possible* infringement that can still protect X in the situation.
- Agents must seek to *minimize the negative effects* of Y's infringement and to ensure that the *positive effects will outweigh the negative effects* of Y's infringement.
- Agents must *act impartially* with respect to all stakeholders and affected parties.

Now consider weighing and balancing in a conflict between principle X, beneficence,[16] which supports a public health measure of mass vaccination to reduce the impact of a serious contagious disease, and principle Y, respect for autonomous choice in consenting to or refusing a vaccination. This conflict may arise in a pandemic because of the urgent need to reduce the spread of a contagious disease, like COVID-19, and the severity of cases of infection, hospitalizations, and deaths, combined with a well-grounded judgment that mass vaccination would be the most effective public health measure in this pandemic.

Ensuring mass vaccination may sometimes require overriding autonomous choices about vaccination. Consider a range of possible behavioural interventions to secure mass vaccination: persuasion; removing barriers or disincentives to vaccination, such as costs; providing positive incentives, such as financial rewards; and mandating vaccination with sanctions for non-compliance. In selecting interventions to achieve compliance with the public health measure of mass vaccination, effective means that do not infringe respect for autonomy have presumptive priority. The conditions of probable effectiveness and necessity do not require that all possibly effective means that do not infringe respect for autonomy actually be tried and judged as failures before resorting to coercive interventions; it may be sufficient to have a well-grounded belief that other possible means will not be effective in the particular circumstances.

Even when mandatory vaccination is deemed to be justified, the infringement or breach of respect for autonomy must be the least invasive and least intrusive action consistent with the efforts to achieve the public health goal. It is also important to minimize the negative effects of infringements of respect for autonomy (e.g., by providing treatment and compensation for vaccine-related injuries) and to ensure that the positive effects of this public health mea-

16 Of course, this beneficence-based goal may also reflect the principles of non-maleficence and justice.

sure and the coercive mandate outweigh their negative effects, not simply for those who are vaccinated but also for the society. Some of the restrictions on autonomous choices and actions during the recent COVID-19 pandemic, especially lockdowns and vaccine mandates, generated long-term negative effects, including magnified suspicion of science (e.g., regarding pandemics and vaccinations) and resistance to public health measures (see, for example, Macedo & Lee, 2025). Such possible or probable effects need to be taken into account in the consequentialist judgments that are part of any assessments in such conflict situations. Finally, impartial treatment is required for all affected stakeholders. This needs close attention because societal responses to pandemics have often breached impartiality by making some groups scapegoats, targeted for blame and for special restrictions and burdens.

## Conclusions

These two essential processes – specification and balancing – for addressing the gap between general principles and concrete situations may not be as far apart or as insulated from each other as is often supposed. On the one hand, as John Arras suggests, balancing may play a greater role in specification than is ordinarily recognized.

> Indeed, what motivates and guides the modification and specification of abstract principles, what compels one to lard them with qualifying clauses, if not precisely the sort of countervailing values and principles encountered by the balancer? Thus, whether one calls this balancing or specification, the respective weights of competing considerations must be sorted out. (Arras, 2017, pp. 16–17)

On the other hand, in agreement with Richardson, we can say that, in principle, every publicly justifiable balancing of principles in concrete situations can be rendered as a specification (see, for example, Richardson, 2005, pp. 220–21). This reflects the formal requirement of universalizability in ethical judgments – a justifiable ethical judgment in a particular set of circumstances holds for all relevantly similar circumstances (Hare, 1989; and many of his other writings). Many disputes hinge, however, on which similarities and dissimilarities are morally relevant.

In reviewing Tom Tomlinson's *Methods in Medical Ethics – Critical Perspectives* (2012), Søren Holm observes that all the methods Tomlinson discusses can "illuminate important moral features of the problematic situation," but that "they run out as decision making tools long before we reach a definite answer." (Holm, 2013) This observation, even if overstated, serves as an apt reminder that we may need to adjust and moderate our expectations of being able always and completely to close or bridge the gap between general principles and particular circumstances in bioethics. Some dilemmas just may not be resolvable this way.[17]

Even though action guidance is an important and ineradicable aim of moral principles and rules and of ethical theories and methods in various practical areas, we need to avoid or temper the unrealistic hope of fully closing or bridging the gap to arrive at definite and definitive answers in each and every situation, whether in a clinic or a public policy forum. Specification and constrained balancing offer promising possibilities for – at least partially – closing or bridging the gap in most situations. But, as we have seen, they also have limitations, whether alone or jointly. Put simply, their contributions sometimes only *illuminate* rather than *dictate* answers.

While we should pursue these two processes vigorously and rigorously, final answers are often elusive, and judgment is frequently required. Incomplete gap closure in some cases should not considered a fatal flaw of principlist approaches and of processes of specification and balancing. Even when definite answers are not reached, the pluralistic framework of bioethical principles, extended to concrete and conflict-filled cases through specification and constrained balancing, can help to structure and orchestrate our bioethical deliberations and discourse. Principles mediated through processes of specification and constrained balancing can guide action by illuminating paths, not only by indicating the right and wrong steps.

## References

Arras, J. D. (2017). Principlism: The Borg of Bioethics. In J. Childress & M. Adams (Eds.), *Methods in Bioethics: The Way We Reason Now*. Oxford University Press. https://doi.org/10.1093/acprof:oso/9780190665982.003.0001

---

17 Despite his strong expectations for specification, Richardson also concedes that "not all conflicts among moral principles are resolvable." (2005, p. 217)

Beauchamp, T. L. (2011). Making Principlism Practical: A Commentary on Gordon, Rauprich, and Vollmann. *Bioethics*, 25(6), 301–303. https://doi.org/10.1111/j.1467-8519.2011.01908.x

Beauchamp, T. L., & Childress, J. F. (1994). *Principles of Biomedical Ethics* (4th ed.). Oxford University Press.

Beauchamp, T. L., & Childress, J. F. (2019). *Principles of Biomedical Ethics* (8th ed.). Oxford University Press.

Beauchamp, T. L., & Childress, J. F. (2020). Response to Commentaries. *The Journal of Medicine and Philosophy*, 45(4–5), 560–579. https://doi.org/10.1093/jmp/jhaa011

Beauchamp, T. L., & Childress, J. F. (2024). *Prinzipien der Bioethik* (J. Pelger, Trans.; D. Lanzerath & A. Halsband, Eds.). Alber. (Original work published in 2019)

Childress, J. F. (1997). Moral Rhetoric and Moral Reasoning: Some Reflections on Evangelium Vitae. In K. Wm. Wildes, S.J., & A. C. Mitchell (Eds.), *Choosing Life: A Dialogue on Evangelium Vitae* (pp. 21–36). Georgetown University Press.

Childress, J. F. (2020). *Public Bioethics: Principles and Problems* (Chapter 11, pp. 252–271). Oxford University Press. https://doi.org/10.1093/med/9780199798483.003.0012

Clouser, K. D., & Gert, B. (1990). A Critique of Principlism. *Journal of Medicine and Philosophy*, 15(2), 219–236. https://doi.org/10.1093/jmp/15.2.219

DeGrazia, D. (1992). Moving Forward in Bioethical Theory: Theories, Cases, and Specified Principlism. *Journal of Medicine and Philosophy*, 17(5), 511–539. https://doi.org/10.1093/jmp/17.5.511

DeMarco, J. P., & Ford, P. J. (2006). Balancing in Ethical Deliberation: Superior to Specification and Casuistry. *Journal of Medicine and Philosophy*, 31, 483–497. https://doi.org/10.1080/03605310600912675

Furlan, T. J. (2024). Principlism, Uncodifiability, and the Problem of Specification. *Cambridge Quarterly of Healthcare Ethics*, 1–22. (online ahead of print) https://doi.org/10.1017/S0963180123000622

Gillon, R. (1994). Medical Ethics: Four Principles Plus Attention to Scope. *BMJ*, 309(6948), 184–188. https://doi.org/10.1136/bmj.309.6948.184

Gillon, R. (2015). Defending the Four Principles Approach as a Good Basis for Good Medical Practice and Therefore for Good Medical Ethics. *Journal of Medical Ethics*, 41(1), 111–116. https://doi.org/10.1136/medethics-2014-102282

Gordon, J.-S., Rauprich, O., & Vollmann, J. (2011). Applying the Four-Principle Approach. *Bioethics, 25*(6), 293–300. https://doi.org/10.1111/j.1467-8519.2009.01757.x

Hare, R. M. (1989). Principles. In *Essays in Ethical Theory*. Clarendon Press.

Holm, S. (2013). There is Method in the Madness. *Clinical Ethics, 8*(1), 1. https://doi.org/10.1177/1477750913483486

Jonsen, A. R., & Toulmin, S. (1988). *The Abuse of Casuistry*. University of California Press. https://doi.org/10.1525/9780520352797

Kagan, S. (1989). *The Limits of Morality*. Clarendon Press.

Liberto, H. (2014). The Moral Specification of Rights: A Restricted Account. *Law and Philosophy, 33*(2), 175–206. https://doi.org/10.1007/s10982-013-9183-4

Macedo, S., & Lee, F. (2025). *In Covid's Wake: How Our Politics Failed Us*. Princeton University Press. https://doi.org/10.2307/jj.19583515

Montague, P. (2015). Specification and Moral Rights. *Law and Philosophy, 34*(3), 241–256. https://doi.org/10.1007/s10982-014-9222-9

Nussbaum, M. C. (1990). *Love's Knowledge: Essays on Philosophy and Literature*. Oxford University Press. https://doi.org/10.1093/oso/9780195074857.001.0001

Parent, W. L., & Prior, W. J. (1996). Thomson on the Moral Specification of Rights. *Philosophy and Phenomenological Research, 56*(4), 837–845. https://doi.org/10.2307/2108283

Pilsner, J. (2006). *The Specification of Human Actions in St. Thomas Aquinas*. Oxford Theological Monographs. Oxford University Press. https://doi.org/10.1093/0199286051.001.0001

Pope John Paul II. (1995, March 25). *Evangelium Vitae*. Retrieved July 1, 2025, from https://www.vatican.va/content/john-paul-ii/en/encyclicals/documents/hf_jp-ii_enc_25031995_evangelium-vitae.html

Ramsey, P. (1967). *Deeds and Rules in Christian Ethics* (Scribner Studies in Contemporary Theology). Charles Scribner's Sons.

Ramsey, P. (1968). The Case of the Curious Exception. In G. H. Outka, & P. Ramsey (Eds.), *Norm and Context in Christian Ethics* (pp. 67–135). Charles Scribner's Sons.

Ramsey, P. (1980). *Ethics at the Edges of Life: Medical and Legal Intersections*. Yale University Press.

Ramsey, P. (2002). *The Patient as Person: Explorations in Medical Ethics* (2nd ed.). Yale University Press.

Rauprich, O. (2011). Specification and Other Methods for Determining Morally Relevant Facts. *Journal of Medical Ethics, 37*(10), 592–596. https://doi.org/10.1136/jme.2010.039214

Richardson, H. (1990). Specifying Norms as a Way to Resolve Concrete Ethical Problems. *Philosophy & Public Affairs, 19*(4), 279–319.

Richardson, H. (2000). Specifying, Balancing, and Interpreting Bioethical Principles. *The Journal of Medicine and Philosophy, 25*(3), 285–307. https://doi.org/10.1076/0360-5310(200006)25:3;1-H;FT285

Richardson, H. (2005). Specifying, Balancing, and Interpreting Bioethical Principles. In J. F. Childress, E. M. Meslin, & H. T. Shapiro (Eds.), *Belmont Revisited: Ethical Principles for Research with Human Subjects* (pp. 205–227). Georgetown University Press.

Ross, W. D. (1930). *The Right and the Good*. Clarendon Press.

Shea, M. (2020). Principlism's Balancing Act: Why the Principles of Biomedical Ethics Need a Theory of the Good. *The Journal of Medicine and Philosophy, 45*(4–5), 441–470. https://doi.org/10.1093/jmp/jhaa014

Solomon, D. (1978). Rules and Principles. In W. T. Reich (Ed.), *Encyclopedia of Bioethics*. The Free Press.

Stoppard, T. (1978). *Every Good Boy Deserves Favor and Professional Foul*. Grove Press.

Stoppenbrink, K. (2022, October 10). *Principles, Rules, and Their Exceptions: Making Sense of Specification* [Conference presentation]. The Future of Principlism: Symposium with Tom Beauchamp and James Childress, University of Tübingen, Germany.

Strong, C. (2000). Specified Principlism: What Is It, and Does It Really Resolve Cases Better than Casuistry? *Journal of Medicine and Philosophy, 25*(3), 323–341.

Tomlinson, T. (2012). *Methods in Medical Ethics: Critical Perspectives*. Oxford University Press. https://doi.org/10.1093/acprof:oso/9780195161243.001.0001

Veatch, R. M. (2005). Ranking, Balancing, or Simultaneity: Resolving Conflicts among the Belmont Principles. In J. F. Childress, E. M. Meslin, & H. T. Shapiro (Eds.), *Belmont Revisited: Ethical Principles for Research with Human Subjects* (pp. 184–204). Georgetown University Press.

Veatch, R. M. (2020). Reconciling Lists of Principles in Bioethics. *Journal of Medicine and Philosophy, 45*(4–5), 540–559. https://doi.org/10.1093/jmp/jhaa017

Veatch, R. M., & Guidry-Grimes, L. K. (2020). *The Basics of Bioethics* (4th ed.). Routledge. https://doi.org/10.4324/9780429507519

Zylberman, A. (2021). Moral Rights without Balancing. *Philosophical Studies, 179*(2), 549–569. https://doi.org/10.1007/s11098-021-01670-9

# Bioethics as Practical Reasoning

## On the Question of Method

*Roman Wagner*

## Introduction

The rediscovery of bioethics requires a reflection on the methods of bioethical thought. The aim of this article is to raise the question of method and to provide a rough outline of how practical bioethical thinking can be conceptualized. This topic has different facets. Firstly, the status of philosophical ethics as a science is linked to the question of methodology. A widely held position is that a scientific discipline must develop methods that make its judgments and claims intersubjectively comprehensible and critically verifiable whether the knowledge gained in the respective discipline is valid. Such a method is the basis for the objective validity of scientific knowledge and ought to prevent the influence of idiosyncratic intuitions and opinions that are not formed rationally. Secondly, the question of method is central to the connection of normative ethics – i.e., first-level ethical theory – and applied ethics. If the aim of normative-ethical theory is to guide action in specific situations, it must be shown how abstract ethical models and specific cases are related. Finally, the question of method is relevant for ethical teaching. In particular, where philosophers use insights from philosophy in interdisciplinary discourse to offer ethical training courses that are intended to enable students from different disciplines to act in a morally justifiable manner in their everyday professional lives, it is necessary to reflect on which methods can be used to make ethical judgments in everyday life on the basis of ethical theories. To that end, the second section will discuss an understanding of ethics as a form of practical reason and practical deliberation. The third section focusses on one type of ethical theory – principlism – in light of the practical deliberation account of ethics. The topics of Chapter three are first principles, principle-pluralism and moral sensitivity and reflective equilibrium.

## Ethics and practical reason

One way to shed light on the question of ethical method is to understand ethics as a form of practical reason (Lovibond, 2004). The object of practical reason is human action. Practical reason serves to answer what in philosophical discourse is called the *practical question*: "What should I do?". This question differs from the basic question of theoretical reason, which is concerned with what we can know, or which judgments are true. In this understanding, the task of ethics is to identify principles of practically reasonable deliberation in such a way that all practically reasonable beings can be guided by them in their actions. Practically reasonable actions are based on valid reasons and in virtue of their validity they justify the action. Accordingly, those who act in a practically reasonable manner are justified in their actions. In this sense, the question of the method of ethics is related to the question of the justification moral action.

To ask for the justification of an action is to ask for the *reasons* a person had for acting in a certain way. While a distinction is sometimes made in the debate on action theory between *normative*, *explanatory* and *motivational* reasons (cg. Smith, 1994, pp. 94ff; Alvarez, 2010), it is clear that in the context of the question of justification, only normative reasons are decisive. Normative reasons are the elements of both theoretical and practical reason. In the theoretical realm, a reason justifies a belief; in the practical realm, it justifies an action. If practical reason serves to answer the practical question of what we ought to do, practical normative reasons reveal why we ought to act as we do. To understand how we ought to act according to the prescriptions of ethics, we need to know what the reasons for are acting in a certain way. One way of discussing this internal connection between reasons and actions is to conceptualise action as having the structure of and being determined by a practical syllogism.

The practical syllogism is a form of practical judgment in which two premises and a conclusion are brought together. While it is disputed how the elements of the syllogism should be classified ontologically – as mental or neural events, as facts, or as ends (Alvarez, 2010) – and whether or not the relationship between the premises and the conclusion can be understood as a causal relation (Davidson, 1963), there is widespread agreement that the first premise expresses the goal of the action, while the second premise identifies the means that serve to realise this end. The term "goal" is defined in a wide sense here. A goal does not necessarily have to be understood as a kind of teleological structure. Maxims or desires or other types of conative states are goals in this broad understanding. The only important thing is that the first premise differs from the second in that it is practical. Unlike the second premise, which is theoretical, it does not take the form of a truth-apt statement, but the form of a normative judgment about what to do.

The premises of this kind of reasoning are *reasons for an action*. As reasons, they reveal what – at least from the perspective of the person acting –spoke in favour of acting as they did and which means she took to be instrumental in reaching her goal (Scanlon, 1998, Chap. 1). Because reasons speak in favour of an action, they *justify* it, and thus play a normative role in determining it, i.e., they exhibit a distinct kind of causality, the causality of practical reason. Note that in practical reasoning of this kind, there is rarely a single deduction standing for itself. Usually, there is a chain of practical syllogisms united in an iterative structure, where the conclusion of one syllogism is the first premise of the following one (Gersbach, 2016, pp. 63f.). As a simple example, consider a syllogism starting from the first premise that I should exercise in order to stay healthy. A second premise of a syllogism of this kind might be that lifting weights would be a way to exercise. This factual premise could be right or wrong – in this case it turns out to be right. The conclusion of this premise, then, might be that I should buy weights, as, in our example, I don't yet own any. This conclusion is the starting point of the next part of the syllogistic chain, namely that I should buy weights, which, in combination with the factual premise that in order to buy weights I should go to the store, yields the next conclusion that I should, somehow, find a way to get to the store and so forth.

If this understanding of ethics as a form of practical, reasoned deliberation is taken as basic, different normative-ethical theories can be understood as attempts to reveal the form and principles of practical reason. Following this line of thought, the principles presented by normative-ethical theories – deontology, utilitarianism, principlism and in a certain reading even virtue ethics – can be interpreted as presenting the ultimate starting points of practical deliberation, i.e. the first premise of any ethical practical syllogism. According to this reading, the foundational principles of ethics can be understood as the most general first premises of practical thought. These principles constitute the realm of morality in practical reasoning and are taken to be the last possible answer to the question to the normative authority of ethics. In other words: these principles are taken to be inherently normative and binding for any moral subject. If, for instance, respect for autonomy is one of the foundational principles of ethics, then, taking this principle as the ultimate first premise of a syllogistic chain, we can decide how to treat patients in medical settings by referring, in the last analysis, to this principle as the normative ground of practical thought. The principle of respect for autonomy therefore becomes the last answer to the practical question in situations in which it is applicable.

Because first principles are taken to be inherently normative such that they bind all practically rational persons able to reason from principles to specific moral judgments and thereby guide their actions, the normative authority of the first principles echoes through the chain of the practical syllogisms all the way to their conclusion. In this way, the practical question is answered by practical reason providing an authoritative starting point as the justifying reason for action and determining a specific action in a given situation. Therefore, these principles, taken as ultimate first premises of a series of interlocked practical syllogisms together with the idea of practical deliberation as deducing concrete actions from general maxims, could be seen to provide us with what we are looking for: an intersubjectively comprehensible mode of reasoning, in which normative theory and the specific moral questions can be.

## Practical Reasoning in Principlism

In many fields of applied ethics, particularly in medical ethics, principlism provides the framework for practical deliberation (Varkey, 2021). Principlism offers a pluralism of principles which, at least in questions of medical ethics, is based on the four principles of beneficence, non-maleficence, respect for autonomy, and justice. The metaethical model for this approach is David Ross' concept of prima facie duties (Ross, 2002, pp. 19ff.). A prima facie duty is a justifying reason for action whose normative authority depends upon whether there are conflicting reasons, principles or demands. Since there are a number of different prima facie duties that all claim equal validity, it is necessary to examine which duty is relevant in a specific situation. According to this model, there is no supreme principle from which we can deduce how to act, but a plurality of principles of the same rank, i.e., none of the principles is more basic or a priori more important.

Applying the model discussed so far to principlism, the method of ethics seems to be as follows: first, we determine the relevant principles of ethical thought. These principles, then, serve as the first premise in a practical syllogism or an iterated structure of practical syllogisms, leading us from general principles successively to concrete actions. A simple practical deduction could be formulated in such a way that the first premise contains, for example, the principle of respect for autonomy, a second premise states that obtaining informed consent serves as a means of respecting patient autonomy, and finally the conclusion is reached that a particular doctor should obtain such consent in a specific situation. In this way, it seems, practical reasoning can move from the abstract – the general ethical principles – to the concrete, and thus reach specific instructions for action from general considerations. However, practical reasoning within principlism cannot be understood as such a mechanical derivation from given principles. In this understanding of ethical judgment as practical reason, it seems that all we need to teach students of ethics are general rules and certain facts, which then enable them to mechanically or algorithmically deduce answers to practical questions. While this misunderstanding of ethics and practical reason is still widespread, it is not the way that Tom Beauchamp and James Childress, two of the main proponents of principlism, envisaged it, as John Arras notes, when he writes:

> Although Beauchamp and Childress never promised anything more than a useful framework for justifying ethical judgments, and certainly not an algorithm for cranking out univocally correct answers to complex and vexing moral questions, their less morally literate followers often choked the medical literature with papers flatly declaring that this or that principle of bioethics provided the unique solution for this or that problem. (Arras, 2020, p. 4)

The same sentiment is expressed by Tom Beauchamp:

> I *accept* the view that certain broad *fundamental* moral principles give support to numerous other principles, rules, and judgments (as part of their 'foundation' or justification); but support is not entailment [...]. Moral principles are rallying points for justification. They provide vital premises, but before we render them the queen of the applied moral sciences, we had better be sure they have the power to fulfill the assigned function. (Beauchamp, 2010, p. 215)

The problems with the idea of a mechanical application of given principles are manifold. The first problem pertains to the normative authority of the first principles as well as their exact number and structure. Ethical thought, neither within philosophy nor in the everyday context of moral deliberation, should be taken to start from unquestioned premises that are presented as dogmatically given. The second problem is tied to the pluralism of the principles presented by Beauchamp und Childress. Prima facie principles of the same order and normative weight can come into conflict without an a priori way of resolving this conflict. Therefore, for any given case, the starting point of practical deliberation is far from being self-evident. Thirdly, it does not seem to be a convincing model of practical deliberation to assume that it is unidirectional, proceeding exclusively from abstract premises to concrete action. Rather, as the idea of a reflective equilibrium suggests, general principles and concrete cases stand not in a *deductive*, but a *dialectical* relationship, in which both are interdependent, and reciprocally and dynamically determine each other. These problems should not be taken as general criticisms of either the discussed conception of practical deliberation as interlocked practical syllogisms or of principlism, but as elucidations of their exact nature. Only by taking these aspects of practical thought into consideration can we gain an appropriate understanding of practical rationality and moral judgment. To do so, the rest of this paper will sketch two ways of meeting the challenges presented.

## First Principles

The first problem mentioned above pertains to the questions of, firstly, how the normative authority of the first principles can be established and secondly, how we are to determine which principles there are. While there are different ways to determine the authority of first principles – transcendentally as in the Kantian tradition, by way of a proof as in the utilitarian tradition following Mill, by way of a social contract as in the Hobbesian tradition etc. –, the following considerations will be restricted to Tom Beauchamp's justification of his and James Childress' principlist approach. To this end, Beauchamp and Childress, in their "Principles of Biomedical Ethics" and in other publications, developed a normative-ethical position that builds on the framework of common morality.

The metaethical position of common morality is characterised by a number of universally valid moral principles that form the basis of practical moral deliberation as standards for moral action. In contrast to particular morals, i.e. those moral systems that are closely tied to individuals, small groups or societies and are characterised by "concrete, nonuniversal, and content-rich norms", common morality is a system of "general moral standards that are conspicuously abstract, universal, and content thin" (Beauchamp, 2010, p. 177). The principles of common morality derive their content and their normative weight – i.e. the fact that they justify certain actions in a generally valid way – from the basic teleological idea that the purpose of ethics is the promotion of human well-being. In a seemingly Aristotelian definition, Tom Beauchamp writes:

> I start with an assumption about the primary goal – that is, objective – of the social institution of morality. This objective is to promote human flourishing by counteracting conditions that cause the quality of people's lives to worsen. (Beauchamp, 2010, p. 43)

This formal goal explains the content of the principles: they are not the result of a deductive process in which, for example, an ultimate principle – such as the utilitarian principle of maximising pleasurable experiences (pleasures) – serves as a normative basis and from which more concrete principles or specific actions could be further deductively derived. Rather, the principles proposed in principlism result from the historically grown experience that certain maxims of action are conducive to human well-being. This means that the principles proposed by Beauchamp and Childress are not the result of a priori reflections, but that they are the result of critical considerations, additions and modifications (Beauchamp, 2010, 185f.). Part of practical thought, therefore, is the constant reflection on as well as criticism and modification of the starting premises of moral reasoning. In this picture, the problem of the source of normative authority derives from the idea that following the principles provided by common morality is conducive to human well-being. Thus, the starting point of practical reasoning and its normative authority is not dogmatically fixed, but tied to what Beauchamp takes to be the goal of morality.

## Principle-Pluralism and Moral Sensitivity

The second problem also has two aspects. The first of these aspects is understanding which of the first principles are pertinent to a given case, while the second involves the weighing of the principles in cases of conflict. To answer these problems, principlism needs to be supplemented by considerations from virtue ethics. In the tradition of virtue ethics, there is not only an analogue to the principlist problem of a plurality of normative foundations – virtues in the case of virtue ethics – which can come into conflict with one another;

in addition, virtue ethicists are also concerned with the nature of the practically wise person's ability to discern what is morally called for in a given situation. To recognise which principle is relevant in a specific situation, people need the right kind of affective receptivity or, in John McDowell's words, the "reliable sensitivity to a certain sort of requirement that situations impose on behaviour." (McDowell, 1998, p. 53) Therefore, virtue ethics incorporates affects and emotions into moral reasoning as epistemic devices that help the practically rational agent to discern what is morally required of them. Taking insights from the philosophical theory of emotions, emotions can thus be understood as a form of *evaluative judgment* based on an affectively laden perception with both cognitive and motivational aspects (Nussbaum, 2001; Solomon, 2008). By *affectively seeing*, i.e. perceiving and feeling the needs of another person through empathy, a moral agent is able to determine which kind of moral consideration is pertinent to the situation at hand (Tappolet, 2016).

According to this understanding, not only is there no way to determine a priori what to look for in a situation to determine which aspects are relevant, but this kind of skill further requires a certain kind of emotional sensitivity, which can and needs to be trained. As Ronald de Sousa has stressed through his idea of paradigm scenarios, complex human emotions are not just biological reactions to stimuli, but socially formed and trained intelligent responses (de Sousa, 2001). As such, we are neither entirely passive in relation to them nor is any response justified simply by its evaluative nature. Rather, as in the training of theoretical reason, people need to be educated and brought up in such a way that they learn to respond emotionally in a morally justified way, thereby training their ability to discern what is emotionally required of them in a given situation, both regarding which principle is relevant and how different moral demands of a situation should be weighed up against each other.

Note, lastly, that the metaphor of "weighing up principles" can be misleading in that it might suggest a quantitative understanding of different principles. This is not how the process of deliberating which principle is decisive in determining our action should be understood. Another way to express this aspect of practical reasoning can be found in John McDowell's phrasing below that certain considerations and perceptions silence others. McDowell explains:

> The distinction becomes intelligible if we stop assuming that the virtuous person's judgment is a result of balancing reasons for and against. The view of a situation that he arrives at by exercising his sensitivity is one in which some aspect of the situation is seen as constituting a reason for acting in

> some way; this reason is apprehended, not as outweighing or overriding any reasons for acting in other ways [...], but as silencing them. (McDowell, 1998, p. 56)

These very general remarks, of course, need to be supplemented by the rich discussion of practical wisdom, or phronesis, in the Aristotelian tradition, to more clearly explicate the nature of the abilities and skills just alluded to (De Caro & Vaccarezza, 2021). What should have become clear though, is the need to understand moral decision-making as a complex skill that not only, albeit crucially, requires the knowledge of moral principles, but also affective and perceptual abilities, which are the result of habituation and reflection, to recognise what morally relevant situations require of us.

## Reflective Equilibrium

The last point, finally, concerns the complex relationship of general principles and specific moral judgments. The idea here is that practical reason should not be understood as an exclusively top-down determination of specific judgments and the actions based on them through general principles, but rather as a complex dynamic between both parts of practical reason (DePaul, 1993). This is the idea of a reflective equilibrium (Daniels, 1979). According to this idea, general principles are not immune to criticism by way of concrete moral judgments, if a specific judgment challenges the validity of a principle. Strong intuitions about concrete cases can provide a standard against which general principles are to be measured.

Consider a standard case against act-utilitarianism. According to the supreme principle of act-utilitarianism, our actions should generate as much happiness as possible. Now imagine a case where in a hospital there are five people. One healthy person who just wants a check-up, and four terminally ill persons who all need an organ and could survive were they provided with the organs of the healthy person. If the principle of act-utilitarianism is correct, it might be argued that it is morally required to kill the healthy person to save the other four, thereby producing a larger quantity of overall happiness than by letting them die. The usual intuitive reaction to this example is disbelief and horror, followed by an attempt to reinterpret the principle – for instance in a rule-utilitarian way – or the wholesale abandonment of the principle. Rarely, if ever, do people change their intuition that such an act would me morally unjustifiable, even if they think that act-utilitarianism is a convincing account of ethics. This is because intuitively, based on our immediate specific moral judgments, it does not seem justified, much less morally required, to murder a person who visits their doctor for a check-up. Here, the intuitive judgment casts serious doubt on the validity of the general principle of act-utilitarianism, which shows that sometimes normative authority is not found in principles, but in specific moral judgments. Utilitarians, of course, have argumentative options open to them and can respond to this objection, but the point stands: a specific moral judgment can invalidate a general principle – at least in its original formulation –, which shows the complex interrelations of general principles and concrete judgments. As John Arras notes: "Our most confident moral judgments and intuitions (e.g., 'Slavery is wrong') provide a touchstone for the adequacy of our principles; any moral principle that justifies slavery would either be reformulated or rejected." (Arras, 2020, p. 175)

Due to this dynamic, practical reason should not be understood as a simple deduction of specific judgments and actions from general principles. Rather, we need to take into account the complex dialectical relationship between both aspects of practical reason. This element of practical thought also needs to be part of ethical education and our understanding of the methods of ethics. Both, bioethical research as well as its application in everyday practice and teaching need to take account of the fact that ethical judgment cannot be reduced to a mechanical application of principles. The ideas outlined in this paper highlight those aspects of ethical thought that require judgment, experience and attention to the complex dialectical structure of general and specific elements.

## References

Alvarez, M. (2010). *Kinds of Reasons*. Oxford University Press.

Arras, J. (2020). *Methods of Bioethics: The Way We Reason Now.* Oxford University Press. DOI:10.1093/acprof:oso/9780190665982.001.0001

Varkey, B. (2021). Principles of Clinical Ethics and Their Application to Practice. *Medical Principles and Practice*, *30*(1), 17–28. doi: 10.1159/000509119.

Beauchamp, T. (2010). *Standing on Principles – Collected Essays*. Oxford University Press.

Daniels, D. (1979). Wide Reflective Equilibrium and Theory Acceptance in Ethics. *The Journal of Philosophy*, 76(5), 256–282. https://doi.org/10.1017/CBO9780511624988.003

Caro, M. D., Vaccarezza, M. S. (eds.) (2021). *Practical Wisdom. Philosophical and Psychological Perspectives*. Routledge.

DePaul, M. R. (1993). *Balance and Refinement Beyond Coherence Methods of Moral Inquiry*. Routledge.

Davidson, D. (1963). Actions, Reasons, and Causes. *The Journal of Philosophy*, 60(23), American Philosophical Association, Eastern Division, Sixtieth Annual Meeting (Nov. 7, 1963), 685–700. https://doi.org/10.2307/2023177

Gersbach, R. (2016). *Practical Reasoning: Its Elements, Practicality and Validity*. Mentis. DOI:10.30965/9783957438515

Lovibond, S. (2004). *Ethical Formation*. Harvard University Press.

McDowell, J. (1998). *Mind, Value, Reality*. Harvard University Press.

Martha Nussbaum, M. (2001). *Upheavals of Thought. Cambridge University Press*. https://doi.org/10.1017/CBO9780511840715

Ross, D. (2002). *The Right and the Good*. Oxford University Press.

Scanlon, T. M. (1998). *What We Owe Each Other*. Harvard University Press.

Smith, M. (1994). *The Moral Problem*. Blackwell.

Solomon, R. (2008). *True to our Feelings: What Our Emotions Are Really Telling us*. Oxford University Press. https://doi.org/10.1093/acprof:oso/9780195368536.001.0001

Sousa, R. d. (2001). Moral Emotions. *Ethical Theory and Moral Practice*, 4(2), Cultivating Emotions, 109–126. https://doi.org/10.1023/A:1011434921610

Tappolet, C. (2016). *Emotions, Values, and Agency*. Oxford University Press. https://doi.org/10.1093/acprof:oso/9780199696512.001.0001

# Bioethics in China

## Developments and Future Outlook

*Wei Zhu*

Bioethics, as an academic field examining ethical issues in life sciences and medical practice, has developed within a distinctive historical and socio-cultural context in China. Ever since its emergence in the 1980s, Chinese bioethics has undergone remarkable transformation – from initial conceptual introductions to its current state as an institutionalised framework guiding biomedical research and clinical practice. As of today, with the rapid economic growth and remarkable advancements in scientific and technological capabilities, the significance of bioethics in Chinese society has become increasingly prominent.

This paper attempts to systematically trace the developmental trajectory of bioethics in China, analysing how landmark events have shaped China's bioethical governance structures, regulatory framework, and institutionalisation mechanisms. It offers to touch upon the issues and challenges bioethics faces and proposes pathways and approaches to address and respond to these critical concerns.

### The Emergence and Development of Bioethics in China

The evolution of modern bioethics in China can be traced back to the 1980s, marking the early stages of China's reform and opening-up era. During this period, the introduction of Western medical ethics coincided with Chinese scholars' renewed exploration of the value of traditional Chinese medical ethical thought. Notable milestones include the publication of Professor Qiu Renzong's pioneering work *Bioethics* in 1987 (Qiu, 1987), alongside a series of pivotal cases that emerged in China following the 1980s. Since then, theoretical discourses within the field of bioethics and practical responses to real-world challenges have synergistically facilitated the refinement of ethical norms, collectively propelling the advancement of bioethics in China.

## China's First Euthanasia Case

The event that most prominently brought bioethics into China's public consciousness was the 1986 euthanasia case in Hanzhong, Shaanxi Province. In this case, a doctor in Hanzhong City, at the request of family members (one son and one daughter) of a terminal liver cancer patient suffering severe pain, administered compound chlorpromazine, which led to the patient's death. Subsequently, the patient's two other daughters sued both the doctor and their siblings (who had requested the euthanasia procedure). By 1987, local public security authorities had applied to the procuratorate to arrest the doctor and the family members involved on charges of intentional homicide, with a formal indictment filed in 1988. On April 6, 1991, the People's Court of Hanzhong City rendered a judgment:

> [...] the defendant Wang Mingcheng had the idea and repeatedly requested the attending doctor Pu Liansheng to inject drugs to end his mother's life painlessly. His actions clearly belong to the intentional act of depriving his mother of her right to life. However, the circumstances are extremely minor, and the harm is not significant, thus not constituting a crime. Defendant Pu Liansheng, at the repeated requests of Wang Mingcheng, along with other doctors, successively injected drugs to accelerate the death of the critically ill patient Xia Suwen, which played a certain role in promoting Xia's death. His actions are intentional acts of depriving citizens of their right to life. However, the circumstances are extremely minor, and the harm is not significant, thus not constituting a crime. In accordance with Article 10 of the Criminal Law of the People's Republic of China, Pu Liansheng and Wang Mingcheng are declared innocent. (Wang, 1990)

This landmark case triggered the first nationwide upsurge of discussions on "euthanasia", sparking intense cross-country debates on the legality, ethics, and morality of euthanasia. Not only did this case bring bioethics into the public spotlight, but it also directly spurred the convening of the first National Symposium on Euthanasia in 1988 (Meng, 1988). This historic conference brought together experts from diverse disciplines – including medicine, ethics, law, and sociology – for the first time to engage in systematic theoretical deliberations on bioethical issues. Marking the formal establishment of bioethics as an independent academic discipline in China, the symposium laid the groundwork for its subsequent development.

Concurrently, bioethics in China was for the first time recognised as a pivotal discipline in resolving practical challenges and addressing the ethical dilemmas posed by breakthroughs in life sciences and medical technology. In the immediate aftermath of this incident, several National People's Congress members initiated formal efforts to advance the legalisation of euthanasia in China (Geng, 2022).

## Gansu Province's "Regulation on Prohibiting Reproduction by the Mentally Disabled"

During the initial phase of China's reform and opening-up, the nation confronted multifold systemic challenges, with poverty emerging as a paramount socioeconomic hurdle. In the acutely impoverished rural regions of northwestern China (e.g., Gansu Province), the incidence of intellectual disabilities among new-borns exhibited an alarming upward trend, accompanied by discernible patterns of intergenerational transmission. Households with intellectually disabled members consistently demonstrated a higher poverty rate than regional averages. Additionally, within traditional familial norms, intellectually disabled male offspring were often expected to fulfil reproductive obligations – including marriage, procreation, and familial continuation. Consequently, local governance entities posited that mitigating such hereditary intellectual disabilities constituted an effective strategy to redress socioeconomic deprivation and enhance living standards. In 1988, the Gansu Provincial People's Congress issued *Regulation on Prohibiting Reproduction by the Mentally Disabled* in 1988 (Standing Committee of Gansu Provincial People's Congress, 1988). Similarly, Liaoning Province in northeast China promulgated the *Regulation on Preventing Inferior Births* in 1990 (Standing Committee of Liaoning Provincial People's Congress, 1990).

The promulgation of these provincial-level regulations has attracted the attention of scholars, especially those specialising in bioethics research. Field investigations revealed that in Gansu Province, the majority of individuals categorised as "intellectually disabled" are primarily patients with cretinism – a congenital disorder caused by iodine deficiency rather than genetic factors. However, due to the scarcity of medical personnel with systematic genetic expertise in the region, families with three generations of intellectually disabled members were simplistically attributed to genetic inheritance, leading to misclassification of numerous cretinism cases as hereditary intellectual disabilities.

Based on their investigative findings, researchers made dual efforts: first, they alerted local health authorities to the misdiagnosis of intellectual disabilities, clarifying that cretinism incidence can be effectively mitigated through the consumption of iodised salt. In the meantime, they argued that the stipulations in the provincial legislation were unethical. For one thing, the term "intellectually disabled" (operationalised as "dementia") perpetuated stigmatisation, contravening the *Law of the People's Republic of China on the Protection of Persons with Disabilities*. Second, researchers emphasised that the practice of requiring sterilisation of those intellectually disabled or any incompetent individuals should be based on voluntary informed consent from either the individuals themselves or their guardians, and no forced sterilisation should be allowed (Zovko, 2024).

Subsequently, at China's first Academic Symposium on Ethical and Legal Issues of Birth Restriction and Control in November 1991, participating scholars formally recommended to government authorities the abolition of the aforementioned discriminatory regulatory measures. Thereafter, the Ministry of Health disseminated the symposium's proceedings and policy recommendations to provincial health administrations, effectively terminating the legislative momentum that had emerged following the regulatory precedents established by Gansu and Liaoning provinces, rendering such measures legally invalid (Qiu, 1993a).

## The Chaos of Stem Cell Therapy

In the 21st century, translational medicine made significant progress in China. Around 2005, some Chinese medical institutions and biotech companies began offering unproven "stem cell therapies, "which hailed as "hopeful treatments" (Qiu, 2009), attracted attention in the international community soon. Many travelled to China for "stem cell tourism" (Kiatpongsan & Sipp, 2009), seeking help for conditions including amyotrophic lateral sclerosis (ALS), traumatic brain and spinal cord injuries, diabetes (Types I and II), autism, Parkinson's disease, Alzheimer's disease, ataxia, optic atrophy, neurological disorders, multiple sclerosis, stroke, myocardial damage, ischemic heart disease, and liver diseases (Qiu, 2013).

By 2007, the media (such as the September 2007 issue of *Xinmin Weekly*, for instance) noted the phenomenon and began exposing the chaos and confusion in the stem cell therapy (Li & Chen, 2007). According to *Xinmin Weekly*, a biotech company had been offering stem cell treatments to patients since 1999 without providing evidence of efficacy (Li & Chen, 2007). Concurrently, complaints from overseas patients about China's so-called stem cell therapies also brought the chaos and disorder to global attention (Cyranoski, 2009).

It was subsequently revealed that the chaotic situation surrounding stem cell therapy in China was closely tied to capital-driven motives. Fuelled by substantial profits, a complete industrial chain spanning stem cell procurement, preparation, production, and clinical administration in hospitals had been formed. Certain stem cell enterprises and institutions had exploited regulatory loopholes in policies and laws to engage in false advertising, exaggerating the therapeutic efficacy of stem cells and administering unproven clinical "treatments" (Consumer Report, 2024). More problematically, stem cell products lacked reliable quality assurance and traceable origin documentation. This had given rise to unethical practices such as unverified stem cells preparations, substitution of ordinary cells for stem cells in medical procedures, non-standardised preparation processes, cellular contamination, inadequate risk communication to patients, and exorbitant fee structures (Gao & Niu, 2023).

To address these pressing concerns, in 2015, the former National Health and Family Planning Commission (NHFPC) and the China Food and Drug Administration (CFDA) jointly promulgated the *Measures for the Administration of Stem Cell Clinical Research* (NHFPC & CFDA, 2015). This regulatory framework established a comprehensive qualification review and registration system for institutions engaged in stem cell preparation, clinical research, and therapeutic trials. The implementation of these measures has led to demonstrable improvements in standardising previously chaotic practices within China's stem cell therapy sector. To a certain degree, this national-level mandate has played a pivotal role in ethically regulating the development of emerging technologies.

## The Gene-Editing Scandal

Between March 2017 and November 2018, He Jiankui, a faculty member at Southern University of Science and Technology, and his research team conducted an unauthorised clinical trial involving eight consenting couples (comprising HIV-positive males and HIV-negative females). Utilising CRISPR/Cas9 gene-editing technology, the team employed Cas9 protein complexed with specifically designed guide RNA to modify the CCR5 gene in human zygotes, with the purported objective of conferring innate HIV resistance. The controversial experiment culminated in He's November 26, 2018 announcement of the birth of genetically modified twins (codenamed Lulu and Nana), whom he claimed possessed "natural immunity to HIV infection" (Baidu Encyclopedia, 2025).

This unprecedented intervention in the human germline sparked immediate international condemnation from both the scientific community and bioethics scholars, while simultaneously triggering widespread public debate about the ethical boundaries of genetic engineering. The controversy acted as a decisive impetus for comprehensive regulatory restructuring in China's oversight framework for gene-editing technologies.

China's legislative response materialised through a series of coordinated legal reforms. The 2019 Biosecurity Law introduced stringent regulatory protocols governing gene-editing research, while the 2020 Civil Code codified explicit prohibitions against unauthorised genetic interventions (Wang, 2025). Furthermore, Article 336 of the Criminal Law was substantially revised to impose graduated criminal sanctions, stipulating that "Implantation of gene-edited or cloned human embryos into human or animal recipients, or implantation of gene-edited/cloned animal embryos into humans" shall be subject to criminal penalties "when such acts meet threshold severity criteria" (Jia, 2024).

These four landmark cases have served as critical catalysts in the normative development of bioethical governance in China. They not only facilitated a crucial paradigm shift from abstract philosophical discourse to applied ethical problem-solving, highlighting bioethics' capacity to address concrete biomedical dilemmas, but also contributed significantly to the institutionalisation of bioethics in China.

## The Institutionalisation and Current Development of Bioethics in China

The development of bioethics in China has been always accompanied by practical issues arising in scientific fields. As a result, its institutionalisation and ethical oversight have gradually improved over time.

As early as 1999, the National Medical Products Administration (NMPA) promulgated China's first Good Clinical Practice (GCP) for Drug Clinical Trials (NMPA, 1999). This landmark regulation mandated in Article 9 that "medical institutions conducting clinical trials shall establish ethics committees to protect participants' rights and ensure public trust." In December 2016, the former National Health and Family Planning Commission (now the National Health Commission, NHC) issued the *Ethical Review Measures for Biomedical Research Involving Human Subjects* (NHFPC, 2016), which marked a significant expansion of ethical oversight requirements.

Following the 2018 He Jiankui gene-editing scandal, the Standing Committee of the 13th National People's Congress revised and adopted the Drug Administration Law in 2019 (NPC, 2019), marking the first time for ethical review to be codified into law. The Civil Code, implemented in 2021, further clarified the scope and procedures for human clinical trials, reinforcing the institutional role of ethics committees (NPC, 2020). And in 2020, the National Committee for Science and Technology Ethics was established (China News Service, 2020).

In 2023, the NHC and the Ministry of Science and Technology (MOST) promulgated the Measures for Ethical Review of Life Sciences and Medical Research Involving Humans and the Interim Measures for Ethical Review of Science and Technology respectively (NHC, 2023; MST, 2023).

With the enactment of these regulations, it may be said that China's ethical governance framework has now taken shape. While early institutional review boards (IRBs) were primarily established in medical institutions, since 2019, ethical governance mechanisms have been built across the country with more ethics review committees being set up in diverse research institutions, including medical and non-medical institutions, universities, and enterprises.

Key provisions in the 2023 *Measures for the Ethical Review of Life Science and Medical Research Involving Humans* (led by the NHC and three other ministries) state:

> If an institution conducting life science or medical research involving humans has not established an ethics committee or its existing committee lacks the capacity to conduct the review, the institution may entrust a qualified ethics committee (either from another institution or a regional one) to perform the review in writing. (NHC, 2023)

Similarly, the 2023 *Interim Measures for Ethical Review of Science and Technology* (issued by the MOST and ten other ministries) specify:

> Higher education institutions, research organisations, healthcare providers, and enterprises are responsible for their own ethical review management.

> Institutions engaged in life sciences, medicine, artificial intelligence, or other sensitive areas must establish science and technology ethics (review) committee. Others may form such committees as needed. (MST, 2023)

These regulations explicitly mandate the establishment of science and technology ethics committees in both medical and non-medical fields subject to ethical review. This regulatory framework provides explicit ethical regulation and guidance for interdisciplinary or cross-sectoral research, thereby preventing recurrences of incidents such as He Jiankui gene-editing scandal.

At present, China's existing ethical governance system is basically compromised of "ethics committees of four different types of committees": national-level ethics committees, provincial-level ethics committees, regional ethics committees, and institutional ethics committees. Statistics show that there are currently 9,771 ethics committees registered with China's National Health Commission, of which 9,571 are affiliated with healthcare institutions (Liu, 2023). This figure does not include research ethics committees established by universities and other scientific research organisations. All regional or institutional ethics committees are required to register and file records on the registration platforms of either the National Health Commission or the Ministry of Science and Technology. China's bioethics governance framework has now been comprehensively established and refined across the nation.

## The "Localisation" and Value Debates of Bioethics

Parallel to the institutional development of bioethics in China, debates persist regarding what discursive framework Chinese bioethics should adopt, its relationship with Western bioethics, and whether China should reconstruct its own bioethical paradigm.

One perspective argues that Chinese bioethics should be localised and reconstructed using China's unique cultural content and language. According to scholars holding this view, the cultural background and quintessential value of Chinese bioethics differ from its Western counterpart in that we deem harmony as its core value base, reflecting a communitarian or collectivist approach, while the Western culture and tradition hails independence and individualism. Some have even proposed "familism" as a counterpart to Western individualism (Fan, 1997).

Proceeding from this concept of contrasting Eastern and Western values, some scholars have suggested emulating the Western bioethical paradigm but replacing its Western content with Chinese elements. For example, they have proposed replacing the "four principles" of Western bioethics with Confucian-inspired principles of harmony, benevolence, justice, and integrity (Fan & Wang, 2009). A more essentialist view posits that it is the traditional Chinese ethical thoughts that constitute the core value of Chinese bioethics, and that a Chinese bioethical framework conceptualised this way then be applied to the study of bioethical issues (Zhang, 2008).

Contrary to the aforementioned views, another universalist point of view stands that bioethical principles represent the universal human assets transcending culture. Turning a blind eye to the shared values and principles under the guise of cultural preservation will harm patients, research participants, and stakeholders, and therefore, is an ethically indefensible position (Qiu, 1993b). For instance, advocating familism in clinical decision-making – using family consent to replace individual consent – an absurd excuse for respecting Chinese culture – has led to fatal treatment delays, sparking public outrage (Zhu, 2009).

Proponents of this universalist perspective argue that differences between Eastern and Western values are merely variations in the application of universal principles in different cultural contexts. Take the "four principles" as an example. In different cultures, their order of importance may differ. In China, it is often the case where the principle of beneficence/non-maleficence is prioritised over respect for autonomy, a preference and ordering rooted in the Chinese cultural and based on the holistic consideration of the relationship between the individual and society. This does not mean, however, that Chinese society rejects other principles (Qiu, 1993b).

It is to be noted that the peripheral aspects of the core values of the four principles may not remain the same with the change of the cultural scenarios. For example, the role of the family in medical decision-making can vary across cultural settings, regions within the same culture, or individuals holding different values, leading to significant differences in clinical decision-making models. This does not imply that families in the East or China always hold primacy in clinical decisions. Therefore, what the universalists hold true to themselves, is that differences in values between the East and West are not fundamental or irreconcilable (Qiu, 1993b).

Between these two positions lies a more moderate view, which argues that there actually exists "overlapping consensuses" – principles affirmed by all traditional belief systems – among different moral traditions. This "middle party" advocates for the development of a set of "intermediary principles" that are compatible with both Chinese traditional ethics and the areas of overlaps identified through the method of reflective equilibrium (Luo et al., 2013).

While academic discourses continue to diverge on key questions – such as whether to advocate for bioethics with distinct Chinese characteristics and the extent of universality in ethical principles, one fact remains incontrovertible: all parties involved in the debates have dedicated themselves to exploring the practical application of existing theoretical frameworks, aiming to tackle and respond to the unique ethical dilemmas emerging in Chinese society. In this intellectual endeavour, the Confucian essence of "harmony without uniformity (和而不同)" (Confucius, 500BC) provides a particularly compelling theoretical framework, offering both historical depth and contemporary relevance.

Likewise, the four fundamental principles – respect for autonomy, non-maleficence, beneficence, and justice – are also universally applicable across nations, regardless of social, historical, experiential, or cultural differences. These values echo what is deeply rooted in Confucian tradition. Mencius' notion of "To do no harm is the essence of benevolent practice" (无伤，仁术也) (Mencius, 150 BC), while Xunzi's notion of "A benevolent person must respect others "(仁者，必敬人) (Xunzi, 255 BC).

Nevertheless, as Confucius observed, "Human nature is similar; habits diverge widely" (性相近，习相远) (Confucius, 500 BC). This perhaps explains why social, cultural, and historical differences must be considered in the application of these universally proven principles. It is precisely for this reason that the order of importance of these principles may vary in real practice.

## Challenges and Future Development of Bioethics in China

Against the backdrop of rapid breakthroughs in cutting-edge technologies – including translational medicine, gene-editing applications, and AI-driven healthcare – China's bioethical governance framework is undergoing dynamic evolution. Yet several entrenched challenges and emerging complexities demand careful consideration. These include not only the tensions between global ethical norms and localised value systems, but also the structural conflicts between breakneck technological advancement and inadequate regulatory system, as well as the governance dilemmas between centralised policy frameworks and decentralised implementation realities.

First, the advancement of emerging technologies presents significant challenges to ethical governance. Like other countries and regions in the world, China also faces the problem of regulatory fragmentation in overseeing these technologies.

Regulatory fragmentation refers not only to the significant disparities in policies across different countries regarding emerging technologies, which lead to "regulatory arbitrage" (where researchers and companies tend to conduct more controversial studies in regions with looser regulations) (Tigerstrom, 2008). It also manifests domestically through loopholes and grey areas between various regulatory bodies and laws.

The He Jiankui scandal serve a typical example for this systemic fragmentation. The fact that He was able to forge ethical review approvals and conduct his trial from recruitment to implementation without oversight is directly tied to the lack of coordinated regulatory and ethical governance.

Similarly, despite regulatory efforts to curb unethical stem cell practices, violations persist, highlighting inadequacies in current policies like the 2015 *Stem Cell Clinical Research Management Measures*, which urgently require revision. This is to say that though there are regulatory updates, what is needed is a holistic ethical-regulatory paradigm – one that closes legal cracks while ensuring morally grounded governance. A case in point here is the work by government bodies such as the Ministry of Science and Technology (MST), the National Health Commission (NHC), and the National Medical Products Administration (NMPA). Although these government authorities do collaborate in ethical governance (for example, they jointly formulated the 2023 ethical review measures), their jurisdictions differ, leading to regulatory loopholes and coordination challenge, especially for interdisciplinary research spanning multiple domains.

Secondly, emerging technologies present additional challenges to the ongoing development of bioethics. The institutionalisation of bioethics in China has played a pivotal role in advancing the discipline's development and facilitating the orderly governance and compliant progress of medicine, life sciences, and emerging technologies. However, it cannot be overlooked that together with the fruit of institutionalisation, tendencies toward formalism, bureaucratisation, and devaluation of ethical values have emerged.

One manifestation is the over-reliance on abstract ethical principles, which reduces complex moral dilemmas to mere logical inference between competing principles. Some even attempt to replace ethical deliberation with "value-neutral" scientific methods (e.g. cost-benefit analyses, quantitative risk assessment), thereby prioritising technical efficiency at the expense of moral dimensions (Wang & Hao, 2024).

Another critical concern resides in the reduction of ethics to mere legal and administrative compliance. Take, for instance, the decision-making process within research ethics committees, which has become increasingly standardised (i.e. by considering only elements like risk-benefit assessment checklists, informed consent templates, and ethics review checklists). This standardisation has fostered an excessive dependence on bureaucratic procedures, a direct result of "procedural compliance" formalism, thereby overshadowing the need for substantive ethical analysis and dialogic engagement (Zhao, 2024).

Furthermore, administrative authority in ethical governance, while occasionally necessary, poses risks of power imbalances and conflicts of interest in decision-making, ultimately undermining the very goals of ethical governance (Yu, Ling & Li, 2021).

Thirdly, public distrust of emerging technologies poses another challenge for bioethics in China. The occurrence of He Jiankui scandal has further eroded public trust in science and the scientific community at large. While specific survey data remains limited, scholars have noted a marked increase in public scepticism toward gene editing and other emerging technologies in the aftermath of the scandal (Braun, 2019). As a matter of fact, this erosion of trust extended beyond the scientific community to include concerns about the effectiveness of ethical oversight institutions – a lack of confidence that called for systemic reforms.

To respond to these multifaceted challenges, the future development of Chinese bioethics necessitates concerted efforts in the following dimensions.

Institutionally, the government, scientists, and ethicists should strengthen collaboration to consolidate and expand the positive outcomes of existing institutionalisation and ethical governance. Efforts must be made to improve the situation where fragmented management still prevails, to reduce the negative impacts of formalistic and bureaucratic tendencies on ethical oversight and review mechanisms, and enhance systemic coordination.

In governance, it is essential to leverage the soft regulatory function of ethical governance to ensure the full actualisation of ethics committees' independence and professionalism, facilitate high-quality and responsible scientific research, and effectively fulfil the government's regulatory duties. To this end, an adaptive governance framework should be established and operationalised to enable the system to respond with alacrity to emerging technologies. The National Science and Technology Ethics Committee established in 2020 should assume the role of top-tier design in ethical governance to fulfil this overarching objective.

Theoretically, it is imperative to conduct in-depth inquiry into ethical dilemmas arising from the application of emerging technologies within China's unique socioeconomic and cultural milieu. This intellectual endeavour entails not only exploring solutions tailored to China's cultural and social topography but also excavating the endogenous cultural resources and axiological foundations that undergird such solutions.

It is necessary to note that bioethical decision-making in China is largely expert-driven, with limited mechanisms for meaningful public participation. A lack of robust public engagement mechanisms risks producing policies that fail to reflect societal values or address community concerns.

Therefore, it is essential for China to develop science communication programs to enhance the public's understanding of emerging technologies. Meanwhile, strengthening public debates on ethical issues surrounding emerging technologies is equally important. Such mechanisms for public discourse and engagement should be institutionalised to ensure that public voices are not only heard, but also meaningfully incorporated into public policy decision-making.

In conclusion, the evolution of bioethics in China represents a remarkable case study in the globalisation and localisation of ethical thought. The challenges posed by emerging technologies to bioethics in China require collaborative efforts among ethicists, scientists, the government, and the general public to take action together.

## References

Baidu Encyclopedia. (n.d.) *Gene-Edited Babies Incident*. https://baike.baidu.com/item/%E5%9F%BA%E5%9B%A0%E7%BC%96%E8%BE%91%E5%A9%B4%E5%84%BF%E4%BA%8B%E4%BB%B6/23176263. Retrieved July 6, 2025.

Braun, M., & Meacham, D. (2019, January 2). The trust game: CRISPR for human germline editing unsettles scientists and society. *EMBO Reports, 20*, e47583. https://doi.org/10.15252/embr.201847583

China News Service. (2020, October 21). *China Has Established the National Committee on Science and Technology Ethics*. https://www.chinanews.com/gn/2020/10-21/9319022.shtml

Confucius. (500 BC). *The Analects* https://wenku.baidu.com/view/02b471319c3143323968011ca300a6c30d22f1dc.html

Consumer Report. (2024, October 18). *"Saving" Lives Turns into "Taking" Lives: Stem Cell Scams Emerge One After Another, and the Elderly Are a High-Risk Group for Being Deceived*. https://www.toutiao.com/article/7427009422582481427

Cyranoski, D. (2009). Stem-cell therapy faces more scrutiny in China. *Nature*, 459(7244), 146–147. https://doi.org/10.1038/459146a

Fan, R.P. (1997). Self-Determination vs. Two Incommensurable Principles of Autonomy. *Bioethics, 11*(3–4), 309–322. https://doi.org/10.1111/1467-8519.00070

Fan, R.P., & Wang, M.X. (2009). Construct Chinese Bioethics and Promote Health Reform and Development. *Chinese Medical Ethics, 22*(6), 13–14.

GAO, Y., & Niu, Y. (2023, December 12). Scams Often Use the Banner of Stem Cells. Life Times. https://www.lifetimes.cn/article/4Fj28G3ADpX

Geng, X.Q. (2022, March 10). *Deputy to the National People's Congress: Proposes Legalizing Euthanasia. China Youth Daily Client*. Beijing Internet Publishing. https://news.cyol.com/gb/articles/2022-03/10/content_YAWvLTm96.html

Jia, Y. (2024). The Criminal Law Regulation of Gene-technology Utilization Behaviors. *Legal Science*, 4. https://law.ucass.edu.cn/info/1985/7322.htm

Kiatpongsan, S., & Sipp, D. (2009). Monitoring and Regulating Offshore Stem Cell Clinics. *Science*, 323(5921), 1564–1565. https://doi.org/10.1126/science.1168451

Li, Z., & Chen, B. (2007). Investigation into the Truth of Stem Cells. *Xinmin Weekly, 38*, 24–30.

Liu, G.S. (2023, June 2–3). n. t. [Conference Presentation]. ECD 2023, Shanghai.

Luo, B.X., Chen, Q.L., & Zhang, Y. (2013). *Philosophical Reflections on Bioethics from a Chinese Perspective*, (123–124). China Renmin University Press.

Meng, X. W. (1988). A Brief Account of the National Symposium on Euthanasia. *Morality and Civilization*, (5), 18–19.https://doi.10.13904/j.cnki.1007-1539.1988.05.009

Mencius. (150 BC). *Mencius · Liang Hui Wang I*. https://mengzi.5000yan.com/

Ministry of Science and Technology, et al. (2023, September 7). *Measures for the Review of Science and Technology Ethics* (Trial). https://www.gov.cn/gongbao/2023/issue_10826/202311/content_6915814.html. Accessed on July 3, 2025.

National Health and Family Planning Commission & China Food and Drug Administration. (2015, July 20). Measures for the Administration of Stem Cell

Clinical Research (Trial). https://mp.weixin.qq.com/s?.... Accessed on July 3, 2025.

National Health Commission, et al. (2023). *Notice on Issuing the Measures for Ethical Review of Research Involving Human Life Sciences and Medical Sciences*. https://www.gov.cn/zhengce/zhengceku/2023-02/28/content_5743658.htm.

Qiu, J. (2009). Trading on Hope. *Nature Biotechnology, 27*, 790–792. https://doi.org/10.1038/nbt0909-790

Qiu, R.Z. (1987). *Bioethics*. Shanghai People's Publishing House.

Qiu, R.Z. (1993a). Summary of the National First Academic Symposium on Ethics and Legal Issues of Childbearing Restriction and Control. *Chinese Health Law* (5), 44–46.

Qiu, R.Z. (1993b). Bioethics in Developing Countries—A Chinese Perspective. *Chinese Medical Ethics*, 4, 5–12.

Qiu, R.Z. (2013). Behind the Vogue for "Stem Cell Therapy": Ethical and Regulatory Issues in Clinical Translation of Stem Cell. *Science and Society, 3*(1), 8–25. https://doi.org/10.19524/j.cnki.10-1009/g3.2013.01.002

Standing Committee of Gansu Provincial People's Congress. (1988, November 23). Regulations on Prohibiting Childbearing by Persons with Dementia and Intellectual Disabilities. November 23, 1988. https://www.110.com/fagui/law_162951.html. Accessed on July 3, 2025.

Standing Committee of Liaoning Provincial People's Congress. (1990, January 13). Regulations of Liaoning Province on Preventing Dysgenesis. https://law.lawtime.cn/d526536531630.html. Accessed on July 3, 2025.

The National Medical Products Administration (NMPA, 1999). Good Clinical Practice (GCP) for Drug Clinical Trials. *China Medical Herald* (1), 5–9.

The National People's Congress. (2020, May 28). Civil Code of the People's Republic of China [EB/OL]. https://www.gov.cn/xinwen/2020-06/01/content_5516649.htm. Accessed on July 3, 2025.

The NPC Standing Committee. (2015, April 24). Law of the People's Republic of China on Drug Administration [EB/OL]. https://www.gov.cn/xinwen/2

Tigerstrom, B.J. (2008). The challenges of regulating stem cell-based products. *Trends in Biotechnology, 26*(12), 653–658. https://doi.org/10.1016/j.tibtech.2008.08.004

Wang, H.J., & Hao, Y.Q. (2024). The Obscuration and Disclosure of the Principle of Fairness in Digital Governance. *Academics Journal, 308*(1), 97–105.

Wang, H.L. (1990). On the First "Euthanasia" Case in China. *People's Justice* (9), 38–40. https://doi.org/10.19684/j.cnki.1002-4603.1990.09.022

Wang, K. (2025, March 19). *On the Private Law Regulation of Human Germline Genome Editing*. Sohu News. https://news.sohu.com/a/873035319_254324

Xunzi. (255 BC). Xunzi. On the Way of Ministers. https://hanyu.baidu.com/shici/detail?pid=eb6435b476ad75180de56279eaf600bd. Accessed on July 3, 2025.

Yu, X., Ling, Y., & Li, L. (2021). Ethical Governance of Emerging Science and Technology: Issues and Strategies. *Science and Society, 11*(4), 51–65.

Zhang, S. Q. (2008). Is a Confucian Bioethics Possible? *Morality and Civilization*, 4, 52–56. https://doi.org/10.13904/j.cnki.1007–1539.2008.04.017

Zhao, W.Y. (2024, July). The Legal Realization of the Medical Ethics Review System. *East China Law Review*. https://mp.weixin.qq.com/s? Accessed on July 5, 2025.

Zhu, W. (2009). *Informed Consent in Bioethics*. Fudan University Press.

Zovko, J. (2024, December). Current Biethical Challenges: A Conversation with Renzong Qiu. *Distinctio, 3*(2), 7–33. Also published in Chinese: *Jianghuai Tribune* 2025(1). https://doi.org/10.16064/j.cnki.cn34-1003/g0.2025.01.002

Impactful Bioethics

# A Path Forward – and Outward

## Repositioning Bioethics to Face Future Challenges[1]

*Vardit Ravitsky*

Bioethics has never been one thing. It is not a discipline with a research methodology. It does not have unifying theoretical or ideological commitments. What unifies the field is a set of challenges. Bioethics is also inherently evolving; it responds to biomedical developments against a backdrop of shifting social contexts. If anything, it is an ever-expanding collection of approaches, allowing rich explorations of an ever-changing set of problems.

Within this evolving landscape, The Hastings Center has played a constitutive role from the very early days. Looking back at the scope of its work over the last five decades, starting with the influential work of the Center's founders, Daniel Callahan and Willard Gaylin, one can clearly see that its vision has always been expansive and inclusive. I am honored to begin my role, as of September 2023, as president of this internationally respected organization and to stand on the shoulders of renowned leaders and scholars who have shaped its history and inspired my own work for years.

As The Hastings Center considers strategic priorities for its research, public engagement, and impact, I welcome the opportunity to share some reflections regarding where we have been and where we are going. Someone once told me, when discussing the expanding scope of bioethics, "If The Hastings Center says it's bioethics, then it is." This view underlies the sense of responsibility I feel as the Center contemplates the scope and emphasis of its future scholarship and activities. I therefore share these thoughts as a first step, offering my own vision in order to invite an open and wide-ranging conversation

1 Reprinted from Vardit Ravitsky (2023). A Path Forward – and Outward: Repositioning Bioethics to Face Future Challenges. *The Hastings Center Report*, 53(5), 7–10, by permission of John Wiley & Sons and The Hastings Center. https://doi.org/10.1002/hast.1510

about the future of bioethics and the role that the Center can and should play within it.

In the 1960s and '70s, bioethics was a nascent field, led by philosophers and theologians, focusing on the protection of individuals from powerful and often paternalistic systems. In the 1980s and '90s, an increasingly diverse cohort of scholars became involved, but the core of the field's interest remained individuals and their autonomy, with an emphasis on their rights as patients and research participants. Those first decades gave birth to important principles, frameworks, and policies that are the basis of patient care and research practices to this day. In subsequent years, bioethics put greater emphasis on diverse methodologies, such as empirical bioethics; saw emerging specializations, such as neuroethics; and developed more nuanced theoretical tools, such as relational accounts of autonomy.

Multiple versions of the story of bioethics have been told, and a definite history of the field is yet to be written. What seems clear, however, is that with the ongoing emphasis on individual autonomy, bioethics gave inadequate attention to the fact that issues related to the common good are just as relevant to health and well-being as those related to individual interests. In recent years, our field at large has started to recognize that many of the challenges bioethics confronts result from structural issues, such as racism or poverty, that can be addressed only at the systemic level, not at the bedside. As Mildred Solomon, The Hastings Center's president emerita, put it in the May-June 2023 issue of this journal, we started focusing on "problems for which society needs guidance ... to protect our shared environment, or, more specifically, the physical and the social, political, and economic environments that we all depend on."

In this essay, I wish to explore what the future holds if bioethics continues its evolution to become a field that embraces systemic, collective-level challenges; has a global scale and focus; emphasizes human flourishing; and seeks to have increased societal impact.

## Exploring Possible Futures of Bioethics

What should the future of bioethics look like? What should our field focus on? Should it merely deepen and intensify the well-established focus of mainstream bioethics, or should it expand and reposition itself? And if the latter, in what ways?

In recent conversations with colleagues, some have argued that venturing out into systemic challenges that impact human health only indirectly, such as climate change or migration, would overstretch our boundaries, dilute our expertise, and make us less effective. We spent decades, they argued, developing an expertise and honing skills and tools that allow us to do important work in the well-defined areas of patient care, health care delivery, biomedical research, emerging biotechnologies, and the policies guiding all these. Other fields, they argued, should worry about other challenges. We should continue to focus on health care and biomedical research.

In return, I have been arguing that bioethics should and must continue to evolve and expand – that without doing so, it will compromise its ability to do timely needed work and will become less relevant in today's world. Developing the field in this way would actually entail a retrieval and reinvigoration of some of the field's founding figures' insights that were eclipsed early on in our history. It would require expanding beyond individualistic and health care-focused approaches toward notions such as the common good as found in Callahan's work, ecological and global bioethics as found in Van Rensselaer Potter's work, and "the imperative of responsibility" for the whole of nature and future generations as found in Hans Jonas's work.

In my own work on emerging reproductive and genomics technologies I have seen the importance of tackling issues related to inequity, lack of access, and impact on future people. My public engagement during the Covid-19 pandemic highlighted the tragedy of neglecting to address global justice. And as past president of the International Association of Bioethics, I have come to believe that building bioethics capacity globally can make a real difference in helping us address urgent challenges, pay appropriate attention to diverse perspectives, and recognize what matters to people in their own cultural contexts. I thus offer a vision for the future of bioethics that would allow the field to better engage with such challenges.

*From individual to collective-level issues.* Bioethics has been recognizing the limitations of trying to address issues affecting individuals without recognizing that they are embedded in familial, cultural, organizational, and societal contexts that must be considered. We became interested in the ethical dimensions of social determinants of health and of health disparities. We also started acknowledging that resource-allocation challenges are present in every aspect of health care, not just in deciding who gets a kidney or a ventilator, and that our conceptual tools for addressing issues of justice, fairness, and equity are underdeveloped and need to become much more sophisticated.

We have been moving from a focus on negative rights and the protection of the individual against systemic forces to a consideration of positive rights, to asking what humans owe each other. We even expanded our vision from research ethics principles focused on protection from exploitation to those addressing the right to be included in research, and even to solidarity as an underlying value that invites us to consider a possible responsibility to participate in research. These shifts in our attention encourage us to have an overall focus on collective-level challenges.

The Covid-19 pandemic was a dramatic wake-up call for bioethics. The daily and excruciating tensions between individual freedoms and the common good, as they played out in heated debates surrounding lockdowns, curfews, school closures, or vaccine mandates, required sophisticated tools of public health ethics. Theories of justice and resource-allocation frameworks were needed to feed into policies surrounding triage protocols, national vaccination priorities, and the debate regarding vaccine nationalism versus global vaccine equity. Bioethics contributed to the fast-changing response to the pandemic, but the crisis also exposed multiple ways in which the field was not ready to tackle these collective-level challenges. Bioethicists should consider the lessons this pandemic offers about the theoretical and practical tools the field should further develop and refine.

*From local to global.* The pandemic showed us that viruses do not recognize national borders and that, as the World Health Organization insisted, "[n]o one is safe until everyone is safe." It gave new, epidemiological, meaning to the notion of the global village. Other challenges that are coming our way, such as those stemming from the digital economy and the integration of artificial intelligence (AI) into every aspect of human lives, are giving additional meanings to the notion of an interconnected world.

But beyond these empirical factors lie the fundamental normative concepts of global justice, equity, solidarity, and what all human beings owe each other. In that sense, the impact of global disparities on human flourishing ought to become a core issue for bioethicists. We need to move beyond the focus on the values of individuals and of the different communities and cultures in which individuals are situated to those that undergird a truly global bioethics. As a field, we started addressing these, but most of the work still lies ahead.

Thinking globally also means learning to take diversity seriously. It is one thing to develop tools for culturally sensitive care within a predominantly Western liberal democracy. It is quite another to promote bioethics exchange across political, cultural, and religious frameworks that hold deeply diverse values and commitments. In a 2023 *American Journal of Bioethics* article, for example, colleagues and I have proposed principles for engaging the global bioethics community in conversations across truly diverse perspectives, via the hosting of international conferences, with an emphasis on antidiscrimination, global awareness, and inclusiveness. While this vision for the future of our field is not a call for ethical relativism, I do suggest that we should explore ways to promote epistemic justice and create global tables where multiple voices have a seat.

*From human health to human flourishing.* Bioethics should move beyond a focus on human health and set the more ambitious goal of exploring the conditions for human flourishing even beyond the WHO's famously broad definition of health as a "state of complete physical, mental and social well-being and not merely the absence of disease or infirmity." Attention to factors such as race, indigeneity, gender, sexuality, and disability are crucial for understanding and overcoming the systems of oppression that stand in the way of the flourishing of all. This more ambitious bioethics should be about removing barriers to flourishing and building societies that promote it.

Some of the issues that plague our societies, such as gun violence, domestic violence, homelessness, or threats to democracy, may not be directly related to biomedicine. Others, such as poverty, racism, war, global warming, or misinformation, are indirectly related to the provision of health care. But all these challenges definitely constrain the ability of individuals, communities, and nations to thrive, to enjoy the right to health, and to "share in scientific advancement and its benefits," as the Universal Declaration of Human Rights envisioned.

The Hastings Center has been taking an expansive approach to bioethics for many years. It is therefore well positioned to help lead this vision of the future of bioethics and to chart a course that broadens the scope of our field and opens the door to new challenges.

*From scholarship to impact.* From the labors of over half a century, bioethics has produced superb scholarship and a literary canon. We have created a rich and nuanced knowledge base, both conceptual and empirical, expressed in articles, commentaries, books, and reports, that was disseminated in all the usual scientific venues. Many of us have used this expertise to contribute to decision-making, through membership in presidential or national commissions, advisory boards, steering committees, and various policy tables. Some of us have been engaging regularly with the media and making genuine efforts to make bioethics more accessible to the general public. However, at the end of the day, mainstream bioethics resides in the academic world. This means that when we train new generations of scholars, when we worry about their job security and career progression, we do not emphasize aspects that are still perceived as "service," that are less valued and recognized than scholarly output.

Going forward, bioethics should, I argue, acknowledge impact as a core mission, one of equal value to scholarship. Impact can mean various things – contribution to policy development, to implementation of recommendations, to public engagement and education, and to mainstream and social media. Such contributions should not be seen as peripheral to our mission. They should be key considerations in how we train bioethicists, how we formulate our research questions and write our grant proposals, and how we evaluate our achievements.

Bioethics will continue to ask philosophically intriguing questions, explore thought experiments, extrapolate possible scenarios, and prepare anticipatory conceptual frameworks. Such work will remain a unique and important part of our DNA. But impact is a critical part of our raison d'être, and we should find ways to consider it all along the pipeline of our knowledge creation and use. Impact is not just about visibility; it is about added value. It should not be a side product but, rather, the driver of many of our endeavors. We now know that misinformation kills. We now see the urgent need to create spaces for genuine exchange in an increasingly polarized world. We saw during the pandemic how bioethics principles were needed daily for policy decisions. Going forward, we should acknowledge the importance of impact and design our field to meet its challenges.

*From a field to a hub.* As a field, we have done tremendous work internally. We mapped the regions of our territory: delineated specialties such as clinical ethics, research ethics, and public health ethics; identified subfields of interest, such as reproductive ethics, animal ethics, and now AI ethics; opened our ranks to an increasingly diverse set of scholars from various disciplines, who employ many methodologies. We constructed our identity. We have research centers, graduate programs, journals, and dedicated conferences. We have a place at many policy tables dealing with health care and biomedical research. It is now meaningful to say, "I am a bioethicist."

Now, bioethics needs to be about building bridges that reach beyond our territory.

I propose the metaphor of bioethics as a hub. Expanding its mission and scope in the ways I described means that we need even more players. We need to engage with additional partners, disciplines, methods, ways of knowing, and a very broad range of perspectives. This does not mean that all these players should be seen as, or define themselves as, bioethicists. It means that we are recognized enough to use our convening power and become a hub of thinking and activity.

Bioethics has always been a field united by the complex problems it was trying to explore, using toolboxes that evolved as needed. In an increasingly complex and interconnected world, bioethics needs to go beyond interdisciplinarity and become a collaborative force that operates as a hub for multiple viewpoints, conceptual frameworks, values systems, disciplinary approaches, and methodologies. It should have soft boundaries that invite to the table all relevant stakeholders, especially those who are at the margins of what has been considered bioethics to date.

## Forward and Outward

The Hastings Center's mission has been aligned with this expansive vision of bioethics from the very outset. The Center is also uniquely positioned to influence the future path of bioethics, due to its historical foundations and the respect it has earned over decades as a trusted independent source. As our field responds to emerging threats, how should the Center leverage its long-standing expertise and influence to help shift our attention? What role can it play in the effort to orient and reposition our field? I am excited for the opportunity to collaborate with people at and beyond the Center in finding effective answers to these questions.

Moving bioethics forward and outward means proactively seeking epistemic justice and diversifying our field. It requires that we keep an open mind about what the scope of bioethics can and should be as we strive for global human flourishing, to increase the impact of our work, and to find creative ways of using our convening powers. We have made incredible progress, and we are standing on the shoulders of giants who have provided the insights we now need to move forward. Much remains to be done. It is time to expand and reposition our field to face future challenges.

## Acknowledgments

I would like to thank the many bioethicists who have discussed these ideas with me, as well as Joe Fins, Brad Gray, Erik Parens, Greg Kaebnick, Ryan Sauder, Bryn Williams-Jones, Charles Dupras, Jean-Christophe Bélisle-Pipon, and Art Caplan, who provided comments on this essay.

# Bioethics, Ethics, and Policy

*David Archard*

In this chapter I want to explore the relation between bioethics, ethics and policy. In doing so I intend to address the question of how we should define bioethics and say something about the proper relation of bioethics to policy and law, before briefly drawing out the implications for the relation between ethics and other disciplines.

A simplified contrast between a broader and narrower construal of bioethics is a good place to start. On the narrow understanding, bioethics is a sub-domain of practical ethics which is itself a sub-domain of ethics. James Childress and Tom Beauchamp elegantly summarize practical ethics and distinguish it from descriptive ethics in these terms in their seminal text on biomedical ethics:

> Practical ethics refers to the use of moral concepts and norms in deliberations about moral problems, practices, and policies in professions, institutions, and public policy [...] Descriptive ethics is the factual investigation of moral beliefs and conduct. For example, anthropologists, sociologists, psychologists and historians determine which moral norms are expressed in professional practices, in professional codes, institutional mission statements and in public policies. (Beauchamp and Childress, 2019, p. 2)

The early development of bioethics in the 1970s was part of a 'practical turn' in philosophy. The phrase consciously echoes and perhaps gently mocks the 'linguistic turn' of 20 years earlier when philosophers sought answers to philosophical puzzles in resolving the confusions of ordinary language. The practical turn, growing out of a frustration with the sterility and irrelevance of philosophy at a time of important social and political changes, was to critical issues of moral significance. In doing this practical ethics developed several sub-domains, of which bioethics was one. Nevertheless, bioethics has acquired an independent identity encompassing a rich area of topics –including, clinical research; informed consent; the beginning and end of life; the fair distribution of scarce medical resources.

Note that on this narrow construal of bioethics, there is a clear and sharp distinction made between normative and descriptive ethics, with the former being the preserve of philosophy and the latter reserved for social sciences. Note too that the narrower construal of bioethics does not – or at least it need not – mean that no attention is paid to work in other subjects. It is rather that such work is subordinate to and serving where appropriate the findings of normative theory.

The broader construal of bioethics lies in two dimensions: the scope of the relevant contributing disciplines, and the remit of the subject itself. As for the former, bioethics, to quote David Benatar, includes "not only philosophical study of the ethics of medicine, but also such areas as medical law, medical anthropology, medical sociology, health economics, and even some areas of medicine itself" (Benatar, 2006, p. 17). Benatar worries about quality control within this all-encompassing (and ever expanding) subject, since on his view the argumentative rigor, conceptual precision, and clear focus characteristic of good philosophy need not extend to other contributing fields of study, or to work that falls between the subjects. I acknowledge this critical claim without further comment or its endorsement.

As for the scope of the subject of bioethics there has been major change since the 1970s. The most significant elements are as follows. An early emphasis upon bilateral relations between individuals–doctor and patient; researcher and subject – has been supplemented by work on public health, on the appraisal of interventions to eliminate or mitigate diseases, as well as those conditions that foster ill-health, at the level of the population. Second, the non-human – animals and the environment – have been viewed as meriting bioethical attention, and not just because of their impact on human health. Thirdly, bioethics is now global. Health emergencies, such as most obviously the recent COVID pandemic, can be worldwide, and the most expeditious way to address them is at this transnational level. At the same time, considerations of justice – both in respect of the impact of such emergencies and the distribution of ameliorative resources – apply globally.

To this overarching division between a narrow and a broad view of bioethics can be added two further relevant distinctions. The first is one of methodology between 'top-down' and 'bottom-up' approaches to any topic. In the classic form of the first, and on a narrow construal of bioethics, an issue is understood and evaluated by applying a general theory or set of ethical principles to the issue, the application being managed by making use of relevant empirical data or findings. The reasoning is syllogistic: a universal ethical claim (for instance: the killing of innocent human beings is wrong) combines as a major premise with a statement of relevant non-ethical facts, the minor premise (for example: the destruction of a fetus is the killing of a human being) to yield a normative conclusion: abortion is wrong. This reasoning attracted the pejorative epithet 'armchair' philosophizing, in that it required nothing more of the bioethicist than the generation of conclusions from already available general moral principles using those non-moral facts that others could supply. The philosopher need never leave the upholstered comfort of their study.

By contrast, 'bottom-up' practical ethical reasoning starts from the problem that needs to be understood and appraised, working up from a full appreciation of its character and salient moral features to a concrete judgment. The bioethicist cannot, on this approach, simply take down the general principle from the study's ethical shelf, as it were, and non-moral information, from another shelf, to draw a concluding judgment. They must work to recognize what is morally important and relevant from a proper appreciation of the issue, taking *all* its features into account, and develop – 'upwards' from there – a moral judgment. This is not an application of a moral theory to a problem; rather it is the formation of an informed moral view that throughout combines ethical reasoning with a grasp of the facts of the case.

It is easy to see how the many disciplines under the umbrella of bioethics, broadly construed, might cooperate in bottom-up reasoning, whereas on a top-down approach the findings of non-normative disciplines are simply taken as and when required for use by the bioethicist whose work is the primary source of the final judgment. It should be added that these findings are not necessarily what is characterized by Beauchamp and Childress as descriptive ethics. However, the subjects they list are the source of the findings that inform the minor premises of syllogistic top-down bioethical reasoning.

The second distinction that must be mentioned is in the status or function of any bioethical judgment on an issue. Here the contrast is between what can be called a consultative and an authoritative judgment. According to the former, the judgment is advisory. Having been sought, it need not be followed. A doctor for instance might bring an issue to the attention of an ethics advisor. The doctor is not obligated or bound to follow the advice given, although it may weigh heavily in the balance of considerations the doctor will take account of in reaching a final decision. An authoritative judgment, on the other hand, is determinative of the outcome. Those, for instance, engaged in medical research must conduct their work as dictated by the judgment. Indeed, in the United Kingdom this distinction can be observed in the respective roles of two types of ethics bodies: clinical ethics committees advise medical practitioners whereas research ethics committees regulate what research can be done. More generally, the ethicist's role can be compared to that of a coach, who helps the sportsperson, an athlete to perform better, or to that of a manager, who instructs the player what they must do.

The three distinctions – a broad versus a narrow understanding of bioethics; top-down versus bottom-up reasoning; and, consultative versus authoritative judgments – should be taken into account when addressing the role of bioethics in the creation of public policy and law. They determine answers to the questions of: *who* does bioethics; *how* bioethical judgments are made; and *what significance* or import those judgments have.

I want now to summarize the views of Jonathan Wolff and Mary Warnock on the relation of normative theory to public policy. Both are philosophers, both have been involved as philosophers in the public domain, and both have interesting things to say about how their role should be understood. Both are sceptical about the real-world relevance and efficacy of certain kinds of ethical writing.

Jonathan Wolff distinguishes between applied and engaged philosophy (Wolff 2020; see also his 2011). Applied philosophy, as the adjective strongly suggests, is philosophy that is top-down applying its general principles to concrete cases with the assistance of germane facts. Found in academic work, it has extensive failings. It is dogmatic in that it presumes agreement with its premises (why we should start from this or that set of assumptions). It underdetermines policy (what follows for a relevant law or regulation from the conclusions drawn). Its recommendations can be implausible (how would that judgment ever be adopted as law or policy). It does not demonstrate how exactly, and why, one moves from those argued for recommendations to the best feasible policy. His preferred approach, that of engaged ethics, has the following features. It is recognizably bottom-up in its reasoning, identifying and understanding the issue at hand, and distinguishing the arguments and values in play. It pays attention to history and comparisons, it creates a profile of possible solutions, evaluates options, and then makes policy recommendations. Its overriding concern is, how can we who want to make policy as philosophers, by recognizing the constraints of policy making in the real world, make a difference.

Mary Warnock was both a philosopher and a distinguished policy maker (Archard, 2024). She chaired two official commissions, of which the most important (and relevant to bioethics) was that on artificial reproduction which led to the creation of the highly influential United Kingdom regulatory body, the Human Fertilization and Embryology Authority. Her starting point was a recognition that some matters – such as the possibility of creating babies by non-traditional means – were controversial, and provoked deep moral disagreement amongst the public. In a liberal democracy everyone's view counts yet on these matters policy and law needed to be agreed. To that end she promoted the idea that a philosopher seeking to make such policy should engage in 'public philosophy' distinguished from the 'private' philosophy that the philosopher might espouse. This distinction is neither fully nor entirely satisfactorily defined in scattered comments throughout her career as a policy maker. Yet, essentially, she meant that public philosophy should address 'the impersonal, or better interpersonal and public question of what is the best state of affairs that can be realized, more particularly what is the best feasible policy that can be justified and secure the support of the public and government' (Archard, 2024, p. 6). It demands a proper democratic regard for the views of all, it seeks general support, it acknowledges disagreement but proposes law that is clear and unambiguous. The law must be acceptable not in that everyone endorses its moral basis but rather in that all should prefer this law to none at all.

Warnock and Wolff share a modest view of philosophy in the process of forming policy. Wolff denies the presumption of 'applied philosophy' that it has a privileged role in this process in supplying the moral foundation of any policy. Warnock explicitly contests the idea, defended prominently by Peter Singer, that moral philosophers are moral experts whose judgments should be given priority. Both thus think that thoughtful, intelligent, well-informed individuals can probably play as good a role as any academic philosopher. If moral philosophers should be listened to it is because, first, ethics is at the heart of policy making. Any legitimate policy must be shown to be morally justified and not just be a purely pragmatic or political achievement. Second, moral philosophers have thought longer, harder, and more diligently – with a professional commitment to argumentative rigour and conceptual clarity – about the issues.

Nevertheless, Warnock and Wolff differ in important respects. Warnock studied at Oxford at a time when moral philosophy was by her own judgment in 'very poor shape' (Warnock, 2004, p. 9) reducing to simple common-sense intuitions of what was right or comprising a naïve emotivist view of ethical judgements as expressions of feeling. Systematic practical normative theory was moribund, political philosophy famously pronounced to be 'dead' (Laslett, 1956, p. vii) By contrast, Wolff is the beneficiary of the re-birth of ethics, political philosophy and jurisprudence through the groundbreaking work of John Rawls, Robert Nozick and Ronald Dworkin amongst others. Wolff may be diffident about how such theory can successfully engage with the real world of policy and law, but he does not doubt the enormous contribution it has played in shaping the values of those whose who seek to engage with that world.

A more significant difference in emphasis between Wolff and Warnock is one that I will characterize in a very broad and oversimplified form. For Warnock, the direction of argumentative travel is from a gap in policy and a fact of moral disagreement about some issue to a set of recommendations that are the product of reasoning in the person of the public. How can *we* as a society agree upon a policy that meets that gap, recognizes our disagreements but secures general support? For Wolff, the direction of argumentative travel is from an issue to a set of feasible recommendations that is the product of reasoning as an individual philosopher but one who is sensitive to the constraint and demands of real-world policy making. How can I as a philosopher make proposals on some matter that are justified as the best possible for the polity within which I work?

Warnock could see herself in this public role because she was directly involved as the Chair of a committee charged with making recommendations to the Government of the day. In this her contribution to the formation of policy was exceptional, if not unique. Others can perhaps only hope that their views feed somehow into any debate about a policy. Such contributions are indirectly influential and most likely made as individuals. Bearing in mind the restricted readership of academic journals that influence is also not significant. Nevertheless, the contrast between thinking about an issue as Warnock does in the person of the public and thinking about it as a private individual is possible for any philosopher.

Moreover, because Warnock approaches a policy gap in this manner, she takes conflict and disagreement seriously. This, it should be stressed, is public disagreement not that between moral philosophers. Wolff does acknowledge that on any matter there are likely to be two sides to the debate. However, he sees the role of the engaged philosopher as a 'forensic' one, taking the respective arguments of each side apart, exposing and dissecting their gaps, erroneous assumptions, and false dilemmas. Although he acknowledges that this is a lengthy and difficult process, his approach strongly implies that any initial disagreement can be minimized, weakened, and perhaps even dissipated. By contrast, Warnock consistently emphasized the strong – and durable – feelings that underpin contrasting public views on a contentious matter. Moreover, she also repeatedly stated that all views should be taken seriously. She took this as required by a democratic regard for all humans as equal. It would be wrong in her mind to discount the views of some.

How should bioethics in seeking to commend policy negotiate such disagreement? At one extreme is an aspiration for consensus. This may well be motivated by a view that we all share a common morality whose core principles – such as those of equality, individual autonomy, and fairness – can be explicated and their significance spelled out. Once this is done then the initial distance between opinions, the opposed sides of any debate, can be narrowed. Even if not eliminated, the resultant disagreement may be such as to permit a law or policy that meets with favour from both sides. Childress and Beauchamp ground their four principles of bioethics in a shared common morality and have been criticised for that foundational presumption. Wolff, as suggested, thinks the forensic skills of the philosopher will show how what is in dispute may rest on false assumptions from one or both sides, thereby presumably facilitating agreement.

Bioethicists should not relinquish their tasks of analytic dissection and of the evaluation of arguments. However, it is optimistic to believe that consensus (or minimal dissensus) can always be secured in these ways. Some disputes are deeply entrenched and rooted in incompatible moral commitments. Abortion is an obvious example, one where the assertions of a woman's right to choose and of a foetus' right to life amount to conflicting, indeed incompatible claims. Wolff thinks that it may be possible – using the forensic skills of the philosopher – to reframe any debate. He cites approvingly (Wolff, 2020, p. 20) Ronald Dworkin's attempt to show that the abortion debate is not about rights, but rather about the value of life. In that debate, the two sides can then be construed as making claims that at base assert the same value, disagreeing only about how it should be understood. This is a valiant attempt to rescue consensus from deep disagreement. However, it is neither clear that the reconstruction of the debate is persuasive nor that, perhaps most importantly, the opposed parties to debate would endorse the reconstruction and reach agreement.

What then remains for the bioethicist faced with enduring and irresolvable disagreement? To John Rawls is owed the idea of 'overlapping consensus,' whereby citizens who subscribe to different fundamental beliefs – those drawn from religion or an ethical theory – can nevertheless agree on those principles of justice that should regulate the structure of their society (Rawls, 1993, IV). This consensus is not an agreement on the underlying basic values, about which they continue to disagree, but rather on those shared principles that govern their institutions. This ideal of 'overlapping consensus' is an extremely important, and influential one. It allows us to envisage, and see as justified, a society whose members exhibit a fundamental and lasting diversity of moral and religious views.

However, it is far from clear how there can be an 'overlapping consensus' when it comes to the laws and regulations that must be put in place regarding some novel development in bioscience or medicine, such as genetic engineering or cloning. Nor would such a consensus always be possible in respect of longstanding contentious matters such as abortion or assisted dying. Now, as Wolff (2020, p. 22) points out there can be significant sea changes in social values which mean that laws once regarded as tolerable only by a minority come to be viewed as entirely acceptable by most. We should also acknowledge that such changes sometimes come in the wake of legal changes. This seems to have been the case with the decriminalisation of homosexuality in the United Kingdom.

Nevertheless, important differences of values persist, and we should take proper account of Warnock's demand that the views of all should be respected. If no form of consensus, overlapping or other, is possible what should a bioethicist recommend? One thought is to urge a compromise. Strictly speaking a compromise is a splitting of the difference between two parties who want different outcomes but who recognise that some agreed outcome is preferable to a lack of agreement. In its classic form of barter a buyer and seller both of whom would prefer an exchange to no sale agree a price that is between what each initially proposes. However, disagreements on medical and bioscientific matters need not be, and most often are not amenable to such splitting of the difference. What, for instance, would this mean in the case of abortion? A determined conscientious pro-life opponent of abortion is unlikely to accept that it should be permitted in some circumstances or up to a certain point in the pregnancy.

Here are two further possibilities that need to be carefully distinguished. Both start from the presumption that there is an ideal policy or law, one that is ranked first among all the possible laws. Such a ranking does not, however, consider and evaluate whether it could be adopted and what its adoption would mean. The first possibility recognises that adoption now and for the foreseeable future of this best law is not the best outcome; the other possibility is that a second-best law is to be preferred inasmuch as it may lead to, or help bring about, the successful adoption of the best law.

To explain further: using the tools of ethical analysis and argument we can rank outcomes. To do so is not quite the same as distinguishing between the ideal and the non-ideal, a distinction much discussed which draws on comments by John Rawls (1999, pp. 7–8, 215–216, 308–309). This is because a ranking may, in principle, run from a first choice through an ordered list of less preferred options, whereas the ideal and the non-ideal are construed as opposed poles of a binary contrast. Adopting the top ranked policy or law may – and this is the first possibility – be counterproductive, that is have harmful consequences that outweigh the benefits of this first choice. There may, for instance, be predictable enforcement costs of an unpopular law. Better then to adopt a sub-optimal outcome whose benefits, once the costs of adoption are taken into account, outweigh on balance those of the top preference. Or – and this is the second possibility – it may be that although there is no prospect of justifying the adoption now of the first-choice law (a lack of public and Government support) a law ranked below that top choice may prepare the ground for successful moves later to introduce and implement the higher ranked law.

These remarks are very abstract and the real-world calculations of what they entail in terms of practical, and political action, are complex and difficult to gauge. Nevertheless, those who engage in making bioethical recommendations do need to be sensitive to their import. As Wolff (2019, p. 8) rightly notes a signal failure of applied philosophy is its pronounced tendency to commend outcomes which are implausible, sometimes wildly so, and which stand no chance of being adopted as policy. Warnock was often criticised – in respect of her human fertility report – of making recommendations that were compromises or solely justified on pragmatic grounds. This is misjudged (Archard, 2017). Consider the celebrated and very influential 14-day limit to experimentation on artificially created embryos. She thought this regulation justified by what she termed an 'amalgam' of reasons, some straightforwardly ethical having to do with what 14 days signified in terms of the embryo's development, others having to do with what might allay public fears about a new science overreaching itself and with the likely extent of any Government support for the law. That this limit is only now after 40 years coming under scrutiny and pressures to change it is tribute to Warnock's insight into what was *both* feasible and morally justified.

All of this brings us full circle. For we can now see how the various disciplines in bioethics broadly construed, and working bottom up, need the cooperation from the outset of ethics with other subjects. We need to be confident about what measures a government will support. We can, as Wolff says, benefit from historical comparisons (how have we come to this topic now and how was it, or similar matters, dealt with in the past). We need to understand public attitudes on this issue and how to engage with the public on what concerns them. We need to understand how clear, precise, comprehensible, and enforceable law might be formulated, and how any novel measures might fit with existing legal provisions. All of this requires that bioethics be a cooperative disciplinary venture, from the bottom up, on any contentious matter. However – and this is a big important qualification – the ethics of bioethics, if it is to be done well, must be recognized as a subject best done by philosophers.

## References

Archard, D. (2017). Compromises, fudges and thresholds. In Nuffield Council in Bioethics (Ed.), *Human Embryo Culture. Discussions concerning the statutory time limit for maintaining human embryos in culture in the light of some recent scientific developments* (pp. 90–93). https://www.nuffieldbioethics.org/wp-content/uploads/Human-Embryo-Culture-NCOB-paper-2017.pdf

Archard, D. (2024). Mary Warnock and 'Public Philosophy.' *Journal of Applied Philosophy, 41*(5), 751–766. https://doi.org/10.1111/japp.12747

Beauchamp, T. L. & Childress, J. F. (2019). *Principles of Biomedical Ethics* (8th ed.). Oxford University Press.

Benatar, D. (2006). Bioethics and health and human rights: a critical view. *Journal of Medical Ethics, 32*(1), 17–20. https://doi.org/10.1111/japp.12747

Laslett, P. (1956) Introduction. In Laslett (Ed.) *Philosophy, Politics and Society. First Series*. Blackwell.

Rawls, J. (1993). *Political Liberalism*. Columbia University Press.

Rawls, J. (1999). *A Theory of Justice* (Revised ed.). Oxford University Press.

Warnock, M. (2004) *An Intelligent Person's Guide to Ethics*. Duckworth Press.

Wolff, J. (2011). Ethics and Public Policy: A philosophical inquiry. Routledge. https://doi.org/10.4324/9780203816387

Wolff, J. (2019). Method in philosophy and public policy: Applied philosophy versus engaged philosophy. In A. Lever & A. Poama (Eds.), *The Routledge Handbook of Ethics and Public Policy* (pp. 13–24). Routledge. https://doi.org/10.4324/9781315461731-2

# Bioethics, Conflict, and Law

*Dieter Sturma*

## Bioethics and Mortal Questions

The field of bioethics was institutionally established during the second half of the 20th century. The ethical challenges posed by modern medicine were the driving force behind this development. Despite the publication of numerous studies on ethics and bioethics in recent decades, there is still no strong methodological connection between philosophical ethics and bioethics. In particular, metaethical discourses and standards for normative justifications are not consistently considered in bioethics. Additionally, comparatively few researchers are qualified in both areas,[1] and there is no widespread tendency in philosophical ethics to abandon the historical and metaethical regions in favour of the lowlands of political and legal regulations.

The term "bioethics" refers to an ambiguous discipline. Its thematic scope varies. While it can represent almost the entire spectrum of applied ethics, it can also be used more specifically to address the challenges of modern medical research and practice (Sturma & Heinrichs, 2015). It is this meaning that predominates in public debates.

From a metatheoretical perspective, bioethics appears somewhat incoherent. There are no standardised methods or procedures of justification. Typically, an approach is adopted from the range of mainstream ethics without providing a methodological explanation for why that position is preferable to the others. Metaethical debates are rare in bioethics. This is most likely because bioethics is an open field for a wide variety of disciplines beyond philosophical ethics.

1 Exceptions include Dworkin (1993), Buchanan et al. (2000), O'Neill (2018), and Beauchamp and Childress (2019).

The relationship between the practice of life sciences and bioethical evaluation is often tense. From a bioethical perspective, scientific realism is only tentatively endorsed. The scientific perspective is not automatically prioritised when answering the question of what exists – a standpoint that is taken for granted in the natural sciences. Disagreement also exists about the limits and scope of the competence of scientific disciplines, and how epistemic uncertainty in research should be handled in normative decisions.

Attempts to influence political and legal decision-making play a significant role in bioethics. Even in democratic societies, ideological positions significantly impact these processes due to their strong presence within political parties and related institutions. The crossroads of science and ethics carry the promise of influence and create opportunities to establish links between life sciences and political and legal decision-making. In the best-case scenario, bioethical practice can contribute to the discourse of giving and asking for reasons in democratic societies.

Bioethical debates are usually public and focus on *mortal questions*. These questions touch on the existential dimension of human life from beginning to end and the role of the subjectivity of persons in the objective world (Nagel, 1979). At their most fundamental level, they refer to the integrity of a person's mind and body. Controversies surrounding the termination of pregnancies, stem cell research, and euthanasia are good examples of these debates. There is no denying that early human life must be protected by law – except by those who reduce it to a mere "cluster of cells." However, how this protection should be legally implemented, and which normative scenarios qualify as justifiable is highly controversial. The controversies generally oscillate between extreme positions. There is not even an agreement on how to address the high ethical value of avoiding harm in specific cases. Depending on one's perspective, situations of suffering are either minimised or exaggerated.

Many statements on *mortal questions* are characterised by excessive demands that interfere with the self-determination and integrity of persons. Ideological or religious dogmas do not speak *for* the threatened woman or *for* the severely impaired human life. We are confronted with a form of normative instrumentalisation that fails to consider the subjective perspectives of those directly affected. The issue is not easing or avoiding suffering but rather implementing guidelines that are not supported by the majority of the society, and it is unclear whether all members of the religious community approve of the dogmas and the related institutional practices. The fact that normative instrumentalisation expands and deepens existing situations of suffering is often overlooked. Denying the termination of pregnancy, even in cases of rape, leads to long-lasting distress that affects not only the victim but also her entire social environment.

## Pluralism and Dogmatism

Dogmatic positions often dominate debates on the challenges posed by the life sciences. Here, the term "dogmatic" refers to an authoritarian standpoint that largely avoids the symmetrical exchange of reasons and relies on fabricated or unquestioningly adopted narratives that cannot withstand critical analysis. Dogmatic positions could be part of a symmetrical exchange of reasons in terms of content, but this would require eliminating dogmatic vocabulary entirely and replacing authoritative standpoints with rational justifications.

Dogmatic positions create conflicts that take on the form of battles between good and evil. This is evident in debates about the sanctity of life, stem cell research, termination of pregnancy, and euthanasia. Despite the ideological *furor* in the debates, one should bear in mind that their intensity is at least partly related to the fact that they seek fundamental answers to *mortal questions*. Everyone has specific attitudes and opinions on these questions regardless of the epistemic limits and ideological dependencies of the standpoint. When it comes to answering *mortal questions*, what unites us is also what divides us.[2]

The large number of dogmatic responses to *mortal questions* gives the corresponding debates a polemical tone. Different opinions about specific technical practices are turned into dramatic decisions about life and death. This makes it difficult for an open exchange of ideas to develop, particularly in cases where the focus is on the beginning and end of human life and its technical modification. In these areas, fundamentalist positions persist, and they are experiencing a politically driven resurgence in many Western countries.[3]

---

2 Cf. Dworkin (1993, p. 28): "The idea that [...] binds us all together, that our lives have intrinsic, inviolable value, also deeply and consistently divides us, because each person's own conception of what that idea *means* radiates throughout his entire life."

3 Fundamentalist religious dogmas concerning the beginning and end of human life cannot be derived directly from texts that are considered sacred. In fact, these dogmas are based on interpretations that are often not shared by related religious communities. The process of interpretation is usually obscured by reference to a higher authority. Already, Immanuel Kant took offense to this approach: "Our age is the genuine age of *criticism*, to which everything must submit. *Religion* through its *holiness* and *legisla-*

Admittedly, public discourse is never entirely free of ideological influences. These influences can be minimised with the help of scientific research, but only if there is a consensus within the scientific community that can be communicated to the public and if the naturalistic fallacy is avoided when incorporating scientific findings into normative discourse.

In bioethical discourse, we often see appeals to the myth of the given, which holds on to the idea of naturalness. This myth implies that technical developments in the life sciences violate naturalness and interfere with creation. It primarily manifests as dogmatic assumptions and the rejection of conflicting worldviews.

Naturalness is a disappearing phenomenon in cultural history. Since ancient times, the concept of second nature has addressed the social and cultural transformation of persons and societies. The concept refers to the intellectual and technical ability of human life to gradually detach from its natural state. The behaviour of a person and the development of human life as a whole cannot be explained by presupposing an unchanging human nature. One consequence of social development not being entirely determined by natural conditions is its impact on biological reproduction and leading life as a *person*.

Besides visions of naturalness, the slippery slope argument plays a prominent role in the myth of the given. Since terms like "naturalness" are open to criticism for epistemological *naïveté* and dogmatism, versions of the myth of the given use the slippery slope argument to justify unconditional protection of human life in an attempt to block undesirable social developments.

A slippery slope argument dramatises the introduction of a technical process that initially poses no unacceptable risks. This argument envisions a series of inevitable and irreversible consequences with a great potential for harm that ultimately result in a nightmare scenario, which is supposed to tip the scales in favour of *immediately* halting the technical process in question and its normative evaluation. The slippery slope argument seeks to reach a final decision, closing off the discourse of giving and asking for reasons. It claims to have epistemic access to future courses of action when evaluating empirical research. Slippery slope arguments are discourses about empirical facts conducted without empirical evidence.

---

*tion* through its *majesty* commonly seek to exempt themselves from it. But in this way they excite a just suspicion against themselves, and cannot lay claim to that unfeigned respect that reason grants only to that which has been able to withstand its free and public examination." (Kant, 1781/1998, A xi fn.)

Considering these scenarios, we must point out that it is epistemically impossible to extrapolate an actual causal chain into the future under changing circumstances. Based on our limited knowledge of initial conditions and the corresponding laws, we can make more or less plausible assumptions about future developments. However, we never leave the realm of probabilities, which becomes less defined the farther ahead we try to look. Vague probabilities do not provide a sound basis for decision-making. Ethical and legal discourse is an open field in which topics, concepts, and methods arise and vanish unpredictably.

Another shortcoming of the slippery slope argument is its refusal to acknowledge the internal connection between autonomy and revision. It does not consider the possibility of adopting and developing reasons for or against a particular procedure. Instead, it paternalistically declares moral competence for future persons and societies. Objections and opposing views are excluded from the start without further examination. The slippery slope argument is characterised by a deep mistrust of the ability of persons to reevaluate and revise decisions and actions for good reasons in later steps. In this version of the myth of the given, future persons are denied the opportunity to decide for themselves.

Given the deep traces of violence throughout human history, it cannot be ruled out that the dystopian scenarios evoked by slippery slope arguments will await us in one form or another. But bleak outlooks do not contribute to ethical decision-making in the present. It is ethically unjustifiable to prevent the reconsideration of decisions in light of new insights and better reasoning.

The fact that normativity cannot be based on naturalness does not mean that there are no constraints when dealing with life technically. However, these constraints are not found in nature. Semantically, it is impossible to establish a concept of human nature or naturalness without reference to the second nature of human life, i.e., the developing epistemic, social, and technical abilities of persons. All of our thoughts and concepts about what occurs over the course of events take place within the space of reasons, which is the logical place for explanation and justification.[4] As the historically later, the space of reasons is

4 Cf. Sellars (1997, p. 76): "The essential point is that in characterizing an episode or a state as that of knowing, we are not giving an empirical description of that episode or state; we are placing it in the logical space of reasons, of justifying and being able to justify what one says."

the necessary epistemological condition for the realm of causes. This asymmetrical relationship between the space of reasons and the realm of causes implies that the limits of technical interventions in nature, and particularly in human nature, are blurred.

The absence of norms in nature can lead to the hasty conclusion that human life offers boundless opportunities for action and development. However, the absence of clearly defined limitations does not justify arbitrariness of any kind. Actions can always be evaluated as better or worse, and identifying harmful practices reveals normative constraints *within* human life. These evaluations indirectly outline the contours of justifiable scientific and technological developments.

While criticism of the naturalistic fallacy and the myth of the given is essential, it can create a fundamental divide between what is and what ought to be. The unmediated division between facticity and normativity must be avoided at all costs. Like everything else that exists, decisions and actions are integral to the course of events. There are no isolated niches. This trivial fact is easily overlooked in dualistic worldviews. When both descriptive and normative premises are introduced into an argument, justifications can be developed for normative judgments based on indirect correspondences between descriptive findings and normative evaluations.

Public debates on *mortal questions* generally leave existing conflicts unresolved. Thorough reviews of justifications rarely change the situation. In the end, political regulations that often have little support from mainstream science or the general public address the normative challenges of the beginning and end of human life. Under these circumstances, it is understandable to expect that an improved ethical and bioethical discourse will pave the way for a greater level of agreement.

## Ethics as Conflict

There is no *ethical* justification for denying persons dignity, in the sense of mental and physical integrity, or autonomy, in the sense of being able to lead their lives. This great and simple principle is a permanent source of conflict in unjust social environments. Pluralism and the contingency of living situations also contribute to ethics as conflict. They generate agent-relative reasons in the lives of persons that are only partially comprehensible to others.

In democratic societies, the presence of ethics as conflict is obvious. Formal equality is the basis of democracy, despite the social asymmetries and the many answers to the question of what democracy consists of. This equality is already violated when someone else makes decisions that affect the mental or physical state of a person without involving her. The inability to communicate one's will does not restrict the principle of formal equality, but rather necessitates special provisions for protection and care.

In all their various forms, democracies share the constitutional principle of legally protecting the equality and dignity of every person. However, even in democracies, minorities can influence political and legal decisions that affect the potential suffering of everyone in the society. In recent decades, we have witnessed the breakdown of consensual legal regulations answering *mortal questions*. This development ultimately reflects the absence of a consensus in ethics. Different moral convictions cannot be harmonised because they originate from higher-order evaluations that are firmly embedded in the empirical identity of a person and therefore charged with emotion.

In the event of a legally binding ruling on challenges posed by *mortal questions*, conflicting beliefs do not disappear. This conflict sparks constant calls for revision, which take effect when political and legal constellations change. We can see this process in the United States with the conservative-dominated Supreme Court overruling *Roe v. Wade*. In doing so, the Supreme Court ended the legal regulation accepted by the majority of the society yet strongly criticised by religious communities with significant political influence. Fundamentalist positions that reject reproductive rights contribute to the global movement against the self-determination of women.

Even in a pluralistic society, there are profound differences regarding the justifiability of normative demands. At least, justifications based on personal integrity can use reasons that do not depend on dogmatic assumptions. This is not the case with beliefs about persons created in God's image. The necessary condition for justifiability is that the reasoning in an ethical evaluation can be understood in semantic and formal terms by those who do not share the underlying standpoint. This is not possible with dogmatic worldviews.[5]

---

5 Thomas Nagel has expressed skepticism about the potential influence of ethics in addressing *mortal questions* (Nagel, 1979). Such influence would require a willingness to consider arguments that challenge one's worldview. Unfortunately, as Nagel points out, this requirement lies outside the reach of ethics and law. Current developments seem to be proving him right.

Normative conflicts persist within a person, between persons, and between persons and institutions. Decisions and beliefs arise from assessments involving various factors, whose value may increase or decrease relative to other factors. Accordingly, the judgments and decisions of persons and institutions depend on conflicting and often incompatible intellectual approaches (Hampshire, 1983, pp. 140–169).

Mainstream ethical theories, such as virtue ethics, contractualism, deontological constructivism, and utilitarianism, use different principles and criteria for normative evaluations. These include catalogues of virtues, altruism, moral feelings, autonomy, bans on instrumentalisation, impartial standpoints, human rights, rational considerations of consequences, and hedonistic cost-benefit analyses. There are also different forms of justification for addressing conflicts. Among these are specific normative models like social contracts and rational discourse. However, these concepts and methods cannot resolve ethical conflicts. They are too widely dispersed, even without dogmatic positioning, to be integrated into a unifying framework. At best, there would be minor overlaps. But it is impossible to develop a methodological and substantive framework that could unify reasonable yet divergent normative approaches into an overarching theory.

## Democracy, Ethics, and Law

In a pluralistic society, ethical conflicts and diverse normative judgments are expressions of democracy, not just temporary historical phenomena.[6] For this reason, an ethical response to normative diversity requires identifying some *minimum content* of morality[7] for normative deliberation. Here, we can draw on

---

6 Cf. Rawls (1993, p.36): "The [...] diversity of reasonable comprehensive religious, philosophical, and moral doctrines found in modern democratic societies is not a mere historical condition that may soon pass away; it is a permanent feature of the public culture of democracy. Under the political and social conditions secured by the basic rights and liberties of free institutions, a diversity of conflicting and irreconcilable – and what's more, reasonable – comprehensive doctrines will come about and persist if such diversity does not already obtain."

7 Even positivist analyses concede a minimum content of morality. Hart refers to the *minimum content of natural law* (Hart 1961/2012, p. 193), describing it as the indispensable universal element of everyday moral experience, which is necessary for maintaining the normative order of social practice.

the existing division of labour between ethics and law in democratic societies. Due to the close historical and systematic relationship between morality and law, ethical and bioethical evaluations can remain within their original normative domain.

Both ethics and law can begin with the systematic recognition of a person as the source of normative considerations when identifying the minimum content of morality. Justifiable normative judgments cannot override the validity of human rights and the integrity of the person. Accordingly, ethical discourse must take the form of a symmetrical exchange of reasons. While symmetry is rarely achieved in practice, recognizing it allows for continuous corrections and improvements.

When discussing *mortal questions* and technical changes to human life, there are many concepts and arguments that do not depend on a specific ideological standpoint. Alongside the concept of human rights, these include the influential principles of respect for autonomy, nonmaleficence, beneficence, and justice.[8] There is no ideology-free justification for not recognising the autonomy of persons, the avoidance of harm to persons, as well as benevolence, care, and justice towards persons.

The epistemic and normative challenges posed by scientific and technological developments are of a global nature. In a pluralistic world, it is unrealistic to expect these challenges to be addressed with a unified approach. Instead, the focus should be on creating an intellectual environment in which reasons are reciprocally accepted. Ethical assessments depend not on decisions between good and evil but rather on the fair and non-repressive treatment of conflicts, particularly since divergent positions tend to persist even after regulations have been established.

When defining values and criteria, it is important to acknowledge that they can be prioritized differently. This leads to *reasonable disagreements*,[9] particularly in bioethical contexts. For instance, some positions advocate for both the protection of life and technical therapeutic progress, but they assign different levels of importance to each. Therefore, the objective of justifiable normative

8 See Beauchamp and Childress (2013, pp. 99–326). The principles that the authors reconstructed from the moral certainties of everyday experience still shape the methodological foundations of bioethical research.

9 We are dealing with reasonable disagreements when persons consider the same reasons but weigh them differently, leading to different conclusions; cf. Rawls (1993, pp. 55–58).

judgments cannot be to achieve overall agreement, but rather to formally structure social life in the presence of conflict. The only *ethical* option for dealing with conflicts is to rely on legal *constraints*. They have a binding force that ethical decisions lack.

The close relationship between morality and law, along with its political implications, has been thoroughly analysed by Ronald Dworkin. He rejects the positivistic separation thesis, which asserts that law must be independent of morality, and argues that ethical considerations are integral to legal justifications in law's empire (Dworkin, 1986). Based on his constructive moral realism,[10] he develops a theory of the only right answer, refuting the widespread assumption in legal positivism and legal pragmatism that judges have room for discretion. Discretion opens the door to reasons outside the law's empire. To maintain the integrity of law's empire, Dworkin asserts "that there is often a single right answer to complex questions of law and political morality." (Dworkin, 1977, p. 279)

Rejecting discretion has far-reaching consequences when it comes to normative questions in bioethics. Even in the face of normative diversity, it is wrong to abandon the notion of right legal answers to bioethical challenges. These answers can be found in the internal connection between morality, law, and democratic politics. According to Dworkin, democratic societies are characterised by formulating morally justifiable political goals and implementing them in ethical, legal, and political practice over time. "Law is effectively integrated with morality: Lawyers and judges are working political philosophers of a democratic state" (Dworkin, 2011, p. 414).[11]

From Dworkin's analyses, one can infer that morality resides in the history of normative innovations and has objective forms of expression in law. The diversity of justifiable legal and political systems ultimately traces back to

---

10 In Dworkin's view, morality is a distinct dimension of our experience with its own sovereignty. He therefore considers it an open question how we ought to react morally to what there is and what is going on, regardless of physical or psychological constraints. According to Dworkin, morality itself presides over its judgments, and we cannot climb out of morality to judge it from the outside, see Dworkin (1996, pp. 122–129).

11 Cf. Dworkin (1982, pp. 193–194): "Each judge must regard himself, in deciding the new case before him, as a partner in a complex chain enterprise of which these innumerable decisions, structures, conventions, and practices are the history; it is his job to continue that history into the future through what he does on the day." When it comes to shaping social practices, Dworkin is particularly concerned with the challenges in bioethics and biolaw, see Dworkin (1993).

normative sources, in which the concepts of human rights and procedural justice play central roles. Therefore, a person must never be exploited or ignored, morally, ethically, legally, or politically, no matter how much injustice and repression they have already endured. Though reality may tell us otherwise, there is no such thing as customary law for exploitation and neglect.

The Achilles heel of law in democratic societies is the direct and indirect political influence exerted on legal decision-makers. This is particularly evident in the appointment of judges by political parties. Current political shifts exemplify how the erosion of the independence of the legal system precedes the transformation of democratic societies into autocratic or dictatorial regimes. The political and legal consequences in the case of reproductive rights are evident in the United States and many European countries. Since there is no normative resolution for reasonable disagreements, legal constraints must be developed under conditions of procedural justice. Throughout this process, it is crucial to ensure that there is not even the slightest hint of non-transparent influence. Otherwise, those with different views will not accept the decision-making process from the start.

In democracies, normative evaluations should not be based on positions that are neither scientifically substantiated nor representative of society. It is crucial to ensure that bioethics and biolaw do not serve any particular worldview. Both must always be more than an extension of ideological interests. This is only possible if shared methodological standards are established. Strengthening its scientific foundation while avoiding instrumentalisation for ideological or religious purposes will allow bioethics to play an important role in a culture of knowledge and democratic decision-making. Scientific and technical challenges must be met with normative innovations that do not allow for the myth of the given or the ideological takeover of law. The ideal outcome of a discourse immune to these attempts would be a balance between scientific, technical, and normative innovations.

The scientific perspective is the most plausible ontological starting point for decision-making in democratic societies. However, it cannot claim a privileged role. In a democracy, science cannot retreat into arcane knowledge. Scientific findings must be communicable to be adequately considered. A cross-disciplinary assessment of the possibilities and limitations of practical knowledge has to be at the heart of the interdisciplinary division of labour. In this context, it is important not to lose sight of the fact that scientific research is conducted under conditions of epistemic uncertainty. This applies not only to the largely probabilistic nature of our empirical knowledge but also to the epistemic limits and practical effects of our actions. Epistemic uncertainty has a significant impact on normative decisions. However, legal constraints can be adjusted to changing circumstances. This is the fundamental distinction between normative constraints and dogmatic positions.

## References


Beauchamp, T. L. & Childress, J. F. (2019). *Principles of Biomedical Ethics* (8th ed.). Oxford University Press.

Buchanan, A., Brock, D. W., Daniels, N., & Wikler, D. (2000). *From Chance to Choice. Genetics and Justice*. Cambridge University Press. https://doi.org/10.1017/CBO9780511806940

Dworkin, R. (1977). *Taking Rights Seriously*. Harvard University Press.

Dworkin, R. (1982). Law as Interpretation. *Critical Inquiry, 9*(1), 179–200. https://doi.org/10.1086/448194

Dworkin, R. (1993). *Life's Dominion. An Argument about Abortion, Euthanasia, and Individual Freedom*. Alfred. A. Knopf.

Dworkin, R. (1986). *Law's Empire*. Harvard University Press.

Dworkin, R. (1996). Objectivity and Truth: You'd Better Believe It. *Philosophy and Public Affairs, 25*(2), 87–139. https://doi.org/10.1111/j.1088-4963.1996.tb00036.x

Dworkin, R. (2011). *Justice for Hedgehogs*. Harvard University Press. https://doi.org/10.2307/j.ctvjf9vkt

Hampshire, S. (1983). *Morality and Conflict*. Harvard University Press.

Hart, H. L. A. (with Green, L., Bulloch, P. A., & Ratz, J.). (2012). *The Concept of Law* (3rd ed.). Oxford University Press. https://doi.org/10.1093/he/9780199644704.001.0001 (Original work published 1961)

Kant, I. (1998). *Critique of Pure Reason* (P. Guyer, & A. W. Wood, Eds., Trans.). Cambridge University Press. https://doi.org/10.1017/CBO9780511804649 (Original work published 1781)

Nagel, T. (1979). *Mortal Questions*. Cambridge University Press.

O'Neill, O. (2018). *From Principles to Practice. Normativity and Judgement in Ethics and Politics*. Cambridge University Press. https://doi.org/10.1017/9781316286708

Rawls, J. (1971). *A Theory of Justice*. Harvard University Press. https://doi.org/10.2307/j.ctvjf9z6v

Rawls, J. (1993). *Political Liberalism*. Columbia University Press.

Sellars, W. (1997). *Empiricism and the Philosophy of Mind*. Harvard University Press.

Sturma, D., & Heinrichs, B. (Eds.). (2015). *Handbuch Bioethik*. J.B. Metzler. https://doi.org/10.1007/978-3-476-05323-7

# Biopolitics with Bioethics
## Critical Companions

*Sarah Cunningham-Burley*

### Introduction

The biosciences and medical technology are increasingly shaping our lives: biopolitics, and the social sciences more generally, can help us understand this sociotechnical landscape and the power dynamics within it. We also live in a world of deep divisions including about what counts as knowledge and expertise, what counts as good or bad or right or wrong. Bioethics can help us to explore some of the dilemmas as we grapple with matters of life, health and well-being, and to find practical solutions to conflicts that arise in an ever more complex, technoscientific world. Biopolitics and bioethics, in collaborative and constructive dialogue with each other, can forge a future for bioethics that is critical, engaged and impactful. This chapter will discuss both why this is necessary and how we may achieve it. Bioethics can make both conceptual and instrumental contributions; the former relates to bioethics' role in the understanding of the issues society has to confront and the latter refers to how this field of practice can influence policy including changing institutional behaviour (Nuffield Council on Bioethics, 2024, p. 17).

Charles Bosk in his book *What would you do? Juggling bioethics and ethnography* concludes that "social scientists have a disciplinary discomfort with normative questions" (2008, p. 239). And yet, sociology developed to understand the world and the drivers of social change in order, at least partly, to make society better. As de Vries notes, sociology classically had an explicit concern with the moral foundations of society (2004, p. 280), and the discipline continues to reflect on the role of the normative in its theorising, methods and subject matter. Sociological empirical work reveals the roles of norms and values, as well as systems and structures, that shape human action at every level – the individual, the group and the institution. Values suffuse all claims to knowledge and processes of knowledge production, whether explicitly or implicitly, and values are also subject matters for investigation in a sociology of normativity. Over recent years we have witnessed both a normative turn in sociology and an empirical turn in bioethics. These theoretical and methodological developments can, and perhaps should, serve as bridges between the disciplines. This would lay the ground for collaboration between sociology and bioethics with the aim of understanding, explaining and generating solutions to the complex social and ethical issues in biomedicine and beyond. Along with the insights from sociology and biopolitics, a deeply interdisciplinary bioethics can help characterise the range of possible futures that developments in biomedicine may bring, and suggest which of those futures is the most socially and ethically acceptable, why and to whom.

The chapter gives a brief account of biopolitics as a theoretical and empirical endeavour, one that seeks to explain the pervasiveness of the "bio" in contemporary life, arguing that this can help map the very context within which bioethics sits. It will then provide a brief overview of the uneasy relationship between bioethics and the social sciences before going on to examine the empirical and participatory turn in bioethics, considering how this may contribute to a bioethics that can reclaim its wider focus on collective and structural issues (Ravitsky, 2025). Bioethics cannot be separated from biopolitics, and a reflexive turn in both can help shape a future for bioethics that is empirically grounded, sociologically inflected and participatory.

## Biopolitics – Science and Society

In brief, and oversimplifying a complex domain, biopolitics explores and explains how individuals and populations are regulated through the management of life, manifested as biopower over bodies and life processes, which are increasingly biologised. Biopolitics can be broadly characterised as how populations, individuals and behaviours are governed. It is not one overarching theory, and others have provided excellent accounts of its origins, diversity, import and impact (cf. Mills, 2017; Lemke, 2011; Means, 2021). As Mills (2017) has written, biopolitics is a 'fecund' concept with a range of perspectives and interpretations, yet it has been and remains a highly influential concept as recent accounts of the Covid pandemic attest to (Lorenzini, 2021). Most closely associated with Foucault, it refers to the centring of life in the context of politics and governmentality. This descriptive and explanatory theory posits that life itself is the subject and object of power, where life is controlled and shaped through state and commercial power in neo-liberal states.

As Mills has noted, there are diverse conceptualisations of biopolitics in contemporary scholarship, and she settles on two broad categorisations as a way of overcoming any conceptual confusion. These are "empirical-descriptive" or "critical-normative" (2018, p. 1). Foucault's genealogical work is a key example, where biopolitics and biopower emerged historically, placing "the new political subject of the population at the centre of governmental calculations" (Mills, 2017, p. 2). Biopower is thus entwined with liberalism, emerging from the 18th century. Kakuk (2017, p. vii) notes a broader use of biopolitics, as an umbrella concept referring to public policies and the applications of biotechnologies and the life sciences – an approach that lends itself well to consideration by bioethics.

The strength of the critique of biopolitics as a descriptive and explanatory approach lies in its diversity, characterising whole societies or even epochs in a way that sheds light on political systems and how populations and the individuals comprising them are controlled, enabled to live or not, and in what way. Rather than being a totalising theoretical lens, it is a conceptually and empirically enabling one. It can help identify the deep ways in which life itself – today increasingly understood as within and beyond bodies – is subject to modification and control that shapes and is shaped by political and economic systems as well as everyday practices, identities and citizenship (Rose & Novas, 2005).

Biopower is essential to biopolitics and how this is practiced through diverse strategies and experienced with diverse impacts. Means (1969, p.2) notes that "rather than operating solely, or even primarily through coercion and/or regulation, biopolitics constituted the basis of liberalism as an act of governmentality that recognised freedom itself as a crucial terrain of rule". Biopower can be both coercive and insidious, blurring autonomy and control and operating at multiple levels within an overarching political system. It shapes the very way in which we understand life and ourselves, and can speak directly to bioethics where decisions about, for example, new reproductive technologies or assisted dying, define the parameters of life and death.

Life and politics are both biologised (Bird & Lynch, 2019). The genomic turn in contemporary healthcare and biomedical science, and thus biopolitics, is a key contemporary example with which bioethics is deeply engaged. Biopower can also be an enabling power, as Bishop and Jotterand explore through the work of Foucault, with "new freedoms and vitalities" (2006, p. 206). This offers promise for a constructive relationship between biopolitics and bioethics and for generating policies and practices that could challenge power relations for the benefit of all.

Biopolitics can also help us to understand inequalities and vulnerabilities as Lorenzini explores: "The *differential exposure* of human beings to health and social risks is, according to Foucault, a salient feature of biopolitical governmentality" (2021, p. 43). Biopolitics differentially and unequally organises life, and social and racial inequalities are embedded in its practices. This is because the biologisation of life is not an equaliser, far from it, as the Covid pandemic starkly revealed, despite pleas for and manifestations of solidarity and the collective good.

## Bioethics, Social Sciences and Biopolitics

Critiques of bioethics abound from within and outside the field (cf. Evans, 2012; Hedgecoe, 2004; Petersen, 2011) and there is little need to recapitulate them here. Bioethics is not unitary, it has evolved as a field of practice and scholarship in different contexts and within different institutional locations. One criticism of bioethics has been that it fails to focus sufficiently on structural factors affecting the development of medical science, health related innovation and the social production of health and disease. This perceived lack of engagement in societal level issues forms part of the critique of bioethics from sociology, and the social sciences more widely, although this assessment is also challenged by some. This critique and dialogue with and about bioethics has not always been productive of collaboration. Turner (2009) notes that bioethics and social studies of medicine have overlapping concerns and challenges the traditional characterisation of the divide between them. Turner identifies that there is much in common across social science and bioethics including overlapping subject matters, from everyday health care interactions and dilemmas to institutional practices, to (bio)medicalisation and health equity. He notes, nonetheless, that "Bioethicists need to understand the institutional structures, social arrangements and large social worlds within which ethical issues emerge" (Turner, 2009, p. 37).

However, bioethics sits uneasily in relation to biopolitics despite both being at the intersection of biomedicine, biotechnology, health care and societies. Ten Have argues that mainstream bioethics became the "dominant manifestation of biopolitics itself" (2017, p. 95) and is itself a form of biopower. Similarly,

Bishop and Jotterand posit that bioethics has always been a biopolitics because a bioethical view will reflect "*political* assumptions concerning the nature, goals and values that should guide the biomedical sciences" (2006, p. 205). In being part of biopolitics – shaping how life and lives are governed – bioethics has been characterised as focussing too much on autonomy and on a narrow approach to minimising harms, thus enabling the reproduction of existing power relations by tinkering with rather than challenging the status quo. For López (2004), this intrinsically links bioethics to contemporary forms of biopower and control by means of science and technology through notions of freedom of choice (itself a manifestation of contemporary biopolitics).

In engaging more closely with the scholarship of biopolitics, and the social sciences more generally, bioethics would move from being a bioethics 'in biopolitics' to a bioethics 'with biopolitics', bringing biopolitics' analytical insights into its deliberations and outcomes. This mirrors the challenges that medical sociology has had to address as a 'sociology in medicine' and a 'sociology of medicine' (Strauss, 1957). The former operates within the field of medicine, often focussing on applied health care contexts and on the social determinants of health; and the latter explores medicine as professional practice, a system of knowledge and a form of power. Similarly, authors have characterised a 'sociology in and of bioethics', with de Vries noting that "sociologists *in* bioethics are lending their skills to the bioethical project, sociologists *of* bioethics 'operate from independent positions', – they are outsiders" (2004, p. 283). These characterisations would be better conceived as continua, with movement back and forth and in-between these different positions. Such iteration would serve to enhance understanding of the complex landscape of science, technology, health, illness and society and to influence the way it impacts on individuals and society. This recognition that external critique can be useful to enhance internal (within the system) analysis and influence, can help to shape a critical bioethics future. For example, understanding the axes of biopower through the work of Foucault, as focussing on the body, governmentality and political practice (Takács, 2017) is very instructive for bioethics, as it highlights the different levels of potential spheres of influence.

Kakuk (2017), in the conclusion to his edited volume on bioethics and biopolitics, notes that an expanded version of bioethics is a reflective one. An expanded agenda should involve an internal critique – questioning of the discipline's own processes of knowledge production and its influence. He states "where bioethics could learn from critical biopolitics is in the appreciation that much of what we take for granted in ethical discussion is the product of social and political processes that are historically specific and contingent" (Kakuk, 2017, p. 134).

Reflexive practice involves transparently examining one's own positionality, values and assumptions, and how these shape the construction of knowledge (cf. Finlay & Gough, 2008; Lumsden, 2019). This will help bioethics to be cognisant of its position 'within biopolitics', recognising that this will be culturally and institutionally specific. The strength of bioethics is that it can operate within the very terrain it is seeking to understand and influence, yet in doing so it could also cultivate itself as a partial outsider – building on the critique that biopolitics and much of the social studies of medicine, health and illness brings – a 'bioethics of biopolitics'. This is both a conceptual and instrumental task, and the normative goals of bioethics are different from much of the social sciences. Yet, De Vries et al. have noted that effective and just social policy can be best achieved through bringing social science and bioethics together to advance our understanding of bioethical issues (2006, p. 665).

## Empirical Engagements

Much has been written about the role of empirical research in or for bioethics, that is bioethics itself conducting empirical research to connect ethical inquiry with empirical description, or to draw on ethnographic and other social science methods to understand substantive issues relevant to such inquiry (cf. Herrera, 2008; Ives et al., 2017; Haimes, 2002; Hedgecoe, 2004). Some of the calls for this empirical turn stem from a dissatisfaction with a top-down application of ethical theory or principles (Borry et al., 2004), although the extent of that itself has been subject to debate with Herrera (2008), for example, challenging this charge and stressing the diversity within bioethics, including its engagement with social scientific, empirical work.

Following the argument that bioethics is enhanced through engaging with biopolitics and other sociological approaches to medicine and healthcare, empirical engagement in and for bioethics can bridge the theoretical, methodological and substantive concerns of both bioethics and biopolitics, and create space for dialogue as findings are discussed, interpreted and acted upon. Sociology and bioethics will, of course, generate, interpret and use empirical data differently, yet the empirical world is what connects across 'disciplines' including the biopolitics and bioethics. As Borry et al. (2005) outline, there are barriers to such engagement and dialogue. They identify three: communication in interdisciplinary dialogue; the absence of social science as partners in bioethics; and the perceived 'natural' barrier that the 'is' and the 'ought' creates between social science and bioethics.

Empirical investigation within bioethics can serve several purposes including considering everyday moral practices (Scully et al., 2006). It can involve diverse voices and look at how various groups experience technology and think about its development. It can also help us understand the operation of biopower and biopolitics, through how individual and groups engage with matters of health, healthcare and related scientific and technological developments. The empirical world should not be investigated solely for the purpose of testing ethical theories – to provide philosophers with some kind of real-world justification for their position, but rather empirical bioethics iterates between theory and method. As situationally specific and historically contingent, getting close to the diversity of the empirical world is essential for bioethics. As Ives et al. note:

> Paying attention to the empirical world means learning from it, and using the empirical to inform our thinking about which values are and should be important. In other words, the empirical…should be integrated into the process of working out what our values ought to be (2006, p. 6).

Ashcroft has noted: "Empirical bioethics can perhaps best be understood as a sort of politics – a set of ways of arguing and making decisions and representations to maintain a sort of civic stability while changing it in the interests of the competing or co-operating agents making up society" (2003, p. 12). As a sort of politics, empirical bioethics can be a positive turn in the context of wider biopolitics (after all, the biopolitical is not all bad), although Ashcroft's position seems more critical. By being part of the socio-technical, biopolitical landscape, bioethics' empirical engagement can bring in multiple voices to help surface and even adjudicate over competing interests and agents. But, as noted above, bioethics should always reflect on what it is doing, why and whose interests are being served, and the sense it is making of the perspectives and voices that are being included. Empirical research from social sciences and bioethics jointly should provide a rich, nuanced approach to understanding the intersection of biopolitics and bioethics; the lived experience of those engaged in biomedical science, whether as professionals or others; surfacing values and everyday ethics; as well as revealing the wider structural factors that shape our experience and the development of science and technology.

Relatedly, bioethics has not been immune to a wider participatory turn, so evident in science policy and practice, generated in part by concern over science/society relationships. Public understanding of and engagement in science and science policy has itself been subject of critique through critical public understanding of science scholarship (cf. Irwin & Michael, 2003; Irwin, 2006), illustrating again how important it is to be aware of the institutional drivers of calls for more participation, asking why it is becoming embedded in governance now and with what effects. A participatory approach brings multiple voices into dialogue and deliberation and it can inform policy by demonstrating how publics can deliberate and come to policy solutions, and the values underlying this process. However, it is also important to be clear about its role, ensure participant expectations are clarified and demonstrate how such engagement informs ethical analysis for policy impact. Public engagement does not necessarily come up with the right or correct solution but can deliberate options, and reveal the contours of values, direct experience of health-related technologies and contemplate future developments. It can signal an ethically robust and socially acceptable way forward.

But public engagement is also a part of biopolitics – an institutionalised activity that can serve strategic purposes (what do the public think? how can we maintain trust?); yet it can also challenge and resist. It can ensure those marginalised by biopolitical power can enter discussions about how best to regulate, or otherwise respond to, biomedical innovation. Public engagement opens up biopolitics and bioethics, linking citizens'/publics' views, hopes, concerns and deliberations into recommendations for embedding ethics into policy. Two examples from the Nuffield Council on Bioethics programmes of work can illustrate this, thus showing how bioethics can shape the bioeconomic ecosystem of science and technology.

The first of these is work on Genome Editing of Farmed Animals (Nuffield Council on Bioethics [NCOB] 2021; 2022b). The work builds on research funders efforts to "embed bioscience in society guided by social values and response to societal priorities" (2022b, p. 1). The NCOB report concludes that innovation in agricultural biotech should, therefore, be guided by a coherent vision of the future food and farming system. Participants in the dialogue "felt policy and regulation should guide the technology to socially desirable ends, and the purposes and principles involved in such assessment should be explicit" (2022b, p. 81). Those social values and societal priorities centred animal welfare and animal health, something that had a direct impact on UK legislation that came to include animal welfare. Importantly, the dialogues concluded that animal health should be the first priority, followed by human health. The participants also wanted to ensure a longer view was not ignored in favour of short-term pragmatic decisions. This all shows an awareness of wider power structures of biopolitics and the impact this may have on farming, food production and animal and human wellbeing. They also took a broad view of the role of regulation, which should be about promoting public good not just protecting from harm, reflecting an extended version of bioethics:

> participants want positive policy interventions in the food and farming system, not simply minimal protections beyond which it would be left to be shaped by market forces. The food system affects all people in fundamental ways. Both research and development, and the implementation and diffusion of new breeding technologies should be treated in this light (NCOB, 2022b, p. 4).

The second example relates to ageing – highly relevant to those societies with ageing populations. Biotechnology is seen as one way to intervene in what is seen as a problem especially for health and social care systems, as well as for individuals themselves as they age. Although a different substantive focus to the previous example, there are common themes in terms of the social values and societal priorities which again speak to an intuitive and lived experience understanding of biopolitics (NCOB, 2022a; 2023). The future of ageing programme at the NCOB including both creative workshops at community level with older people, as well as public dialogues with older and younger people. In addressing the question of the role of science and technology in responding to the challenges of ageing, participants also took a broad view of what this might mean for shaping the future of ageing in positive and negative ways

As with the dialogues on gene editing and farmed animals, participants took a holistic view and challenged stereotypes of ageing that might also drive some research and innovation. They stressed autonomy to make decisions, the importance of intergenerational engagement, equitable access and fair distribution of impactful biotech, accountability and safety:

> People felt strongly that a range of voices should be heard in research and innovation, from bench to bedside, including in the prioritisation, design and delivery of research, and that a more diverse range of people should be supported to take part in research (2022a, p. 3).

The NCOB report on the Future of Ageing drew on these findings and other research to identify key principles for ageing research and innovation: flourishing, trustworthiness, equity, challenging ageism, sustainability and shifting power. This latter point directly addresses biopolitics by asking 'How can older adults control the way the technology or intervention works for them and how will it enhance their control over how they wish to live their lives'? The report states:

> A key question for any researcher to ask is, therefore, to what extent will the particular technology, or medical intervention, enhance the control that older adults have over their lives, and support them in more equal relationships with those around them? (NCOB, 2023, p. 118).

As the 2022 dialogue report's foreword notes this "calls for a new framing of how science, technology and policy might address how to age well" (2022a, p. 3). While the broader contours of biopower remain unchanged, this framing does represent a shift in the distribution of such power and the potential of agency to challenge it– and to create a more socially just, healthy future.

## Conclusion: The Future of Bioethics and Biopolitics

This brief journey into the relationship between biopolitics (and social science more widely) and bioethics suggests that bioethics' reach, conceptually and instrumentally, can be deepened and extended through theoretical and empirical attention to how life itself, and the biological in particular, is controlled and shaped through the exercise of biopower. Power is enacted at different levels including on the individual body, identity and citizenship and through political and economic practice and governmentality. Conceptually, biopolitics elevates bioethical analysis to include the complex landscape of contemporary biomedicine and the bioeconomy, and then building the deliberations for possible political solutions to bioethical concerns to achieve instrumental impact.

As Lorenzini points out, we also need to be aware of the everyday practices of biopolitical power, "the fact that disciplinary and biopolitical power mainly functions in an automatic, invisible and perfectly ordinary way – and that it is most dangerous precisely because we do not notice it" (2021, p. 42). Bioethics can help surface that insidious hand of power, through its emphasis on its impact on individuals and groups, and through its embracing of empirical and participatory work. This may help challenge instances of epistemic injustice (Fricker, 2007) by including those most marginalised or disadvantaged through current practices.

Yet, bioethics is in uneasy dialogue with biopolitics, not least because it is part of the very biopolitical sphere it must also critique at the same time as engaging within it. Bioethics in and of biopolitics is one way of conceptualising this, mirroring the role of sociology in and of medicine, or the sociology in and of bioethics. Rather than treating these as binary positions, the reality is more iterative. While frequently eschewing the normative, sociologists still engage with values, sometimes implicitly and sometimes explicitly including through normative recommendations in their conclusions. In other words, the normative is never far away in the social sciences. Sociology might usefully turn to bioethics for frameworks to help articulate those values and evaluate any normative judgements it makes. This tightrope of being 'inside and outside', the 'in and of', might be made easier through a different framing – a 'working with' characterisation. Bioethics *with* biopolitics, or biopolitics *with* bioethics, suggest a more symmetrical relationship. Pickersgill (2011), reflecting on engagement with research and public bioethics, acknowledges "the liminality of bioethicists – that their 'proper' place is neither completely within nor completely outwith biomedicine" (p. 4). This can be a creative and productive position as we look to the future of bioethics.

Any renewal of bioethics is also about how to anticipate and shape the future too, and there are methodologies that can help us in that task. Horizon scanning can help identify future developments in health, medicine, biosciences and health care and what the associated ethical and social contexts and impacts are or would be. This enables us to challenge assumed trajectories in a timely way that can therefore influence the direction of travel. This can be achieved through research, engagement, consultation and deliberation for a truly inclusive, interdisciplinary bioethics – embedding a bioethics with biopolitics in shaping the future of health relevant science and technology.

## References

Ashcroft, R. E. (2003). Constructing Empirical Bioethics: Foucauldian Reflections on the Empirical Turn in Bioethics Research. *Health Care Analysis, 11*(1), 3–13. https://doi.org/10.1023/a:1025329811812

Bird, G., & Lynch, H. (2019). Introduction to the politics of life: A biopolitical mess. *European Journal of Social Theory, 22*(3), 301–316. https://doi.org/10.1177/1368431019838455

Bishop, J. B., & Jotterand, F. (2006). Bioethics as Biopolitics. *Journal of Medicine and Philosophy, 31*, 205–212. https://doi.org/10.1080/03605310600712760

Borry, P, Schotsmans, P, & Dierickx, K. (2005). The Birth of the Empirical Turn in Bioethics. *Bioethics, 19*(1), 49–71. https://doi.org/10.1111/j.1467-8519.2005.00424.x

Bosk, C. L. (2008). *What would you do? Juggling Bioethics and Ethnography.* University of Chicago Press.

De Vries, R. (2004). How Can We Help? From "Sociology in" to "Sociology of" Bioethics. *Journal of Law, Medicine & Ethics, 32*(2), 279–292. https://doi.org/10.1111/j.1748-720X.2004.tb00475.x

De Vries, R., Turner, L., Orfali, K., & Bosk, C. (2006). Social Science and bioethics: the way forward. *Sociology of Health and Illness, 28*(6), 665–677. https://doi.org/10.1111/j.1467-9566.2006.00535.x

Evans, J. H. (2012). *The History and Future of Bioethics: A Sociological View.* Oxford University Press. https://doi.org/10.1093/acprof:oso/9780199860852.001.0001

Finlay, L., & Gough, B. (Eds.). (2008). *Reflexicity: a practical guide for researchers in health and social sciences.* John Wiley and Sons. https://doi.org/10.1002/9780470776094

Fricker, M. (2007). *Epistemic Injustice: Power and the Ethics of Knowing.* Oxford University Press. https://doi.org/10.1093/acprof:oso/9780198237907.001.0001

Haimes, E. (2002). What can the social sciences contribute to the study of ethics? Theoretical, empirical and substantive considerations. *Bioethics, 16*(2), 89–113. https://doi.org/10.1111/1467-8519.00273

Ten Have, H. (2017). Can Bioethic Escape from Biopolitics? In P. Kakuk, (Ed.), *Bioethics and Biopolitics. Theories, Applications and Connections* (pp. 95–107). Springer. https://doi.org/10.1007/978-3-319-66249-7_7

Hedgecoe, A. M. (2004). Critical bioethics: beyond the social science critique of applied ethics. *Bioethics, 18*(2), 120–143. https://doi.org/10.1111/j.1467-8519.2004.00385.x

Herrera, C. (2008). Is it time for bioethics to go empirical? *Bioethics, 22*(3), 137–146. https://doi.org/10.1111/j.1467-8519.2007.00621.x

Irwin, A., & Michael, M. (2003). *Science, Social Theory and Public Knowledge*. Open University Press.

Irwin, A. (2006). The Politics of Talk: Coming to Terms with the 'New' Scientific Governance. *Social Studies of Science, 36*(2), 299–320. https://doi.org/10.1177/0306312706053350

Ives, J., Dunn, M., & Cribb, A. (Eds.). (2017). *Empirical Bioethics: Theoretical and Practical Perspectives.* Cambridge University Press. https://doi.org/10.1017/9781139939829

Kakuk, P. (Ed.). (2017). *Bioethics and Biopolitics. Theories, Applications and Connections*. Springer. https://doi.org/10.1007/978-3-319-66249-7

Lemke, T. (2011). *Biopolitics: An Advanced Introduction* (E. F. Trump, Trans.). New York University Press. (Original work published 2007). https://doi.org/10.18574/nyu/9780814753378.001.0001

López, J. (2004). How Sociology can save bioethics... maybe. *Sociology of Health & Illness, 26*(7), 875–896. https://doi.org/10.1111/j.0141-9889.2004.00421.x

Lorenzini, D. (2021). Biopolitics in the Time of Coronavirus. *Critical Inquiry, 47*(S2), 40–45. https://doi.org/10.1086/711432

Lumsden, K. (2019). *Reflexivity. Theory, Method and Practice*. Routledge. https://doi.org/10.4324/9781315692319

Means, A. J. (2021). Foucault, biopolitics, and the critique of state reason. *Educational Philosophy and Theory, 54*(12), 1968–1969. https://doi.org/10.1080/00131857.2021.1871895

Mills, C. (2017) *Biopolitics*. Routledge. https://doi.org/10.4324/9780203732588

Nuffield Council on Bioethics. (2021). *Genome editing and farmed animal breeding: social and ethical issues.* https://www.nuffieldbioethics.org/publication/genome-editing-and-farmed-animal-breeding-social-and-ethical-issues/

Nuffield Council on Bioethics. (2022a). *Future of ageing: Public Dialogue.* https://www.nuffieldbioethics.org/publication/future-of-ageing-public-dialogue/

Nuffield Council on Bioethics. (2022b). *Public dialogue on genome editing and farmed animals.* https://www.nuffieldbioethics.org/publication/public-dialogue-on-genome-editing-and-farmed-animals/

Nuffield Council on Bioethics. (2023). *The future of ageing: ethical considerations for research and innovation.* https://cdn.nuffieldbioethics.org/wp-content/uploads/The-future-of-ageing-ethical-considerations-in-research-and-innovation.pdf

Nuffield Council on Bioethics. (2024). *Making Ethics Matter. Strategic Direction 2024–2025* https://cdn.nuffieldbioethics.org/wp-content/uploads/NCOB-5-Year-Strategy-Making-Ethics-Matter-FINAL.pdf

Petersen, A. (2011). *The Politics of Bioethics*. Routledge. https://doi.org/10.4324/9780203830338

Pickersgill, M. D. (2011). Research, engagement and public bioethics: promoting socially robust science. *Journal of Medical Ethics, 37*(11), 698–701. https://doi.org/10.1136/jme.2010.041954

Ravitsky, V. (2025), in this volume. (Reprinted from "A Path Forward – and outward: repositioning bioethics to face future challenges", 2023. *Hastings Center Report, 53*(5), 7–10. https://doi.org/10.1002/hast.1510)

Rose, N., & Novas, C. (2005). Biological Citizenship. In A. Ong & S. Collier (Eds.), *Global Assemblages: Technology, Politics and Ethics as Anthropological Problems* (pp. 439–463). Blackwell Publishing. https://doi.org/10.1002/9780470696569

Scully, J. L., Shakespeare, T., & Banks, S. (2006). Gift not commodity? Lay people deliberating social sex selection. *Sociology of Health & Illness, 28*(6), 749–767. https://doi.org/10.1111/j.1467-9566.2006.00540.x

Strauss, R. (1957). The Nature and Status of Medical Sociology. *American Sociological Review, 22*(2), 200–204. https://doi.org/10.2307/2088858

Takács, Á. (2017). Biopolitics and Biopower: The Foucauldian Approach and Its Contemporary Relevance. In P. Kakuk (Ed.), *Bioethics and Biopolitics. Theories, Applications and Connections* (chapter 1, pp. 3–15). Springer. https://doi.org/10.1007/978-3-319-66249-7_1

Turner, Leigh (2009). Bioethics and Social Studies of Medicine: Overlapping Concerns. *Cambridge Quarterly Journal of Healthcare Ethics, 18*(1), 36–42. https://doi.org/10.1017/S0963180108090063

# Inclusive Bioethics

# Participation and Bioethics

## The Inserm Ethics Committee (IEC) Perspective

*Hervé Chneiweiss*

## Introduction

The involvement of the public in bioethical decision-making has become a central concern in contemporary research ethics. In this chapter, we explore this dynamic through the lens of the Institut National de la Santé et de la Recherche Médicale (Inserm) Ethics Committee (IEC). Inserm is the public scientific and technological French national institute dedicated to biomedical research and human health, and is involved in the entire range of activities from the laboratory to the patient's bedside. We will focus on how participatory ethics intersects with institutional responsibilities, scientific innovation, and democratic deliberation. Drawing from the philosophical insights of Paul Ricœur and the practical engagements of the IEC, particularly within the European HYBRIDA project and its work on genome editing, we outline key themes and dilemmas.

## Ricœurian Ethics as a Framework for Participation

Paul Ricœur's ethics, centred on the "aim of the good life, with and for others, in just institutions" (Ricœur, 1990), offers a foundational approach to understanding participation in bioethics. Participation is not only a procedural requirement, but a moral imperative rooted in respect for the autonomy and dignity of others. In medical research, this means affirming one's own freedom while recognising and enabling the freedom of others. Participation becomes a dialogical process, guided by trust, mutual recognition, and a shared pursuit of justice. The IEC embraces this vision, seeing bioethics not merely as a gatekeeping mechanism but as an active site of engagement, learning, and co-construction of norms.

## Building Trust: Lessons from the HYBRIDA Project

The HYBRIDA project (HYBRIDA, 2024), focused on the ethical implications of organoid research, has emphasised that trust is the essential precondition for meaningful participation. The IEC has identified four foundational domains of trust-building: Respect: towards fellow scientists and participants in research; Analysis and Evaluation: of both technologies and ethical frameworks; Information and Training: to empower all stakeholders with knowledge; Dialogue and Cooperation: across disciplines and with society at large. These dimensions align with Ricœur's ethics and are operationalised in the IEC's contributions to HYBRIDA, aiming to bridge the gap between scientific innovation and social perception, emotional or cultural resonance.

Beyond the variety of entities that fall under the umbrella term "organoids" and the many applications of organoids, there is uncertainty related to the precise definition of the term: what does "being similar" to something actually mean? Researchers generally refer to them as "models", because they are essentially biotechnological avatars built to study specific tissue features of interest. Organoids are typically hybrid entities, both biological, alive, self-organised structures arising from natural stem cells, and artificially and technologically human-made (use of specific culture media and physical forces). In addition, current organoids do not have the same properties and functions as an organ. It is therefore incorrect to refer to organoids as mini-organs, and communicating incorrect information constitutes misconduct. Misnaming would be both prejudicial for the advancement of science and for the trust of the public.

Mini-deliberative workshops were conducted within HYBRIDA, gathering each time around 20 people in Italy, Greece and Denmark (see https://hybrida-project.eu/deliverables/ WP4 Co-creation). This allowed identifying several issues raised by the public that will need addressing at some point: whilst there was general support for biomedical research and innovative technologies to find new treatments and improve public health, informed consent and responsible governance were highlighted as concerns throughout the deliberations. Addressing these is essential to safeguard ethical use. Proper guidelines for organoid research are needed to ensure that any economic interests do not prevail over patient safety and to prevent exploitation. Commercialisation of organoids is essential for their implementation in biomedical and preclinical research, but it is a sensitive issue, with participants expressing concern on use, ownership and remuneration. These points led HYBRIDA to propose clarification in donor consent forms, keeping in mind that contemporary biomedical research on organoids should not add to existing healthcare inequalities. Potential misuse and breach of the privacy of personal data in connection with data storage and donation was also another concern raised by the public.

The HYBRIDA consortium reviewed different models of informed consent. Proper informed consent regarding the deposition and use of human biomaterials faces two specific challenges when it comes to organoid research. First, given the unknown future direction of research, it is impossible to anticipate all the potential information and uses that might derive from a given biological sample. Second, integration of the material collected in biotechnological constructs that are shared among laboratories makes it difficult to envision how donors would be able to withdraw their consent, even though it is one of their fundamental rights as stipulated in the Declaration of Helsinki.

In order to address these two specific challenges, one solution might be to use dynamic consent, which provides for continuous information to pass between the donor and users on new projects, allowing the donor to agree for the reuse of their biological samples. This solution involves obtaining the donor's initial consent for the collection and storage of their biological samples in a biobank, along with ongoing information provision, which requires complex logistical implementation. Because re-contacting donors raises practical and ethical problems, an alternative might be to adopt the consent for governance model where consent and agreements for the reuse of biological samples would be entrusted to an independent third party representing the donor. In addition, the donor should be further informed in anticipation of the potential use of their donation so that they can allow or decline specific uses. HYBRIDA is thus proposing a Donor's Tissue Research Under Secure Transparent Ethical Donation (TRUSTED) that anticipates the conditions of use of biological samples according to the donor's preferences. Donors should complete a questionnaire at the time of donation as part of the consent procedure which also specifies the restrictions they would like to impose on any future use of their tissues, trusting the initial researchers and the secondary users, and, if necessary, with the support of a third party, to ensure that these wishes are respected. The TRUSTED would facilitate implementation of the use of biological material, while respecting both the donor's participation and the researcher's investment. We believe that future European regulations regarding informed consent lie beyond the scope of HYBRIDA but we nonetheless call for European action based on our analysis to compile appropriate and updated regulations.

## The Genome Editing Case: An IEC Engagement

The IEC's early involvement in the ethics of genome editing exemplifies its proactive and participatory approach. The rapid trajectory from basic research to clinical application, following the 2012 publications by Charpentier and Doudna (Jinek et al., 2012) and Zheng (Cong et al., 2013), prompted urgent ethical reflection. The IEC anticipated global tensions over the clinical translation of genome editing. Its opinion stressed the unprecedented convergence of technologies – low-cost sequencing, advanced bioinformatics, human embryo access, and CRISPR-Cas9 – culminating in ethical challenges at a speed rarely seen before. In May 2015, the IEC released one of the first ethical opinions on human genome editing (Inserm Ethics Committee, 2015), highlighting the following key concerns:

### Germline Editing in Humans

The IEC's position was among the first institutional calls for a moratorium on germline editing until international public deliberation could mature. The application of CRISPR-Cas9 to human germline cells or to human embryos raised significant issues: incompatibility with Article 13 of the Oviedo Convention and Article 16–4 of the French Civil Code forbidding any human heritable genome modification; unsolved scientific uncertainties, that remain until today, making irresponsible for a scientist to edit the genome of a human embryo; lack of societal deliberation. The IEC argued for a precautionary approach, stating that germline modification should remain prohibited until uncertainties are addressed and robust public engagement occurs (Inserm Ethics Committee, 2015). This position was later echoed by the United Nations Educational, Scientific and Cultural Organization's (UNESCO) International Bioethics Committee (2015) and at the Three Academies Summit in Washington (December 2015).

## Gene Editing in Animals

IEC raised concerns about genome editing in so-called "harmful" species, especially the potentially irreversible effects on biodiversity. This was particularly critical for gene drive, a technique designed to rapidly spread specific genes through populations, often proposed to combat diseases like malaria, which kills over 500,000 people annually. Such research carries unique ethical responsibilities given its capacity to alter entire species and ecosystems.

Key ethical principles were identified. First, research must promote collective welfare, proceeding only if it is scientifically rigorous, ethically sound, and approved by competent authorities. Second, it requires transparent governance, robust risk assessment, and adherence to international biosafety norms, with ecosystem-level impacts carefully anticipated. Third, transparency and accountability are essential throughout the research process.

A major concern was that these projects, largely developed in the Global North, were intended for application in the Global South. This led to a fourth principle: the need for meaningful engagement with local populations, including indigenous communities and civil society, through inclusive, culturally sensitive, and well-resourced processes. Finally, such work must ensure co-development and co-ownership of knowledge, fostering equitable global participation in decision-making. These principles were shared internationally (National Academies, 2016) and further articulated by funders – including Inserm – at a science policy forum (Emerson et al., 2017).

## Plant Genomes and MOGEs

Our opinion also mentioned the emergence of Molecularly Oriented Genetically Edited (MOGEs) plants that may reignite challenges previously seen in GMO debates. The IEC stressed the need to revisit regulatory frameworks to reflect new technical realities and societal values. Environmental implications of genome editing require integrated assessments that combine ecological science with participatory risk evaluation.

In each of these three main domains, the elephant in the room was the communication challenge, balancing on the one hand ambitious but highly uncertain promises of miraculous treatments at these very early stages, and on the other hand excessive fear of human genome manipulation impacting population on a wide scale. Preventing exaggerated claims, hype as well as fears, regarding clinical applications is a major ethical imperative for maintaining public trust and realistic expectations.

## From IEC Report to ARRIGE: Fostering a Global Debate

The call for global governance was not abstract. The IEC's engagement through the Association for Responsible Research and Innovation in Genome Editing (ARRIGE) and in forums with UNESCO, World Health Organisation (WHO), and regional ethics bodies (e.g., Brazzaville 2018 with six Central African committees) highlighted real asymmetries in access to information, decision-making power, and infrastructures. These gaps demand proactive strategies rooted in capacity building, transparency, and subsidiarity. Moreover, the ARRIGE charter emphasised not only ethical reflection but also operationalisation: providing informal guidance, promoting shared risk management approaches, and developing "toolboxes" for scientists, regulators, and citizens across diverse sociopolitical settings.

Between 2016 and 2018, to support the creation of ARRIGE, the IEC – strongly supported by Katherine Littler, then at the Wellcome Trust – initiated and participated in numerous international events aimed at fostering inclusive global discussions around genome editing (details available on the IEC website). A key milestone was a European meeting held in Paris on March 16, 2016, which led to significant reflections and policy discussions on genome editing. This meeting resulted in a short note published in *Nature*, presenting a European position on CRISPR-Cas9 and related technologies (Hirsch, Lévy, & Chneiweiss, 2017). Subsequently, a comprehensive white paper was published in *Transgenic Research*, offering a broader European perspective on promoting responsible research in genome editing (Chneiweiss et al., 2017). Travelling from Vienna to Buenos Aires, from Geneva to New Delhi, from Paris to Brazzaville, produced an inclusive process that culminated in a major gathering in Paris on March 23, 2018, leading to the official creation of ARRIGE – a global network dedicated to ensuring the safe, ethical, and inclusive governance of genome editing (Montoliu et al., 2018, see arrige.org). Central to its mission is the development of global cooperation, grounded in the principles of transparency, equity, and justice, ensuring that genome editing technologies are used in a manner that benefits all of society.

## The Jiankui He Scandal and the Global Governance Turn

The 2018 scandal involving unauthorised human genome editing in China marked a turning point in the global governance of genome editing. The IEC and the ethics committee of the French National Centre for Scientific Research (CNRS's COMEST) issued a joint statement that strongly criticised the scientific irrelevance of the intervention – specifically the editing of the CCR5 gene, which lacked robust evidence of benefit – highlighted its medical irrelevance, as the embryos were not at actual risk of HIV infection, and condemned severe ethical violations concerning informed consent and protocol transparency. This shift also reignited ethical reflections on the limits and conditions of genetic enhancement of the human person. Such episodes demand a reconsideration of the boundaries between therapeutic intervention and enhancement and call for a renewed ethical framework sensitive to emerging biotechnological capabilities (Chneiweiss, 2019). In parallel, ARRIGE underscored the necessity of promoting responsible genome editing research, insisting on robust ethical, legal, and social oversight to ensure the alignment of scientific practice with societal values (Hirsch et al., 2019).

This event catalysed a series of international governance efforts, most notably the establishment of the WHO Expert Advisory Committee on Human Genome Editing. The Committee published three major reports emphasising the need for clarity, transparency, and accountability; responsible stewardship across legal, scientific, and public funding dimensions; and the promotion of inclusiveness, fairness, solidarity, global health equity, and the equal moral worth of all individuals.

## UNESCO Engagement and the Global Citizens' Assembly

Between 2018 and 2021, UNESCO's International Bioethics Committee (IBC), with support from a Japanese government grant, organised a series of four roundtables aimed at fostering global public engagement on the ethical and societal challenges of genome editing. This initiative marked the 25th anniversary of the IBC and emphasised Article 28 of the Oviedo Convention: the duty to conduct public debate on fundamental biomedical developments. These roundtables addressed the implications of gene editing across a wide spectrum – science, environment, health, economy, democracy, and civic participation. Importantly, this initiative predated the public revelation of the now-infamous genome editing case in China, underscoring that UNESCO had already recognised the urgent need to democratise the conversation around emerging biotechnologies.

Yet, just as the program was unfolding, the world learned of an unauthorised experiment involving the genetic editing of human embryos in China. The Global Citizens' Assembly on Genome Editing (2019) was launched in this context. As summarised by Dryzek et al. (2020), the Global Citizens' Assembly represented a methodological innovation in participatory governance. Participants deliberated over five days on real cases (plants, animals, humans), supported by expert witnesses, and co-produced recommendations. This inclusive, multilingual, and culturally situated process grounded ethical guidance in real-world diversity.

In an unprecedented exercise in democratic deliberation, over 200 citizens from seven regions across France, half being 17-y or so (last college school year), came together to reflect on one of the most complex ethical challenges of our time: genome editing. Organized by IEC with the support of the regional ethics councils (Espaces éthiques régionaux, ERE), this French component of the Global Citizens' Assembly sought to bring lay voices into the heart of debates too often reserved for scientists, legal experts, and policymakers.

The structure of the process was both ambitious and carefully designed. Spanning five days, the assembly began with a foundational session on norm-setting, providing participants with a common ethical and scientific vocabulary. Over the next three days, citizens were invited to deliberate (small groups of 6 to 8) on the uses of genome editing in plants, animals, and humans – each domain raising distinct but interconnected concerns. The final day was devoted to formulating recommendations addressed to policymakers.

Two overarching questions guided the process: should genome editing proceed? And if so, under what principles and conditions should its governance be organised?

What emerged was a nuanced and thoughtful set of positions. Citizens expressed conditional support for genome editing, particularly when deployed for therapeutic purposes. They favoured curative uses that could be adapted to medical research or clinical practice, provided there was room for legal flexibility and regulatory oversight. There was strong consensus that such interventions should only be carried out by authorised professionals and be embedded in a robust framework that includes patient consent, data protection through medical confidentiality, legal regulation of eligible diseases, and compensation mechanisms for potential adverse effects. Ensuring equal access to treatment emerged as a key condition of ethical acceptability.

However, the participants also drew clear lines. They rejected genome editing when it risked exacerbating social inequalities or entailed discriminatory practices, particularly in contexts like banking, insurance, or employment. They were sceptical of the necessity of genome editing when other, less invasive or already proven alternatives (such as vaccines, drugs, or organ transplantation) were available. Most firmly, they opposed heritable modifications – highlighting the risks these posed to future generations and the unknowns they introduced into the human gene pool. The spectre of homogenisation and loss of genetic diversity concerned many, as did the possibility of a drift toward aesthetic enhancements aligned with narrow societal norms, threatening the value of self-acceptance and human variability.

Yet the deliberations also left open a series of important and unresolved questions. Citizens asked: who defines which diseases are eligible for gene editing interventions? By what criteria? How can society prevent the misuse of such powerful technologies? What kind of consent is meaningful or even possible for children, embryos, or future generations who cannot speak for themselves? How should the benefits and risks be evaluated – not only for individual patients, but also for their descendants and society at large? What level of technical and ethical oversight is needed to prevent drift or abuse? And finally, how should enhancement be treated in a world where competitive pressures – whether in sports, education, or the workplace – could tempt individuals to cross ethical boundaries?

In short, this citizens' assembly did not produce easy answers, but it did demonstrate that the public is capable of grappling with the profound ethical questions posed by genome editing. Their contributions reflected a desire not to reject science, but to anchor it in values of justice, precaution, dignity, and democratic oversight. As such, the recommendations of these citizens offer not only a snapshot of public opinion but a vital resource for those shaping the future of biotechnology.

## The Main Question Today: Access to Approved Treatments

As the age of genome editing transitions from scientific promise to clinical application, a new ethical dilemma has emerged – one that no longer centres on permissibility alone, but on access, equity, and affordability. In recent analyses, ethicists have argued that the defining challenge of the post-genome-editing era lies not in whether we should modify the human genome, but in how to ensure that the resulting therapeutic breakthroughs are accessible and sustainable. The traditional focus of bioethics – drawing boundaries around what is permissible – has shifted toward questions of infrastructure, cost regulation, and social justice (Chneiweiss, 2023).

This shift is particularly evident in the landscape of gene therapy. As of now, over 100 clinical trials involving gene editing – including base editing and epigenome editing – are listed on ClinicalTrials.gov. These trials address a range of rare and serious conditions, often for patients with few therapeutic options. Several gene therapies have already received approval, targeting diseases such as sickle cell anaemia, beta-thalassemia, transthyretin amyloidosis, and familial hypercholesterolemia. However, each treatment carries a staggering cost of $2 to $3 million per patient.

The situation is similar for CAR-T cell therapies, such as Yescarta or Kymriah, used in certain blood cancers, which are priced at around $400,000 per treatment. Even more experimental approaches, like xenotransplants involving genetically modified pig hearts or kidneys, raise questions not only about long-term safety but also about future pricing models and healthcare system integration.

In this context, affordability and access have become central ethical concerns. Without public infrastructure and policy frameworks to regulate costs and ensure equitable deployment, these innovations risk reinforcing existing inequalities. Therapeutic potential alone is not enough – societies must also address the conditions under which these technologies are made available, to whom, and on what terms.

Recognising this urgency, the French Academy of Medicine has called for the development of public platforms and infrastructure capable of supporting fair access to these high-cost therapies. This position underscores a broader realisation: that medical innovation must be accompanied by social and institutional innovation. If genome editing is to fulfil its promise, it must do so within systems that are transparent, inclusive, and designed to serve the public good.

The future of genomic medicine will thus be shaped not only by breakthroughs in science, but by political and ethical decisions about who benefits, who pays, and how society defines fairness in the age of biological intervention.

## Conclusion

Participation in bioethics is not a decorative element of responsible research but a structural and normative requirement. Through the lens of Ricœur's ethics and the experience of the Inserm Ethics Committee, we see how trust, cooperation, and just institutions enable meaningful inclusion in decision-making about life sciences. The path forward demands vigilance, dialogue, and an unwavering commitment to the life lived "with and for others."

## References

Cong, L., Ran, F. A., Cox, D., Lin, S., Barretto, R., Habib, N., ... & Zhang, F. (2013). Multiplex genome engineering using CRISPR/Cas systems. *Science*, 339(6121), 819–823. https://doi.org/10.1126/science.1231143

Chneiweiss, H. (2023). Genome editing for the clinics: First successes and new issues. *Med Sci (Paris)*, 39(8-9), 589–590. https://doi.org/10.1051/medsci/2023110

Chneiweiss, H., Hirsch, F., Montoliu, L., Müller, A. M., Fenet, S., Abecassis, M., Merchant, J., Baertschi, B., Botbol-Baum, M., Houghton, J. A., Kritikos, M., Mifsud, J., Bartnik, E., Rath, J., Druml, C., Friedrich, B., Carvalho, A. S., Lanzerath, D., & Saint-Raymond, A. (2017). Fostering responsible research with genome editing technologies: A European perspective. *Transgenic Research*, 26(5), 709–713. https://doi.org/10.1007/s11248-017-0028-z

Chneiweiss H. *Back from Hong Kong or ethics at the time of a genetic increase of the human person*. Med Sci (Paris). 2019 Mar;35(3):263-265. https://doi.org/10.1051/medsci/2019033

Dryzek, J. S., Nicol, D., Niemeyer, S., Pemberton, S., Curato, N., Bächtiger, A., & Vergne, A. (2020). Global citizen deliberation on genome editing. *Science*, 369(6510), 1435–1437. https://doi.org/10.1126/science.abb5931

Emerson, C., James, S., Littler, K., & Randazzo, F. (2017). Principles for gene drive research: Sponsors and supporters of gene drive research respond to a National Academies report. *Science*, *358*(6367), 1135–1136. https://doi.org/10.1126/science.aap9026

Hirsch, F., Lévy, Y., & Chneiweiss, H. (2017). CRISPR-Cas9: A European position on genome editing. *Nature*, *541*(7635), 30. https://doi.org/10.1038/541030c

Hirsch F, Lemaitre C, Chneiweiss H, Montoliu L. *Genome Editing: Promoting Responsible Research*. Pharmaceut Med. 2019 Jun;33(3):187-191. https://doi.org/10.1007/s40290-019-00276-1

HYBRIDA Embedding a comprehensive ethical dimension to organoïd-based research and resulting technologies (2021–2024) www.hybrida-project.eu

Inserm Ethics Committee. (2015). *Opinion on Human Genome Editing*. [IEC Publication].

Jinek, M., Chylinski, K., Fonfara, I., Hauer, M., Doudna, J. A., & Charpentier, E. (2012). A programmable dual-RNA–guided DNA endonuclease in adaptive bacterial immunity. *Science*, 337(6096), 816–821. https://doi.org/10.1126/science.1225829

Montoliu, L., Merchant, J., Hirsch, F., Abecassis, M., Jouannet, P., Baertschi, B., Sarrauste de Menthière, C., & Chneiweiss, H. (2018). ARRIGE arrives: Toward the responsible use of genome editing. *The CRISPR Journal, 1*(2), 128–129. https://doi.org/10.1089/crispr.2018.29012.mon

National Academies of Sciences, Engineering, and Medicine. (2016). *Gene Drives on the Horizon: Advancing Science, Navigating Uncertainty, and Aligning Research with Public Values*. Washington, DC: The National Academies Press. https://doi.org/10.17226/23405

Ricœur, P. (1990). *Soi-même comme un autre*. Paris: Éditions du Seuil.

UNESCO International Bioethics Committee. (2015). *Report of the IBC on Updating Its Reflection on the Human Genome and Human Rights*. Paris: UNESCO.

WHO. (2021). *Human Genome Editing: Recommendations*. https://www.who.int/publications/i/item/9789240030060

# Bioethics in Africa

## A Contextually Enlightened Analysis of Three Cases[1]

*Nancy S. Jecker, Caesar Atuire*

### Introduction

Across sub-Saharan Africa, bioethics is an emerging field of scholarly inquiry, informed by contextual features distinct to the region. A cultural mix comprised of Euro-American influences, indigenous traditions, Christian faiths and Muslim communities, a bioethics for the sub-Saharan region must be responsive to this cultural milieu. This paper asks, what values and methods can best promote the practice of bioethics in Africa? We set forth a strategy that leans one way or another in response to contextual features of a particular setting. Since our aim is to be responsive to context, we begin with a series of cases and develop values and methods in response to each case as we work through its ethical analysis. Section I introduces a case involving setting priorities for public funding of services that produce large benefits for a small group of people, using the example of dialysis in Ghana. Section II presents a situation involving determining the permissibility of a double standard of quality for healthcare devices in rich and poor nations, using the example of explanting pacemakers from deceased people in wealthy nations for use by people in low- and middle-income nations. Section III describes a scenario where international groups clash with religious and spiritual healers over the chaining of people with severe mental illness at prayer camps and healing centers in Ghana. Section IV articulates a three-pronged strategy for engaging in bioethics brought to light by the case analyses and defends it against

1 Reprinted from Nancy S. Jecker, Caesar Atuire (2022). Bioethics in Africa: A contextually enlightened analysis of three cases. *Developing World Bioethics, 22(2)*, 112–122, licensed under a CC BY 4.0 license. https://doi.org/10.1111/dewb.12324 Please note that the published version includes figures that are not part of this reprinted version.

objections. Throughout the paper, we tag certain views 'African' and others 'Western' to indicate ethical beliefs commonly found in these regions and less commonly found elsewhere. We do not mean to imply that all Africans hold a certain ethical stance or that all Westerners do; nor do we mean to suggest that people outside these regions do not hold the views in question.

## Dialysis for End-Stage Kidney Disease in Ghana

The first example involves setting priorities for public funding of services that produce large benefits for a small group of people, using the example of dialysis to treat patients with end-stage kidney disease in Ghana. Ghana's National Health Service, instituted in 2004, does not currently cover the cost of hemodialysis for end-stage kidney failure, leaving Ghanaians with this life-threatening condition to face the stark choice of raising private funds and paying out of pocket or foregoing dialysis and dying of their disease. Some patients seek traditional medicine and faith healing, although they are generally advised against it due to lack of evidence that these alternatives are effective (Boateng et al., 2018). The cost of hemodialysis in Ghana is roughly between $50-65 USD per session; yet most (80%) chronic kidney disease patients in Ghana earn less than $125 USD monthly (Tannor et al., 2019). Ghanaians with end-stage disease generally turn to family, community, corporate organizations and religious groups in search of funding. For those who overcome financial barriers, the frequency of sessions they can afford might be suboptimal and the duration of dialysis they can pay for might be limited. Even with some ability to fund dialysis, access is challenging. A country of roughly 30 million people, Ghana had eight nephrologists and 15 centers offering in-center hemodialysis services in 2017, with a total of 103 functioning hemodialysis machines (Tannor et al., 2018). Many who can pay for dialysis must leave the country to obtain it.

What values should guide the distribution of dialysis services for Ghanaians with end-stage kidney disease? Much of the bioethics debate about allocating scarce resources in Western nations focuses on qualities of individuals and makes these the determining basis for a distributive scheme (Jecker & Pearlman, 1992). For example, appealing implicitly or explicitly to a person's age, ability to pay, place of residence, life expectancy, healthy life years remaining, social contributions, or lifestyle choices illustrates a focus on distinguishing features of individuals. One source for this approach is Aristotelian ethics, which characterizes formal justice as requiring that like cases be treated alike, and different cases be treated differently (Aristotle, 2017, Book III, p. 72). Using this standard, the question of how to distribute scarce resources becomes, 'what makes people different in morally relevant respects?'

## Community and Solidarity

An African ethic avoids focusing on individual differences, because doing so pits one individual against another. Instead, it views persons as part of a community and, in some respects at least, inseparable from it. The givenness of communal life is one of a family of concepts in African ethics that fall under the general heading of *ubuntu*. A Nguni word, *ubuntu* has no exact English equivalent, but is often translated as 'humanness' or 'I am because we are.' Although sometimes associated narrowly with Southern and Eastern Africa, we interpret *ubuntu* broadly as an umbrella concept covering the deep structure of African collectivist values (Shutte, 1993). Tersely captured by adages such as, *Motho ke motho ka batho; umuntu ngumuntu ngabantu* ('A person is a person through other persons') (Ramose, 1999, S. 99), an *ubuntu* ethic tends to conceive of community as both ontologically and normatively prior to individuals. According to this way of thinking, persons are *derivative* of a community in the sense that an individual exists only corporally at birth, acquiring full moral standing gradually as they are incorporated into a community. So understood, *ubuntu* places individuals' lives in the context of social roles and relationships and their responsibilities flow from their community membership. Metz renders *ubuntu* as an ethic holding that "the superlative value and dignity of human beings arises by virtue of their capacity for community (Metz, 2011). As a normative principle, he interprets *ubuntu* as holding that "[a]n action is right insofar as it produces harmony and reduces discord; an act is wrong to the extent that it fails to develop community (Metz, 2011). While not without critics (Molefe, 2017), we use Metz's account as a working definition.

A further feature of an *ubuntu* is *ubumwe*, translated from the Bantu as 'solidarity'. Solidarity in the African communal tradition indicates 'we-ness,' meaning a shared feeling and attitude of responsibility towards each other among members of a group (Jecker & Atuire, 2021). When members of a group evince this feeling and attitude, a victory of one group member is experienced as a victory of the whole group. Although inequalities exist, the group takes responsibility to ensure that no member falls beneath a threshold of human dignity and participation in community. Reflecting this, it is common to be expected to assist distant relatives and others perceived to be part of a solidary circle; a phenomenon often referred to by urban Africans as a 'black tax' (Mhlongo, 2019).

How might an *ubuntu* ethic so understood help with the problem of distributing limited dialysis services in Ghana? When allocating scarce resources, an *ubuntu* ethic is broadly communitarian. While some interpret African communitarianism as rooted in political movements oriented toward establishing socialism and an emancipatory politics aimed at independence from European colonialism (Masolo, 2010; Senghor, 1964) we side with Wiredu (1999) and Ramose (2019), who hold that the capacity to commune is not necessarily linked to any particular political order, but to a moral order requiring regard for others' interests and enjoining people to live together harmoniously in whatever form of association they are in. As noted, such an ethic would be disinclined to emphasize differences between medically qualified dialysis candidates, which can engender competition and frustrate living harmoniously in a community and standing in solidarity. Yet how can people stand in solidarity when resources are scarce and some must go without? One reply is that African leaning bioethics underscores what makes people *the same*. In the broadest sense, what makes people the same is their shared humanness.

## Capabilities

A helpful way to further specify 'humanness' is to combine an *ubuntu* ethic with a complementary capability approach found in the West and used already in low- and middle-income nations to track human development (Sen, 1984; Nussbaum, 2011). Capability approaches understand humanness in terms of the central things that human beings can do and be, i.e., their central capabilities; they measure a nation's development by the extent to which its citizens experience capability gains or shortfalls. Working in a capability tradition, Nussbaum offers a normative interpretation of capabilities, which holds that each member of a community should have enough, i.e., sufficient capabilities to live a life of human dignity (Nussbaum, 2011). So understood, a capability analysis evaluates healthcare policies by assessing their impact on people's threshold capabilities, such as their threshold ability to be healthy and well-nourished, have bodily integrity, affiliate with others, and move freely from place to place. An *ubuntu* ethic extends the relational aspects of capabilities in a helpful way. Some have gone so far as to say that "relationality is part of the concept of a capability itself," arguing that falling below a threshold in any of the central human capabilities disrupts relationality by undermining an individual's ability to commune with others (Hoffman & Metz, 2017, p. 153).

Applied to the allocation of dialysis in Ghana, a combined *ubuntu*/capability account can help address priority setting questions at three levels:

**Macro-allocation**
Should Ghana's National Health Service cover all or a portion of the costs of dialysis?

**Meso-allocation**
Should the level of dialysis coverage be high, medium, or low relative to other healthcare priorities?

**Micro-allocation**
Which patients should be prioritized for dialysis services?

The macro-allocation level of setting budgetary priorities within Ghana's National Health Service asks, 'should dialysis be a priority for funding?' One reasonable answer would be to say, 'no.' Even if all one cared about was health, the health of Ghana's population can arguably be better served by investing in public health and preventive health services that have a greater impact on the health of Ghanaians than healthcare treatment does. However, suppose that reasonable investments in public health and preventive healthcare have been made and some level of investment in healthcare treatment will occur; we might ask, at the meso-allocation level, 'which healthcare categories merit priority?' Should dialysis be covered in lieu of some other healthcare services? Here again, a reasonable answer would be not to fund dialysis. The meso-allocation argument might hold that priority should go to more cost-effective measures that benefit more people. For example, from a utilitarian perspective, prenatal care would benefit more people, enabling Ghana to reduce its high rates of under-5 mortality, which currently stand at 47.9 per 1,000 live births (UNICEF, 2021a) –by comparison, under-5 mortality in high-income nations, such as Japan (UNICEF, 2021b) and Sweden (UNICEF, 2021b) during the same year were 2.5 and 2.7, respectively.

While this reasoning may seem initially compelling, we submit that an ubuntu ethic rejects meso-allocation strategies aimed single-mindedly at benefiting the most individuals, because this strategy is compatible with excluding whole groups of people outright, such as those with less common conditions and those requiring expensive lifesaving procedures, like dialysis. If we stand in solidarity, then each group deserves to be recognized.

Yet, standing in solidarity with people who have kidney disease leaves open the question of what form support ought to take. Clearly, we could potentially help more people with kidney disease by intervening early, before progression to end-stage disease. For example, investing in screening and early detection to identify and treat people with known risk factors for chronic kidney disease, such as hypertension, obesity, dyslipidemia (e.g., high cholesterol), and type II diabetes mellitus would help more people than investing in dialysis to treat end-stage disease. So too would educational interventions to enhance the clinical competence of general practitioners as well as research to better understand the unique causes for chronic kidney disease in low- and middle-income countries. In addition to non-communicable causes prevalent in richer countries, evidence implicates other sources in poorer regions, such as infectious diseases, secondary to poor sanitation and lack of safe drinking water; environmental toxins; analgesic abuse; the use of harmful herbal preparations; the use of unregulated food additives; and genetic factors (Jha et al., 2013). Prioritizing research into the etiologies of kidney disease in low- and middle-income African nations would potentially help more people with kidney disease (or at risk of developing it) in the long run.

We submit that a strategy that aligns with an *ubuntu* ethic should avoid two extremes. First, it avoids focusing only on helping the most individuals without considering solidarity and inclusion of people afflicted with different types of diseases. Second, within the group of people afflicted with kidney disease (or at heightened risk of developing it), a strategy that aligns with *ubuntu* avoids focusing narrowly on rescuing people with end-stage disease and instead shows solidarity with the many people earlier in their disease course. To enact these values, we propose making some investment in a wide range of diseases and within each disease category, helping the most people. This approach lends support to prioritizing public funding of patients with kidney disease (or at heightened risk of developing it) and within that category, prioritizing early detection, screening, and disease management. Our proposal, shown in Table 1, distinguishes two ways of 'helping the most': helping the most groups and helping the most individuals.

*Table 1: Two Ways of Helping People the Most*

| | Investment | # Groups | # People |
|---|---|---|---|
| **Help the most people** | 100% Prenatal | 1 | 200 |
| **Help the most groups** | 50% Prenatal<br>50 % Dialysis | 2 | 100 |

Admittedly, even under the best circumstances, some patients will reach end-stage disease and their needs will be unmet by a public system that sets our proposed priorities. In the future, as Ghana develops economically and more resources become available, more subgroups of kidney disease patients should be cared for, including patients with end-stage disease. Yet, in light of present resource constraints, Ghana should not use scarce public monies to make expensive rescue medicine its policy aim. We agree with the sober assessment offered by Luyckx et al. (2013), who note, "realistically, with the resources available, an adequate response to the enormous unmet need for treatment of kidney failure in sub-Saharan Africa will not be possible in the short or medium term."

If dialysis does not qualify for public funding at meso-allocation levels, we do not yet reach the micro-allocation stage and the question of how to select between eligible patients for dialysis. However, in the future, Ghanaians are likely to face this question. When they do, one way or honoring ubuntu's focus on community and solidarity would be to give all medically suitable candidates an equal chance to receive dialysis by means of a random method, such as a lottery, or by means of a weighted lottery favoring those with better prognoses (while still allowing each person some chance to receive dialysis).

## Explanted Pacemakers for Low-Income Countries in Africa

We turn next to a case involving cardiovascular disease. While the case raises a number of ethical concerns, we focus on how to justly allocate scarce resources between and within nations. While cardiovascular disease is a leading cause of mortality worldwide, it is low- and middle-income countries that account for 80% of cardiovascular deaths globally. Many who die in low- and middle-income nations could be saved and their symptoms managed by pacemakers; yet, most individuals residing in poorer nations cannot pay the out-of-pocket cost of $2500 to $3000 USD for pacemakers. A controversial strategy for expanding access is refurbishing devices from deceased people in high-income nations and donating them to people in poorer nations. Suppose a private citizen in the U.S. made aware of a device donation program to bring refurbished pacemakers to Africa wishes to donate a pacemaker from a deceased loved one that has 70% of battery life remaining? Should this be allowed? Since U.S. pacemakers are designed for single-use and by law, are not allowed to be reused in the U.S., refurbishing them for use by people in poorer countries creates a controversial double standard. Critics charge that a double standard violates justice. Yet defenders argue that explanted reused pacemakers produce the greatest good. How might an African ethic contribute to this debate?

## Kinship

To answer this, it will be helpful to pause briefly to further elaborate *ubuntu* ethics. In addition to emphasizing community and solidarity, an *ubuntu* ethic stresses kinship and kin responsibilities as a central guidepost for ethical life. Importantly, the notion of "kin" extends beyond the immediate nuclear family to encompass a wider community. Thus, rather than indicating blood ties, kinship designates, "identity, or sharing a way of life, and solidarity, or caring for others' quality of life." (Metz, 2012, p. 69) An expansive conception of kinship is apparent, for example, in the African practice of referring to those outside the nuclear family by honorifics such as 'sister,' 'brother,' 'uncle' or 'mama.' These ways of referring to people express the underlying inclusivity of African communities and their heavy emphasis on a *human* family, in which anyone can be my sister, brother, uncle or mama (Gyekye, 2004, p. 81).

Although within an *ubuntu* ethic, it is generally held that individuals owe more to persons with whom they stand in special relationships, such as close friends, immediate family members, and members of one's own tribe or ethnic group (Jecker, 2020), most proponents of *ubuntu* still see kinship as extending beyond the boundaries of these relationships. Ramose (2019), for example, appeals to the "permeability" of moral boundaries and the duty to extend mutual caring and sharing to all. Another defender of *ubuntu*, Wiredu, dwells on the Akan moral precept, *Onipa hia moa* ('a human being needs help'), to ground a notion of "sympathetic impartiality." (Wiredu & Gyekye, 1992, p. 201)

Bringing all humanity under the embrace of kinship affords a basis for solidarity among people of different nations. Linking kinship specifically to justice, Atuire et al. (2020) invoke the Ghanaian concept, *biik*, meaning son or filiation, and the corresponding Bulsa sayings, '*nworuk kan nak ku dek biik a paar kobi ya*,' which translates to 'even lightening will never strike its own son to the bone.' (p. 7) They argue that recognizing the filiation of each member of the human community underpins African justice, and is distinct from many Western accounts that base justice on mutual advantage.

## Equality

How might an *ubuntu* ethic elaborated in these ways help address the question of whether using explanted pacemakers for people in poorer nations is ethically permissible? With its focus on bringing people together in a family-like way, an *ubuntu* ethic is at odds with a double standard for rich and poor nations. Unlike charity, which assumes "asymmetric, top-down interactions, where the overall-more-privileged party gives to the overall-less-privileged party," solidarity emphasizes the language of common humanity which underscores "symmetry in the respect which is relevant." (Prainsack & Buyx, 2011, p. xiii) The logic of seeing people as equals suggests we should regard needy people with cardiovascular disease in wealthy nations as equals with their counterparts in poorer nations. The exclusive use of refurbished pacemakers for poorer African nations would signal that refurbished pacemakers are good enough for Africans, but not good enough for people in wealthy countries. This is problematic because it conveys that people in rich and poor nations have unequal moral worth.

To avoid this, a single standard is the approach taken by the WHO, which argues that "there should be no double standard in quality: if an item is unacceptable in the donating country, it is also unacceptable as a donation." The WHO sanctions refurbished pacemakers from wealthy nations, such as the U.S., only if they remain suitable for use within the U.S. Similarly, the U.S. Food and Drug Administration (2015) holds the view that "[p]acemaker re-use is an objectionable practice," noting that it violates single-use requirements and the same requirements should apply everywhere.

However, in reply it could be argued that strict equality is impractical because poor people in the U.S. have access to *new* pacemakers and therefore do not need refurbished ones. Yet, we hold that a better way for people in the U.S. to stand in solidarity with people in low-income nations is to embrace a single standard – if pacemakers are safe enough for people in receiving nations, they must be safe enough for people in donor nations too.

Yet it might be thought that by offering explanted pacemakers to people in poorer nations, sending nations *are* standing in solidarity. They are providing poorer people with a medical service that they would not otherwise have. Yet, in reply, we reemphasize the distinction between solidarity and charity. Charity refers broadly to the aid and humanitarian drives that rely on encouraging citizens and governments of rich countries to come to the aid of poorer countries. To achieve this end, such efforts highlight the differences between the 'privileged' and less 'privileged.' Unlike charity, solidarity is based on recognizing similarities and shared fate. In the African tradition, solidarity is sometimes expressed using the Adinkra symbol of *funtunfunefu* (conjoined crocodiles) [...] which depicts conjoined crocodiles with a common stomach. In this depiction, the crocodiles' fates are entwined – what happens to one happens to both. In the case of explanted pacemakers, a single standard expresses solidarity by underscoring the shared human condition of recipients and donors alike.

[...]

## Dignity

An *ubuntu* ethic might also support a single standard for pacemakers on the basis of respect for human dignity. In the African tradition, human dignity has been understood as consisting of the human capacity for community, which encompasses both the ability to identify with others and to stand in solidarity with them. More broadly, dignity is frequently linked to human rights in the sense that "to observe human rights is to treat an individual as having a dignity" and to violate human rights is to fail to honor this superlative value, frequently by treating a human being merely as a means (Metz, 2011, p. 542). A dignity-based conception of human rights is affirmed in multi-national declarations of human rights (UNESCO, 2006; World Medical Association, 2013), and in national reports, including the U.S. President's Council on Bioethics' Report on Human Dignity and Bioethics (President's Commission for the Study of Ethical Problem in Medicine and Biomedical and Behavioral Research, 2008).

Returning to the topic of pacemakers, how might the concept of dignity help with the analysis? Respect for dignity gives grounds for requiring first, that pacemakers meet a minimum standard of safety and efficacy everywhere. In some parts of the world, where resources are more plentiful, the quality of pacemakers may exceed the minimum of respect for dignity, but nowhere should pacemakers fall below this standard. Second, a dignity analysis requires that safe and effective refurbished pacemakers be made available to people in both richer and poorer nations, yet it allows for the possibility that their actual use may be more common in poorer nations because they have less ability to afford new ones.

In response, a utilitarian might object that if a person can prevent something bad from happening without sacrificing something of comparable moral importance, they ought to do it (National Academies of Sciences, Engineering, and Medicine, 2016). According to this analysis, if pacemakers in wealthy nations would simply be discarded at death, they should be donated without restriction, because doing so prevents something bad from happening at minimal cost. Yet, in reply, this interpretation is consistent with allowing shoddy standards that violate human dignity, since low quality pacemakers could still create more utility than the alternative, which in poor nations, is death or dysfunction from untreated disease.

A further objection is that unequal bargaining power between rich and poor nations will put the governments of poorer nations in the position of "a beggar who has limited choice" and prompt governments in poorer nations to "accept whatever intervention is offered by the party from a rich country." (Ndebele, 2017, p. 28) In reply, we set parameters based on dignity that require using only safe and effective pacemakers, which helps offset the unequal bargaining power between nations. In our estimation, the ideal that should be upheld is not avoiding waste per se, but meeting threshold level human needs.

## Maltreatment of People with Severe Mental Illness in Ghana

We turn finally to a third case, involving maltreatment of individuals with mental illness at the hands of traditional and faith-based healers in Ghana. Maltreatment includes well-documented shackling, flogging, and forced fasting measures. These measures gained international attention in the wake of investigative reports by the BBC (BBC News, 2018), *The Guardian* (McVeigh, 2020), and Human Rights Watch (2019). The reports occurred subsequent to Ghana's 2012 Mental Health Act 846, which explicitly bans maltreatment, affirming that "A person with a mental disorder has the right to enjoy a decent life as normal and as full as possible which includes, the right to education, vocational training, leisure, recreational activities, full employment and participation in civil, economic, social, cultural and political activities" to the extent that they are capable (Republic of Ghana, 2012, p. 23). Despite the law, inhumane treatment of people with mental illness continued in private homes and residential facilities run by traditional and faith-based healers.

Traditional and faith-based healing reflect a plurality of traditions, including: Pentecostal/ Charismatic Christian faith healers, Islamic faith healers, herbalists, shrine priests and priestesses, and medicine men (Kpobi & Swartz, 2018). Typically, traditional healers treat diseases by using local herbs and pouring libations to 'small gods' in shrines, while faith healers or pastors/imams invoke God's power to heal by prayers, fasting, and the sprinkling of water (Ae-Ngibse et al., 2010). Residential facilities, such as prayer camps and healing centers, run by traditional and faith healers offer people with mental illness a place to stay for a short visit or for multiple years. Often, these services furnish food, shelter and clothing, as well as counseling and companionship.

Inhumane treatment at residential facilities arises for a variety of reasons. Rather than being based on cruelty or lack of caring, it often reflects desperation and lack of viable alternatives. In 2017, the WHO (2017) reported that the number of psychiatrists in Ghana was .06 per 100,000 population and the number of mental health nurses was 7.73. In 2016, the National Academies of Sciences, Engineering, and Medicine (2016) identified lack of human resources as a major barrier to accessing mental healthcare in Ghana, due not only to shortages of trained providers but to their heavy concentration in cities, leaving community and rural areas without access (Eaton & Ohene, 2016). When patients are perceived as violent or threatening to a community, yet lack access to psychiatric and mental health nursing care, and associated treatments, such as anti-psychotic medication or intensive in-patient rehabilitation, chaining may seem like the only way to keep a community safe.

Under these conditions, it is unsurprising that a 2019 Human Rights Watch's (2019) report, which examined six residential facilities (prayer camps and traditional healing centers) across Ghana's Greater Accra, Eastern and Central regions, found chaining to be common, including one facility (Nyankumasi prayer camp) where there were "16 men in a dark stifling room, all of them with short chains, no longer than half a meter, around their ankles." Although the Ghana Mental Health Authority sawed the chains off, Human Rights Watch pressed that this was not enough, stating that if the government wants its ban on chaining to be more than "empty words," it must not only ensure chains come off, but ensure mental health services for people who need them (Human Rights Watch, 2019). Mental health researchers concur, saying release from chains "marks the beginning of the journey to the realization of rights and freedoms," not the end (Read & Kpobi, 2021). Progress is difficult without more resources and trained personnel available to furnish essential mental health services. Ghana is not alone; the WHO (2009) reports that mental health services are scarce throughout low- and middle-income regions and attention to human rights for mentally ill people is limited.

## Humility

Pragmatically, most Ghanaians have little choice when it comes to seeking care for mental health conditions and simply use the more readily available pathways (Badu et al., 2019). In 2010, Ghana had one registered traditional healer for every 200 people, compared to one medical doctor for every 20,000 people during the same year (Ae-Ngibse et al., 2010). Moreover, resource considerations aside, traditional and faith healing is seen in a positive light by many Ghanaians. A 2017 Gallup (2017) poll found the country to be among the most religious in the world, with 94% of the population professing belief in God. Many Ghanaians understand symptoms of mental illness as having a spiritual or supernatural etiology, even while remaining open to different treatment modalities. In a qualitative analysis of 81 semi-structured stakeholder interviews across five Ghanaian regions, Ae-Ngibse et al. (2010) reported widespread consensus that mental illness was a form of "spiritual illness" among diverse respondents, including policy makers, health providers, psychiatric service users, teachers, police, academics, and religious and traditional healers. Asamoah et al. (2014) conducted semi-structured interviews with 20 Pentecostal/ Charismatic clergy in Ghana and found widespread belief that mental illness was caused by "diabolic manipulations of the soul" that must be corrected by exorcism, which involves expulsion of malign spirits by means of religious rituals and practices, such as prayer and fasting.

This backdrop offers a better understanding of the larger setting in which maltreatment occurs. While graphic portrayals of maltreatment are disturbing, simply closing down prayer camps or shunning religious leaders who chain residents will not help patients with severe mental illness get better. It would simply leave them bereft of a community, without food, clothing or a place to go. Pastor Isaiah Nchiroba, who runs the Nyinbonya prayer camp and Pentecostal church near Ghana's border with Burkina Faso, told *The Guardian* in 2020 that some health professionals label him as 'mad': "Anywhere I go, even at the hospital, my fellow professionals at different departments call me 'mad nurse'," he says (McVeigh, 2020). Nchiroba treats about 150 patients, 20 of which were chained to trees when *The Guardian's* 2020 report was filed.

Another response that will do little to stem the suffering of people with severe mental illness is insisting on obtaining informed consent from patients or family members on the assumption that inhumane practices would end, because no one would consent to them. Guided by a Western ethic which emphasizes respect for individual autonomy, this position is enshrined in the language of Act 846, which established a Mental Health Review Tribunal, whose functions include investigating complaints about informed consent processes or involuntary admission or treatment abuses. However, in a Ghanaian context, the type of disclosure required by Western biomedical models of informed consent would be difficult to extract from traditional herbalists, whose curative powers lie in tightly held formulas that are not patent protected. Moreover, it is a fair question to ask, what happens if a violent person with severe mental illness or their family refuse chaining? Nchiroba, the Pastor at Nyinbonya prayer camp, says that, "shackling is necessary for those who 'can frighten people and even cause injury…'." (McVeigh, 2020) Perhaps this is why *The Guardian*'s investigative reporting found 'chain makers' common throughout Ghana, present in "every third or fourth village." (McVeigh, 2020)

Our analysis establishes an urgent need for understanding and humility to solve problems. It cautions against what the Akan call, *kintinkantan* ('puffed up extravagance'), depicted in the Adinkra symbol […]. Puffed up extravagance is reflected in some Western reactions, such as of sawing off chains without providing safe alternatives; requiring informed consent signatures without helping to expand services; or shunning healers, rather than joining forces with them to better serve people with mental illness.

[…]

## Consensus Building

An *ubuntu* ethic can guide people with different approaches to mental health by bringing them together to advance the common goal of helping the sick. Emphasizing that the whole community has a stake in the well-being of each member can facilitate not only understanding, but change. An *ubuntu* ethic points to humane alternatives that draw on the strengths of diverse practitioners by building consensus toward achieving shared goals, such as expanding public funding for community-based mental health, including people with mental illness within the life of a community, and forging partnerships between healers and biomedically trained practitioners. While mental health services have been a relatively low priority in sub-Saharan Africa since precolonial times (Kpobi et al., 2014), Act 846 has set the stage for positive change through decentralizing mental health services and endorsing community-based mental health.

Yet delivering on the law's promise requires an influx of funding to train and deploy mental health professionals and increase facilities for treatment within communities. Rather than eliminating resources already in place, we propose expanding them though collaborations with healers to affirm their vital roles and draw on their knowledge of a community. This approach recognizes healers' successes, such as reaching out to stigmatized and abandoned people living on the street and ensuring they are fed, clothed and housed. It recognizes spiritual and faith-based healers' efforts to include people with severe mental illness in social relationships and interactions, which play such an essential role in realizing a better, more dignified, human life. Ae-Ngbhise et al. (2010) report that traditional and faith healers often function "like 'clinical psychologists', providing 'talk therapy', 'counselling' and 'asking questions and providing solutions';" whereas biomedical approaches "just give drugs and then send you away." (p. 561) Seen in this light, healers are assets, offering both a point of entry into healthcare systems, and a pathway for people suffering from mental illness to return to communities and live within them. An *ubuntu*-based strategy of consensus-building does not entail agreement with faith-based or herbal treatment techniques, but instead focuses attention on working in partnership to realize a common goal of helping needy people.

Clearly, the services offered by trained mental healthcare workers must also be part of the mix. The range of conditions represented, which include psychosis or schizophrenia; older people with neurodegenerative diseases, such as dementia; younger people with substance abuse disorders; and individuals with epilepsy, cannot be successfully managed without the treatments biomedically trained healthcare workers prescribe. However, mental healthcare alone is not sufficient. It is ill equipped for reintegrating people into communities or deciphering the complex overlay of cultural and spiritual beliefs that inform their illness. For example, consider the case of older women in the Ashanti and northern regions of Ghana accused of witchcraft who reside apart from others in shrines or witches' camps (Aikins, 2015). When they develop witchcraft related depression, their care must be responsive to the cultural context of beliefs about being bewitched and work with, rather than against, these cultural influences. Responsive treatment requires community alliances.

Building alliances and trust takes time and commitment, but when successful, it can help people suffering from mental illness suffer less. Maltreatment should teach us to recognize that things can go badly wrong when families and spiritual leaders are left to fend for themselves. Without solidarity and backing from government and mental health professionals, individuals with mental illness grow more vulnerable. The Adinkra symbol, *sankofa* ('return and get it') [...] encapsulates our perspective. It shows a bird turning around to find its lost egg, symbolizing looking back to remember mistakes and learn from them. Shackling people with severe mental illness is a mistaken way to help people and its persistence should warn and remind healers, families, healthcare workers and government officials what is at stake and why collaborating with one another is so vital. *Sankofa* can also be understood as looking back to traditional teachings, such as *ubuntu*.

[...]

## Doing Bioethics in Africa

Stepping back from the three examples, what general insights have we gained about doing bioethics in Africa? Since the continent of Africa is comprised of 54 diverse countries with varied ethical traditions and diverse healthcare practices, when we refer to 'doing bioethics in Africa,' it is helpful to distinguish broad differences across the continent.

### A Contextually Enlightened Framework

One way of going about this is to group healthcare practices into three types: Western style biomedical healthcare, traditional medicine, and modern religious spiritual healing (Atuire, 2019). Bioethics in each of these healthcare settings should be responsive to distinct contextual and cultural features. Western style biomedical healthcare, which is widespread throughout Africa, will often be best served by combining Western and African bioethical values and concepts, sometimes leaning Western and sometimes leaning African. Where Western-leaning bioethics is called for, Western frameworks may still require cultural adaptations. A combined bioethics characterized the approach we took in analyzing the first case, involving the use of dialysis for

Ghanaians with end-stage kidney disease. In the first case, we combined an African ethic of *ubuntu* with a Western capability view of justice.

In other settings, Western-leaning approaches may clash with values on the ground and a model that leans African will suit the setting better. Our approach leaned African in the second case, involving the use of explanted pacemakers. Here, we emphasized an African approach to justice that underscored kinship, equality and solidarity between people of all nations, rather than a utilitarian approach that focused on aggregating individual utilities.

Finally, in some situations, where religious and faith based healing is practiced, Western bioethics may not suit the situation of stakeholders, such as patients, families, or communities, and African bioethics should guide. In our third case, where traditional medicine and spiritual healing was practiced in prayer camps and healing centers, we invoked *ubuntu* and applied it at the community level, appealing to humility and consensus building, rather than autonomy-based strategies, like informed consent. The overarching aim in all three examples is for bioethics to be responsive to the varied settings in which it is practiced and to the interests and values of people holding stakes. Table 2 summarizes these three general strategies for doing bioethics in Africa. According to our proposed framework, the underlying rationale for leaning one way or another is contextual- and stakeholder-based.

*Table 2: Doing Bioethics in Africa*

| **Type of Healthcare** | **Type of Bioethics** | | |
|---|---|---|---|
| | Western Leaning | African Leaning | African |
| Western Biomedical | ✔ | ✔ | |
| Traditional Medicine | | | ✔ |
| Religious Spiritual Healing | | | ✔ |

Our proposal carries weighty implications in regions of Africa where the majority of a population prefers or has greater access to traditional, rather than Western, medicine. Referring to Africans who obtain their care primarily from traditional doctors, Murove (2005) claims that what "bioethics" in fact means to them is "peripheral to most of our scholarly discourses on bioethics" and charges that academic bioethics has "turned a blind eye" to African bioethics as it practiced in traditional settings (p. 17). Likewise, Frimpong-Manosh (2019) finds a "restrictive focus on biomedically-related bioethics" problematic in African contexts, because it neglects bioethical issues raised by traditional systems of health and healthcare (p. 32). Nor is this problem isolated to Africa; according to a 2019 WHO (2019) Report, 88% of WHO's 194 member states acknowledge using traditional and complementary medicine. While it is tempting to simply use the Western bioethics at hand, doing so can further entrench Western hegemony and risk exacerbating epistemic injustices associated with a prevailing discussion's framework (Fricker, 2007). We have argued that a better strategy is building capacity for African bioethics and leaning African in settings where this is called for. We envision an African bioethics that is diverse, nimble and context aware.

## Objections

Important objections might be raised against our proposal and we turn next to address these. First, it might be argued that the dominant approach to bioethics is principlism, as discussed by U.S. philosophers Beauchamp and Childress (2019), and it is unclear why principlism is inadequate in an African context. In reply, principlism draws heavily on the discipline of Western philosophy, which omits all of the philosophy of Asia, Africa, India and the Indigenous Americas from its curriculum and thereby "convey[s] the impression – willingly or not – that no other culture was capable of philosophical thought." (Van Norden, 2017, p. xix) To avoid what Solomon (2006) calls the "export problem," (p. 337) or the attempt to transplant Western bioethics to developing regions, what is needed is a view "from below," that is, with less affluent nations and less wealthy members (Farmer & Campos, 2004). The problem with exporting principlism to Africa is that it generates tensions when it is out of synch with African values. For example, principlism's emphasis on autonomy and individual informed consent may clash with African values that emphasize family, community, and respect for elders; it may ignore realities on the ground, such as poverty and illiteracy (Ezeome & Marshall, 2008). Taking seriously these concerns, we submit that bioethics should incorporate ethical values beyond the West when it is practiced in Africa.

A further objection holds that authentic bioethical principles are universally valid and a contextually oriented bioethics ignores this. In reply, our proposal is compatible with a range of metaethical stances. For instance, it is consistent with our contextually enlightened account to hold that bioethical principles are univerally valid but must be contextualized, specified and internalized at a particular time and place they are nonetheless universal (Richardson, 2014). Tangwa (2004) argues along these lines when he claims that scholars can derive universalizable insights from various cultures that enrich bioethics. A contextually enlightened account is also congruent with a metaethical view that rejects universal principles and regards the truth or falsity of an ethical claim as objectively dependent on particular features of a case (Ross, 1930). Setting such debates aside, whichever metaethical stance one adopts, we submit that it will be crucial for bioethics to avoid what Widdows (2007) calls, "moral neocolonialism," or employing a dominant Western moral framework covertly, under the guise of 'universal values.' In practical fields like bioethics, moral neocolonialism can result in practical harms to communities (Bamford, 2018, p. 43).

A third objection holds that by drawing on traditional African beliefs we are engaging with a form of ethnophilosophy, or beliefs indigenous to a culture, and this differs from authentic philosophy, which requires critical appraisal. Wiredu (1984), for example, cautions that a spoken folk philosophy generally consists of "bald assertions without argumentative justification;" it takes the form of "This is what our ancestors say..." (pp. 140, 141). He argues that folk belief cannot be elevated to philosophy without the addition of critical analysis and argument. Likewise, Hountondji (1996) argues that African ethnophilosophy is not rigorously subject to philosophical methods. "One is no more spontaneously a philosopher," he writes, "than one is spontaneously a chemist, a physicist or a mathematician, since philosophy, like chemistry, physics or mathematics, is a specific theoretical discipline with its own exigencies and methodological rules." (p. 47) In contrast to Houtondji, Oruka (1991) defends a form of African ethnophilosophy associated with the Sage tradition (p. 384), a tradition that is largely oral and transmitted through symbols, myths, pithy sayings, stories, and religion. Oruka refers to African sages as philosophers when they are not only "versed in the beliefs and wisdoms of their people," but thinkers, who are "rationally critical...and... recommend only those aspects of the beliefs and wisdoms which satisfy ... rational scrutiny." (p. 386)

In reply, regardless of how this wider debate is settled, the analysis of this paper does not accept at face value the moral beliefs of indigenous people, but instead references written reflections on those beliefs and draws out their implications in practical bioethical domains. Testing ethical concepts and principles by assessing their implications in particular cases represents a form of critical inquiry, sometimes known as 'reflective equilibrium'. (Rawls, 1974) The aim of such deliberation is coherence between general and particular beliefs. By employing the tools of reflective equilibrium, this paper has contributed a critical reflection on African thought, rather than an unreflective description of it.

## Conclusion

In closing, we began by asking, 'what values and methods can best promote doing bioethics in Africa?' We situated this question in the context of three cases: (1) setting just priorities for hemodialysis for end-stage kidney disease in Ghana; (2) using refurbished pacemakers from wealthy nations for people in low- and middle-income African nations, and (3) shackling of severely mentally ill people by religious and faith-based healers in Ghana. Appealing to an African ethic of *ubuntu*, we introduced a family of concepts to shed light on these examples: community, solidarity, kinship, equality, dignity, humility, and consensus building. Throughout our discussion, leaning African or Western led to a more contextually enlightened analysis and demonstrated the advantages of a more culturally attuned bioethics.

## References

Ae-Ngibise, K., Cooper, S., Adiibokah, E., Akpalu, B., Lund, C., Doku, V., & Mhapp Research Programme Consortium. (2010). 'Whether you like it or not people with mental problems are going to go to them': a qualitative exploration into the widespread use of traditional and faith healers in the provision of mental health care in Ghana. *International review of psychiatry (Abingdon, England)*, 22(6), 558–567. https://doi.org/10.3109/09540261.2010.536149

Aikins, A.D.-G. (2015). Mental illness and destitution in Ghana. In E. Akyeampong, A.G. Hill, A. Kleinman (Eds.), *The culture of mental illness and psychiatric practice in Africa*. Indiana University Press

Aristotle. (2017). *Nicomachean ethics* (W.D. Ross, Trans.). Reseda, CA: Enhanced Media Publishing. (Original work published ca. 340 BCE)

Asamoah, M. K., Osafo, J., & Agyapong, I. (2014). The role of Pentecostal clergy in mental health-care delivery in Ghana. *Mental Health, Religion & Culture, 17*(6), 601–614. https://doi.org/10.1080/13674676.2013.871628

Atuire, C. A. (2019). A Prolegomena to Bioethics in Africa. In Y. A. Frimpong-Manosh & C. A. Atuire (Eds.), Bioethics in Africa (pp. 1–29). Vernon Press

Atuire, C. A., Kong, C., & Dunn, M. (2020). Articulating the sources for an African normative framework of healthcare: Ghana as a case study. *Developing world bioethics, 20*(4), 216–227. https://doi.org/10.1111/dewb.12265

Bamford, R. (2018). Decolonizing bioethics via African philosophy. In G. Hull (Ed.), *Debating African philosophy* (pp. 43–59). Routledge. https://doi.org/10.4324/9780429438189

Badu, E., Mitchell, R., & O'Brien, A. P. (2019). Pathways to mental health treatment in Ghana: Challenging biomedical methods from herbal- and faith-healing perspectives. *The International journal of social psychiatry, 65*(6), 527–538. https://doi.org/10.1177/0020764019862305

BBC News. (2018, October 9). Ghana 'prayer camps' chain residents with mental health problems. BBC News. Retrieved May 12, 2021, from https://www.bbc.com/news/av/world-africa-45800263

Beauchamp, T., & Childress, J. (2019). *Principles of biomedical ethics* (8th ed.). Oxford University Press.

Boateng, E. A., East, L., & Evans, C. (2018). Decision-making experiences of patients with end-stage kidney disease (ESKD) regarding treatment in Ghana: a qualitative study. *BMC nephrology, 19*(1), 371. https://doi.org/10.1186/s12882-018-1175-z

Eaton, J., & Ohene, S. (2016). Providing sustainable mental health care in Ghana. In *National Academies of Sciences, Engineering and Medicine, Providing sustainable mental and neurological health care in Ghana and Kenya: Workshop Summary* (pp. 183–232). National Academies Press. ttps://nap.nationalacademies.org/catalog/21793/providing-sustainable-mental-and-neurological-health-care-in-ghana-and-kenya

Ezeome, E. R., & Marshall, P. A. (2009). Informed consent practices in Nigeria. *Developing world bioethics, 9*(3), 138–148. https://doi.org/10.1111/j.1471-8847.2008.00234.x

Farmer, P., & Campos, N. G. (2004). Rethinking medical ethics: a view from below. *Developing world bioethics, 4*(1), 17–41. https://doi.org/10.1111/j.1471-8731.2004.00065.x

Federal Drug Administration. (2015, February 19). CPG Sec. 310.100 pacemaker reuse. Retrieved May 12, 2021, from https://www.fda.gov/regulatory-info

rmation/search-fda-guidance-documents/cpg-sec-310100-pacemaker-reuse

Fricker, M. (2007). *Epistemic injustice: Power and the Ethics of Knowing*. Oxford University Press. https://doi.org/10.1093/acprof:oso/9780198237907.001.0001

Frimpong-Mansoh, Y. A. (2019). Bioethics: Traditional African perspective. In Y. A. Frimpong-Mansoh & C. A. Atuire (Eds.), *Bioethics in Africa* (pp. 31–56). Vernon Press

Gallup. (2017, April 10). Religion prevails in the world. Retrieved May 12, 2021, from https://www.gallup-international.bg/en/36009/religion-prevails-in-the-world/

Gyekye, K. (2004). Epilogue: 'The ties that bind'. In *Beyond cultures: Perceiving a common humanity* (pp. 80–82). Council for Research in Values and Philosophy.

Hoffman, N., & Metz, T. (2017). What Can the Capabilities Approach Learn from an *Ubuntu* Ethic? A Relational Approach to Development Theory. *World Development, 97*, 153–164. https://doi.org/10.1016/j.worlddev.2017.04.010

Hountondji, P. (1996). *African philosophy: Myth and reality* (2nd ed.). Indiana University Press.

Human Rights Watch. (2019, November 27). Ghana: Faith healers defy ban on chaining. Retrieved May 12, 2021, from https://www.hrw.org/news/2019/11/27/ghana-faith-healers-defy-ban-chaining

Jecker, N.S. & Atuire, C. (2021). Out of Africa: A Solidarity-Based Approach to Vaccine Allocation. *The Hastings Center Report* 51(3), 27–36. https://doi.org/10.1002/hast.1250

Jecker, N. S., & Pearlman, R. A. (1992). An ethical framework for rationing health care. *The Journal of medicine and philosophy*, *17*(1), 79–96. https://doi.org/10.1093/jmp/17.1.79

Jecker N. S. (2020). African Conceptions of Age-Based Moral Standing: Anchoring Values to Regional Realities. *The Hastings Center report*, *50*(2), 35–43. https://doi.org/10.1002/hast.1100

Jha, V., Garcia-Garcia, G., Iseki, K., Li, Z., Naicker, S., Plattner, B., Saran, R., Wang, A. Y., & Yang, C. W. (2013). Chronic kidney disease: global dimension and perspectives. *Lancet (London, England)*, *382*(9888), 260–272. https://doi.org/10.1016/S0140-6736(13)60687-X

Kpobi, L., & Swartz, L. (2018). Implications of healing power and positioning for collaboration between formal mental health services and traditional/alternative medicine: the case of Ghana. *Global health action, 11*(1), 1445333. https://doi.org/10.1080/16549716.2018.1445333

Kpobi, L., Osei, A., & Sefa-Dedeh, A. (2014). Overview of mental health care in Ghana. In A. Ofori-Atta & S. Ohene (Eds.), *Changing trends in mental health care and research in Ghana* (pp. 4–12). African Books Collective.

Luyckx, V. A., Naicker, S., & McKee, M. (2013). Equity and economics of kidney disease in sub-Saharan Africa. *Lancet (London, England), 382*(9887), 103–104. https://doi.org/10.1016/S0140-6736(13)60817-X

Masolo, D. A. (2010). *The Self and Community in a Changing World*. Indiana University Press

McVeigh, T. (2020, February 3). 'All we can offer is the chain': the scandal of Ghana's shackled sick. *The Guardian*. Retrieved May 12, 2021, from https://www.theguardian.com/global-development/2020/feb/03/all-we-can-offer-is-the-chain-the-scandal-of-ghanas-shackled-sick

Metz, T. (2007). Toward an African moral theory. *Journal of Political Philosophy, 15*(3), 321–341. https://doi.org/10.1111/j.1467-9760.2007.00280.x

Metz, T. (2011). Ubuntu as a moral theory and human rights in South Africa. *African Human Rights Law Journal, 11*(2), 532–559. https://www.ahrlj.up.ac.za/metz-t

Metz, T. (2012). Developing African political moral-theoretic strategies. *Philosophia Africana, 14*(1), 61–83. https://doi.org/10.5840/philafricana20121419

Mhlongo, N. (2019). *Black tax: Burden or Ubuntu?* Johannesburg, Gauteng: Jonathan Ball Publishers.

Molefe, M. (2017). Relational ethics and partiality: A critique of Thad Metz's *Towards an African Moral Theory*. *Theoria: A Journal of Social and Political Theory, 64*(152), 53–76. https://www.jstor.org/stable/44862872

Murove, M. F. (2005). African bioethics. *Journal for the Study of Religion*, 16–36. https://www.jstor.org/stable/24764253

National Academies of Sciences, Engineering, and Medicine. (2016). *Providing sustainable mental and neurological health care in Ghana and Kenya: Workshop Summary*. Washington, D.C.: National Academies Press. https://nap.nationalacademies.org/catalog/21793/providing-sustainable-mental-and-neurological-health-care-in-ghana-and-kenya

Ndebele P. (2017). Standards of Care in Global Health: Identifying the Right Question. *The Hastings Center Report*, 47(5), 28–29. https://doi.org/10.1002/hast.767

Nussbaum, M. C. (2011). *Creating capabilities*. Harvard University Press

Oruka, H. O. (1991). Sagacity in African philosophy. *International Philosophical Quarterly, 23*(4), 383–393. https://doi.org/10.5840/ipq198323448

Prainsack, B., & Buyx, A. (2011). *Solidarity: Reflections on an emerging concept in bioethics*. Nuffield Council on Bioethics. https://cdn.nuffieldbioethics.org/wp-content/uploads/Solidarity-report.pdf

President's Commission for the Study of Ethical Problems in Medicine and Biomedical and Behavioral Research. (2008). *Human dignity and bioethics*. Retrieved May 14, 2021, from https://bioethicsarchive.georgetown.edu/pcbe/reports/human_dignity/chapter2.html

Ramose, M. B. (1999). *African philosophy through Ubuntu*. Mond Books.

Ramose, M. B. (2019). Motho ke motho ka batho, an African perspective on popular sovereignty and democracy. In L. K. Jeno, M. Idris, & M. C. Thomas (Eds.), *The Oxford Handbook of Comparative Political Theory* (pp. 83–106). Oxford University Press

Rawls, T. J. (1974). The independence of moral theory. *Proceedings and Addresses of the American Philosophical Association, 48*, 5–22. https://doi.org/10.2307/3129858

Read, U., & Kpobi, L. (2021, February 8). *The interdependence of human rights in mental health in Ghana*. Retrieved May 12, 2021, from https://www.youtube.com/watch?v=1fMJWlVMTeQ&feature=share&fbclid=IwAR1tZ8_09WvtjCkhGQJq6kLPKrIN6EEenJlHYoI9UBlEjKaINBtJw97l1hs

Republic of Ghana. (2012). *Mental Health Act, 2012* (p. 23). Retrieved May 12, 2021, from https://www.refworld.org/pdfid/528f243e4.pdf

Richardson, H. S. (2014). Specifying norms as a way to resolve concrete ethical problems. *Philosophy and Public Affairs, 19*(4), 279–310. http://www.jstor.org/stable/2265316

Ross, W.D. (1930). *The Right and the Good*. Oxford University Press.

Sen, A. (1984). *Resources, Values and Development*. Oxford University Press.

Senghor, L. S. (1964). *On African socialism* (M. Cook, Trans.). Praeger Publishers.

Shutte, A. (1993). Traditional African thought. In A. Shutte, *Philosophy for Africa* (pp. 46–58). University of Cape Town Press

Solomon, D. (2006). Domestic disarray and imperial ambition. In H. T. Engelhardt (Ed.), *Global bioethics: The collapse of consensus* (pp. 335–361). Scrivener Press.

Tangwa G. B. (2004). Between universalism and relativism: a conceptual exploration of problems in formulating and applying international biomedical ethical guidelines. *Journal of medical ethics, 30*(1), 63–67. https://doi.org/10.1136/jme.2003.003194

UNICEF. (2021a). *UNICEF Data: Monitoring the Situation of Children and Women*. Retrieved May 12, 2021, from https://data.unicef.org/country/gha/

UNICEF. (2021b). *UNICEF Data: Monitoring the Situation of Children and Women*. Retrieved May 12, 2021, from https://data.unicef.org/country/jpn/

UNICEF. (2021c). *UNICEF Data: Monitoring the Situation of Children and Women*. Retrieved May 12, 2021, from https://data.unicef.org/country/swe/

Van Norden, B.W. (2017). *Taking Back Philosophy. A Multicultural Manifesto*. Columbia University Press.

WHO. (2009). *Mental Health Systems in Selected Low- and Middle-Income Countries: a WHO-AIMS cross-national analysis*. World Health Organization.

WHO. (2017). *Mental Health ATLAS 2017 Country Profile: Ghana*. Retrieved May 17, 2021, from https://www.who.int/publications/m/item/mental-health-atlas-2017-country-profile-ghana

WHO. (2019). *WHO global report on traditional and complementary medicine 2019*. World Health Organization.

Widdows, H. (2007). Is Global Ethics Moral Neo-Colonialism? An Investigation of the Issue in the Context of Bioethics. *Bioethics, 21*(6), 305–315. https://doi.org/10.1111/j.1467-8519.2007.00558.x

Wiredu, J. E. (1984). How Not to Compare African Thought With Western Thought. In R. A. Wright (Ed.), *African Philosophy: An Introduction, 3rd edition* (p. 133–147). University Press of America.

Wiredu, K., & Gyekye, K. (1992). *Person and Community: Ghanaian Philosophical Studies I*. Council for Research in Values and Philosophy.

Wiredu, K. (1999). Society and democracy in Africa. *New Political Science, 21*(1), 33–44. https://doi.org/10.1080/07393149908429850

World Medical Association. (2013). World Medical Association Declaration of Helsinki. Ethical Principles for Medical Research Involving Human Subjects. *Journal of the American Medical Association, 310*(20), 2191–2194. https://doi.org/10.1001/jama.2013.281053

# Pluralism as a Moral Challenge

*Laura Palazzani*

## Moral Pluralism in Bioethics

Since the beginnings of bioethics, V. R. Potter has referred to a "bridge" between "bios" and "ethics" in response to scientific and technological progress in biomedicine, and profound social transformations. The "bridge" to the future was intended, above all, on an interdisciplinary level, between the scientific and humanistic disciplines. Interdisciplinarity means the structural need for comparison, the search for differences and convergence, beyond the mere juxtaposition of knowledge (that is multidisciplinarity). Interdisciplinarity involves the interaction between different disciplines which, while preserving their distinct methodologies and epistemological foundations, require the integration of specialised knowledge in the pursuit of a cohesive synthesis.

In the context of interdisciplinarity, one of the main moral challenges is pluralism, arising from the different theories, principles, and approaches to bioethics. Pluralism is an evident characteristic of bioethics (though not exclusive to it), apparent since the very beginning in both the different topics of bioethics and in a spectrum ranging from 'strong' divergence to 'mild' convergence. Pluralism is more evident in the most sensitive questions (beginning and end-of-life issues), less evident in clinical trials/research ethics, and in emerging technologies; it is also present in the discussion on non-human beings, in both radical and moderate forms (i.e. animals, the environment, future generations).

Within a framework of ethical pluralism, bioethical theories have differed from the outset. Among these theories, seven have proven particularly influential:

(i) libertarianism, which – starting from non-cognitivism, i.e. from the impossibility of knowing a shared objective truth – defends the individual and the principle of subjective self-determination, within the limits of compatibility between everyone's freedom and absence of certain damage to third parties; (ii) utilitarianism, which – starting from the consideration of the inherent inclination of individuals towards seeking pleasure and avoiding pain – promotes social convenience, measured in the cost/benefit analysis with the maximisation of well-being and minimisation of harms for the greater number of individuals; (iii) personalism,– which as a metaphysical view, recognises the intrinsic dignity of the human person in every human being – supports not only the principle of defence of physical life – but also values of freedom, responsibility, justice and solidarity; (iv) communitarianism, which recognises the value of the common good, while also promoting solidarity and cooperation in society as key objectives; (v) principlism, which – given the impossibility of justifying a convergence between the different theories – deems it necessary to refer to general principles, such as autonomy, beneficence, non-maleficence and justice, which must be interpreted and contextualised; (vi) virtue ethics underlines the relevance of moral virtues, which are expressed through behaviour that reflect stable dispositions of character, directed towards morally good aims; (vii) ethics of care and responsibility, which, in different ways, focus on the importance of caring for others in conditions of particular vulnerability in the absence of symmetry and reciprocity (applied both to humans and non-humans, to existing individuals and not yet existing individuals).

## Different Conceptions of Pluralism and Ways to Deal with It

After more than 50 years of bioethical discussions, it is impossible to substantially formulate a framework of universal human values that is in itself recognisable from all the different philosophical perspectives. Many topics remain very controversial, due to lingering irreconcilable differences.

The different perspectives entail different concepts on how to face the challenge of pluralism. The main positions in this regard are the following:

1) In the *relativistic perspective,* pluralism is a fact only to be noted and described; and it is interpreted as a richness to be embraced and not to be overcome. Relativism is limited to considering the plurality that is manifested according to times and places, in the awareness of the impossibility to reduce plurality to unity. Rather, it relies, to some extent, on the positive acceptance of plurality, not hoping for unity, seen either as impersonal indifference or as repressive standardisation.

In this context, the principle of tolerance, understood in a pragmatic sense, takes on a very precise configuration: to tolerate means to embrace every value for the mere fact that it exists and in the very way in which it manifests itself. It follows that all ethics are and must be considered equivalent. Pragmatic tolerance appears therefore like uncritical passive acceptance of all values.

This perspective has been criticised because of the contradiction between the theoretical assumptions of non-cognitivism and the pragmatic principle of tolerance: either one is coherent with the affirmation of the non-existence and the non-knowability of objective truth, recognising that tolerance cannot be a truth, or one should grant both tolerance and intolerance, as there are no objective reasons to prefer tolerance to intolerance. Furthermore, neutrality tends to separate values but it cannot be realised in practice. In conflicts, where opposing values clash simultaneously and contextually, the principle of tolerance becomes inconsistent, giving way to the prevailing of the strongest over the weakest.

2) In an *absolutist perspective*, pluralism needs to be overcome imposing one theory considered as the best and unique through the model of assimilation; absolutisation of one ethical perspective as 'the' perspective means imposing it on others, as being hierarchically superior and hegemonic with respect to other theories considered inferior.

   This position has been criticised as the imposition of one universal perspective implies a form of unjustified 'arrogance' (on which criteria can we say what is the best?) and excluding other ones, without dealing with pluralism but claiming to cancel it, results in asserting the existence of exclusive values lacking any comparison.

3) In between (relativistic description and absolutist imposition) there are intermediate paths outlined in the search of a dialogue between ethical theories. Dialogue not as a negotiation procedure based on agreement but as a progressive hermeneutical effort to grasp (on a qualitative level) 'on principle' shared values/principles beyond the empirical diversities engaging in an active critical comparison. In this context, a very important contribution is the one of bioethics committees.

## The Pluralistic Dialogue Within Bioethics Committees: Seeking Shared Values

Notwithstanding existing differences in ethical theories, bioethics committees have played and continue to play a key role, at national, regional, and international levels, engaging in dialogue, while considering both interdisciplinarity and pluralism. Bioethics committees could be defined as a group of individuals/experts, who are committed to working together towards common goals of public interest, in the field of bioethics, intended as public bioethics.

The reason why bioethics committees have been established is an increasing need for dialogue to identify (if possible) an '*ethical balance*' or '*ethical mediation*', which should not be reduced to a mere compromise or pragmatic agreement, but as a minimum level (or maximum possible level) of shared ethical principles/values on specific topics.

The aim of the committee's discussions is to elaborate opinions with final recommendations that can contribute towards giving the conceptual instruments to governments, in order to understand the often complex, dynamic, changeable issues and their importance and urgency, outlining the possible scenarios or lines of action in social policies to be undertaken at public level. These lines of action should seek a balance between the needs of science and technology to progress and the protection of human beings and societies, while considering the dignity of human beings as a priority, in the context of the human rights framework.

The function of the committees consists in the challenging and sensitive role of ethical intermediation between science and technology, on the one hand, and between society and governments on the other. The task of intermediation can be performed at a descriptive level, a dialogic-dialectic level and, ultimately, also at an advisory level.

The description is generally complex and requires specific and specialist knowledge, in-depth analysis, and constant updating from the different disciplines (medicine, biology, human and social sciences, philosophy, law, economics, politics). Pluralism arises also at the scientific level: even in a scientific context, quite often, there is not just one single interpretation of phenomena.

At a dialogic-dialectic level, the committees represent a space for discussion, which is essential, given its interdisciplinarity and pluralism. In terms of methodology, an ethical balance is achieved, through a constant exchange of insights both between disciplines and with regard to the theories and arguments, identifying the empirical context of the problem, principles and values at stake and weighing them, in the face of real complexity, through balanced critical reflection and dialectic argumentation.

Pluralism (together with interdisciplinarity) spurs discussion and makes the exchange of opinions essential, assuming the diversity of viewpoints and heterogeneousness of values. But while it is true that pluralism constitutes the *raison d'être* of the committees, it is also true that such pluralism cannot be radical and irreconcilable. If this were the case, no debate would be possible, as each ethical sphere would be closed in itself and to communication or discussion: any type of discussion would be useless and sterile, given the principled impossibility formulating a common discourse. Only a type of pluralism that is open, no less than in a minimal way, to the possible convergence of some values, at least 'on principle', leaves room for discussion and dialogue: this way of understanding plurality is the condition for the possibility of 'thinking together', in the conviction that it no longer makes any sense and that perhaps it is not even possible any more to think in an isolated self-referential way.

The dialectic and dialogic approach to questions can only emerge from a vital prerequisite essential for participation in a committee: the epistemological willingness for dialogue or the dialogic intentionality. The interdisciplinary and pluralistic approach succeeds insofar as every concept has been adequately and consistently justified and articulated: dialogue identifies with the willingness to consider the arguments of others through dialectic dimensions, including willingness to question one's own perspective.

Dialogue is only possible by distancing oneself from the extreme positions between non-cognitivism (relativism) and cognitivism (absolutism). Whoever takes part in an ethics committee should be inspired by a dialogic intention, abandoning an absolutist attitude of denying truth (ethics without truth) or affirming the truth (ethics with truth).

Dialogue can only happen in the exchange of reasons: justifying one's own position and letting others justify theirs; listening to and understanding the argument of others, to put one's own standpoint to the test, verifying its consistency and coherence. Discussion facilitates the interpretation of principles/values within a specific context, critically questioning the standpoints involved in a particular situation.

The most challenging and sensitive aspect of a committee's work is the effort to search for minimum (even if not maximum) points of opinion-sharing from this exchange: to see to what extent one's own rationally justified position is shared by others, from different and even opposing standpoints. Dialogue means checking our own position against different and opposite stances, while striving for balance in defining a set of shared or likely to be shared minimum ethical standards.

It is not a matter of reaching a compromise, but rather a mediation: this can be achieved only if one is willing to give something up of one's own theory (safeguarding the fundamental principles/values, considered non-renounceable) in order to seek a point of contact – whenever and as far as possible – with others.

It may also entail partially giving up the 'maximum' expression of one's own theory to find common ground, avoiding irreconcilable conflicts, as far as possible, in the effort to seek a harmonious synthesis, as a result of the spirit of dialogue. In any case, dissenting opinions, personal remarks, or integrative declarations may be attached to the document, when dialogue does not succeed in finding shared recommendations.

Dialogue within a bioethics committee is demanding but nonetheless also very stimulating: at times the sentences and words are chosen carefully, if not also the adverbs, prepositions, and articles. Each element of the text is subject to critical evaluation from every member that, in turn, should offer a constructive contribution.

The aim of the committee's discussions is to elaborate opinions and documents/reports, which can contribute to giving the conceptual instruments to governments and society in a broad sense in order to understand the often complex, dynamic, changeable issues and their importance and urgency, envisaging the possible scenarios/lines of action in social policies to be undertaken at public level, avoiding the shifts of a radical techno-scientism or a just as radical obscurantism.

## The Pluralistic Dialogue in the Horizon of Fundamental Human Rights

The elaboration of minimum ethical elements for regulating techno-science draws inspiration from the horizon of fundamental human rights as a conceptual framework, which form a crucial part of national constitutions and international documents. In recent decades, these documents have undergone a process of dynamic explicit specification and interpretation, in light of emerging issues stemming from scientific and technological development, through declarations issued by international organisations (UNESCO, WHO), conventions, resolutions, recommendations, directives, and regional regulations. The reference to human rights is guaranteed, at national level, by constitutions (Andorno, 2009, 2013; Barilan, 2012; van Beers et al., 2014; Beyleveld & Brownsword, 2002; ten Have & Gordijn, 2014) both in national legislation and case-law (jurisprudence), by international documents as European norms and judgments of the European Court of Human Rights and the Court of Justice of the European Union. In this context, individuals, national legislations, and European regulations are called upon to refer to basic fundamental human rights, placed at a higher level.

The discussion carried out by bioethics committees, along with the elaboration, interpretation and clarification of fundamental human rights, within the various international and national institutional settings, has contributed to entrenching some shared ethical principles, such as: the primacy of the human being and his/her dignity over the sole interest of science or society; the respect for physical and psychological integrity (safety) and the ban on exploitation and commercialisation of the human body, manipulation or arbitrary use of the body and its parts; the need to ensure autonomy as awareness of individuals; the duty of proportionality (beneficence/non-maleficence) in interventions on human beings; the need of equity of access and equal treatment of human beings; the responsibility towards non-human beings and future generations.

However, these shared values and principles do not provide a clear solution to every ethical problem. Some ambiguities and conflicts persist, notably in the context of particularly sensitive and controversial issues. We need to clarify, theoretically and practically, the interpretation of dignity, of proportionality/disproportionality of interventions (based on objective and/or subjective standards), of autonomy (as self-determination or in relation to responsibility towards oneself and/or others), of justice (between liberal-individualism or social-solidarism). In any case, the human rights framework sets limits to interpretation that cannot be overcome.

## The International and Intercultural Dialogue

The universalistic claim of human rights has facilitated the formulation of transcultural standards in the context of cultural pluralism. This is because human rights are conceived as entitlements that persons have because of their human condition, regardless of their age, sex, ethnic origin, socio-economic status, health condition, religion, or political convictions. The recourse to human rights is a way to ground intercultural dialogue that helps bioethics to go beyond the pluralistic fragmentation.

This trend was consolidated at the international level within UNESCO through *Universal Declarations* as the *Universal Declaration on Bioethics and Human Rights* (2005). This document is particularly important as a universal instrument, as it establishes the minimum principles that are universally agreed upon and considered essential for bioethics. The recognised principles are: autonomy and responsibility, equity of access and justice, informed consent and confidentiality, respect for the integrity and vulnerability of the human person, solidarity and international cooperation, responsibility towards the environment and future generations.

As a declaration, this document falls within "soft laws", as a non-binding instrument. As a form of soft law, it may have an influence and is potentially binding, as the initial document that begins a process that may bring states to gradually elaborate binding and enforceable rules for states with biolegal and biopolitical relevance. There is an increasingly felt need to harmonise how issues are dealt with to overcome 'bioethical tourism' (or cross-countries bioethical services).

The need to seek a dialogue among cultures in the discussion on the diversities of the issues and contexts is becoming more and more evident. The objective is to build an inter-cultural bioethics, to avoid the assimilation of some cultures into a dominant one, and to prevent dangerous forms of colonialism, imperialism or bioethical paternalism, which may result in exploitation. It is also to avoid the separation of the various cultures, all considered relativistically equivalent, and the tolerance of any form of bioethics without a critical filter. The objective is instead to foster the development of an intercultural bioethics capable of creating a space for dialogue, in an effort to integrate diversity and enabling the drafting of shared documents that highlight the commitment to seeking common ground.

International and intercultural bioethics expresses the need for cooperation between the so-called advanced/developed countries and the developing ones in order to guarantee a health equity in a dimension that moves away from localisms and considers the right to the protection of health as a universal human right from a global point of view. There is an increasing need for a macro-bioethics, across space (among cultures, States and Continents) and across time (among generations, next and future), an international, intercontinental and intercultural bioethics – in short, a global bioethics.

## A Dialogue with Society: Raising Awareness and 'Bioethics Literacy'

Today, the role of 'active citizenship' and 'citizen participation' is growing in importance in bioethics, along with the need to build (institutional and diverse) platforms for dialogue, which enable dynamic updating and active interaction between experts and non-experts (citizens/individuals).

Interaction aims to adequately inform and educate every individual (the so-called 'technological and scientific literacy' and 'bioethics literacy'), while also seeking, on the one hand, to prevent irrational fear of novelty in science and, on the other hand, a blind trust in it, as both attitudes are emotional, uncritical, and insufficiently justified. The goal focuses on raising social awareness, while enabling citizens to develop a critical consciousness, to ensure their participation, public engagement, and active involvement in ethical reflections on tecno-scientific development.

Developments in techno-science have the potential to affect everyone, bringing about significant changes in our lives, both now and in the future. The fundamental objective is to increase awareness by encouraging the circulation of information and opinions, envisaging discussions with experts and the organisation of debates, where the different arguments on bioethical issues are never only emotional, but always also rational. The public debate on health, should primarily focus on biomedical developments that raise concerns relating to dignity, autonomy, responsibility, justice: these principles are at the very foundation of the European ethical framework, enshrined in the Charter of Fundamental Rights.

The dialogue with society should be inclusive and make the voices of those who are most vulnerable heard, such as children, the elderly, people with disabilities, and minority groups. Public debate cannot only make citizens more aware of their choices, but it can also strengthen their role in the governance of their society.

Citizens should be at the centre of inclusive, participatory and dynamic dialogue, for democratic participation, in a consultative process of democratic deliberation, with the participation of all in collectively making the future we would like to see unfold. The "societal dialogue" is an essential requirement in order to build a "collective responsibility" to overcome the "divides", as the European Group on Ethics in Science and New Technologies at the European Commission underlines in the Statement *Values for the future: the role of ethics in European and global governance* (May 2021). The EGE stresses the need to foster a common space of reasons, civil discourse, and respect for persons as equal and reasonable participants in public debates as a requirement for democracy, the rule of law and human rights. There is a need of ethical dialogue systemically, democratically, inclusively, transparently, and sustainably, as well as a culture of communication and dialogue that recognises openness for discussion. The basis should be the consolidated set of shared values centred around human dignity, autonomy, responsibility, equality, justice, and solidarity.

## The Future of Bioethics: Lessons Learnt

It is essential to learn lessons from the (not so short) history of bioethics and look to the future. There are issues on which our society is still divided, and which call into question how we should respond to these divisions, both as a matter of principle and as a matter of practice. We need to decide what sort of society we wish to be and how we should resolve conflicts over bioethical questions. In our pluralistic society, we need to work out how to establish a basis for dealing with the very practical choices with which we are faced.

The challenges encountered with building a shared ethical space often generate ideological polarisation, leading to a progressive impoverishment of rational analysis. Creating the conditions for a critical and open debate requires knowing how to clarify the reasons underlying the different ethical positions and the values by which they are inspired, but also knowing how to put them to the test with facts, and verify the acceptability of the conclusions to which they lead. This confrontation with concrete ethical questions and issues is the social function that has been carried out by the bioethics committees. The role entrusted to them is to 'do ethics' in an interdisciplinary and pluralistic context and find ways to overcome differences and go beyond them Ethics committees have played this role as an 'ethical laboratory' to deal with pluralistic challenges based on the belief that making the reasons 'of others' explicit, even without any passive acceptance, is a method for identifying the best possible solution, reasonably acceptable to the interested parties even if far from an 'ideal' moral perfection from an individual point of view. The hope is that the work of ethics committees and their procedural methodology will continue, involving society, and inspiring law and politics.

We need to improve what we have done: to educate individuals on bioethics and ethics of techno-science in order to have experts in bioethics (maybe thinking about specialisations, as the fields are increasingly expanding); to educate citizens to develop 'bioethics literacy' to enable participation in discussions; to improve ethics committees as spaces for dialogue, both interdisciplinary and pluralistic; to coordinate ethics committees– at all levels, in the different fields (biomedicine, human and social sciences, emerging technologies), and training ethics committee members on dialogic methodology; and to engage policymakers and all stakeholders in ethics, both on health issues and techno-science.

Pluralism remains a challenge that could be addressed not by choosing one ethics among the different theories in order to determine the rightness and wrongness of choices in bioethics (codifying bioethics in a normative, definitive and comprehensive way), but educating people to identify ethical questions and acquire an epistemological attitude for dialogue: This methodology and procedure for deliberative processes of making choices should be adopted, both on a public and individual level.

This could provide guidance to give answers to the continuously evolving questions in bioethics and ethics of science and technologies, not lagging behind scientific 'progress', but potentially anticipating scenarios, as far as possible, not to be ready to deliver solutions, but at least to approach and tackle dilemmas and questions that animate the discussion. This is very important in light of new, complex technologies in contexts of uncertainty, which need an adequate awareness of the problems, willingness to recognise their complexity and require adopting a systemic vision that integrates and weighs all the variables connected to the different dimensions and different temporal phases that influence the actual consequences of the deliberation process. The goal is to reach the best possible shared moral agreement on ethically sensitive issues, in a pluralistic society, with a view to guiding regulatory production and political decision-making.

## References

Andorno, R. (2009). Human dignity and human rights as a common ground for a global bioethics. *Journal of Medicine and Philosophy*, 34(3), 223–240. https://doi.org/10.1093/jmp/jhp023

Andorno, R. (2013). *Principles of international biolaw. Seeking common ground at the intersection of bioethics and human rights*. Bruylant.

Barilan, Y. M. (2012). *Human dignity, human rights, and responsibility: The new language of global bioethics and biolaw*. The MIT Press. https://doi.org/10.7551/mitpress/9311.001.0001

Beyleveld, D., & Brownsword, R. (2002). *Human dignity in bioethics and biolaw*. Oxford University Press.

ten Have, H. A. M. J., & Gordijn, B. (Eds.). (2014). *Handbook of global bioethics* (Vols. 1–4). Springer. https://doi.org/10.1007/978-94-007-2512-6

van Beers, B., Corrias, L., & Werner, W. G. (Eds.). (2014). *Humanity across international law and biolaw*. Cambridge University Press. https://doi.org/10.1017/CBO9781107257139

# Shaping the Future?

## Emerging Technologies, Value Shifts, and Bioethics

*Aurélie Halsband*

## Introduction

Bioethics as a discipline is increasingly confronted with the evaluation of actions whose implications extend into the long-term future. Issues such as the harmful effects of climate change, the potentially negative outcomes of heritable human genome editing, and the ongoing loss of biodiversity are examples of developments being decided upon today that will significantly impact both the near and distant future. The accelerated pace at which broadly accessible biotechnologies, which can be applied to manifold purposes – such as CRISPR/Cas9 – emerge, raises the frequency of actions with long-term implications that require moral evaluation.

In recent debates, bioethics' capacity to assess emerging biotechnologies in light of their long-term consequences has come under scrutiny. One of the central challenges in this domain is how bioethical evaluations can account for the concerns of those who will primarily bear the risks and burdens resulting from decisions made today – namely, future persons. More specifically, this challenge stems from two types of uncertainty: axiological and factual.

Assessing the precise harms and benefits of emerging technologies is a well-known challenge. Due to these *factual uncertainties*, technology assessments typically rely on risk analysis – acknowledging that specific harms cannot be detailed – and weigh those risks against anticipated benefits, considering only those benefits that are sufficiently justified.[1]

1 Note also the non-identity problem and the related debate on the possibility of creating harms for future persons if the occurrence of these harms is at least co-constitutive for the later existence of these specific individuals.

*Axiological uncertainties*, in turn, arise from the possibility that future individuals may hold different values in assessing the risks and benefits of specific biotechnologies. In other words, in contrast to those of today people born in the more distant future may differ in how they conceptualise risks, in their willingness to accept those risks considering potential benefits, and in how they weigh those benefits. They may share our current values, reject them entirely, or – most plausibly – agree with some while differing on others. I will use the term "values" in a broad sense (Schroeder, 2024, p. 28), designating the varieties of goodness. Axiological uncertainties are thus uncertainties about what future persons will designate as "good" or "bad", acknowledging the different types of values and uses of "good".

However, addressing value change in the ethical assessment of emerging biotechnologies requires bioethics to do more than respond to factual and axiological uncertainties. It also requires bioethics to acknowledge that technologies themselves are significant drivers of value change (Danaher & Sætra, 2023). The increasing pace of emerging biotechnologies, with long-term implications and vast applicability, thus necessitates defining, from the perspective of current generations, which technology-induced value changes we consider desirable:

> We are not only interested in knowing which axiological changes are possible in the future but also which are desirable. Thus, an important reason to anticipate future value changes is to carry out a normative assessment of these technology-driven transformations. (Rueda, 2025)

Such an encompassing moral evaluation of technologies extends beyond simple risk–benefit analysis. As de Melo-Martín (2017, p. 224) argues in the context of reprogenetics, a comprehensive ethical assessment must also consider the values that underlie the development of a technology, the utility of its creation, and the values the technology itself may come to embody.

As a consequence, the discipline of bioethics faces the challenge to provide the methodology apt to ethically assess emerging technologies while reckoning the delineated factual and axiological uncertainties *and* technology-induced value shifts.

In light of these challenges, the second section investigates the phenomenon of value change in the context of emerging biotechnologies. Beyond mere description, the discussion will explore specific moral issues arising from anticipated future value shifts – such as the exclusion of long-term risks for the yet unborn from ethical evaluations. The third section presents four approaches within bioethics that can be interpreted as responses to the phenomenon of value change: informed speculation, design-for-value-change, defining universal values, and striving for moral closure. The fourth section examines the implications for future roles of bioethics as a discipline.

## Value Change Regarding Emerging Technologies as a Moral Issue

The assumption that value changes will occur in response to emerging technologies is supported by investigations into past technology-induced moral shifts. For instance, reproductive medicine has witnessed several such transformations: the introduction of prenatal diagnosis has influenced views on the acceptability of genetic disabilities; ultrasound technology has altered assumptions about the moral status of the human foetus; and hormonal contraception has reshaped the perceived importance of virtues such as chastity.

In his investigation of value change regarding technologies, van de Poel develops an instructive list of five kinds of value change which also applies to value changes outside technology ethics:

1) The emergence of new values;
2) Changes in what values are relevant for the design of a certain technology;
3) Changes in the priority or relative importance of values;
4) Changes in how values are conceptualized;
5) Changes in how values are specified, and translated into norms and design requirements. (van de Poel, 2018, p. 28)

Various factors have been identified to explain why such value changes occur. Robert Baker (2019), for instance, views moral change as driven by paradigm shifts, paralleling the dynamics described in Thomas Kuhn's theory of scientific revolutions. Others highlight more specific contributors to value change, such as "normalization" (Rueda et al., 2025) – a shift in values resulting from habituation to previously disruptive technologies. More generally, mechanisms of techno-moral change such as the expansion of agency through new technological options (Danaher & Sætra, 2023) can in turn prompt shifts in underlying values.

The phenomenon of value changes following the introduction of technologies is not new (Danaher & Sætra, 2023). What is new, however, is, first, the increasing occurrence of biotechnologies that significantly transform moral values, and second, the growing tendency of these emerging technologies to involve potentially harmful long-term consequences. As a result, future individuals and their value frameworks are becoming a central and recurring concern in ethical assessments of technology.

To name just two examples, heritable human genome editing (the modification of human germ cells) and in vitro gametogenesis (the derivation of human germ cells from somatic cells in the laboratory) are emerging biotechnologies believed to induce significant value changes in the future and to have considerable impacts on future persons. Rueda et al. (2022) describe how the prospective use of these technologies could disrupt existing concepts of justice, equal standing, and reproductive choice. Reproductive choice, for instance, may undergo profound transformation, as future parents could be expected to take responsibility not only for the conditions in which they raise their children, but also for their children's genetic makeup. This is because the genetic constitution of their offspring – and, presumably, the associated preconditions for a flourishing life – will significantly depend on the parents' decision to use or refrain from using genome editing on the germ cells or embryos from which their possible future children will originate.[2]

Beyond the systematic challenge of understanding how technology drives shifts in values, this phenomenon also raises significant moral concerns. In the context of genome editing in human medicine, Rueda and co-authors introduce the concept of an "anticipatory gap": a potential mismatch between the current population's attitudes toward the benefits and risks of emerging technologies and the future moral perspectives of those who will ultimately bear the consequences (Rueda et al., 2025, p. 318). As a result, contemporary technology governance may fail to account for the values and priorities of future generations, effectively excluding a key stakeholder group from ethical consideration.

2 Reproductive technologies, which have been assessed in view of their long-term implications and potentially changed values of future persons, are, e.g. in-vitro-gametogenesis (IVG) (Segers, 2023), the combination of IVG with genome editing (Rueda et al., 2022; De Proost & Segers, 2022;Rueda et al., 2023), the combination of IVG with preimplantation genetic diagnosis (PGD) (Greely, 2016), or the combination of artificial intelligence and embryo selection (Tamir, 2022; Halsband, 2025).

The authors touch only briefly on the broader moral implications of this anticipatory gap, but several further concerns deserve exploration. First, overlooking or minimising potential long-term harms of a technology may unjustly shift higher burdens onto future generations. This issue is well-documented in climate ethics, where it is discussed as a form of "moral corruption" (Gardiner, 2010), and in debates over the ethical justification for discounting the future (Davidson, 2015).

Second, neglecting long-term consequences can also lead to missed opportunities: excessive caution or premature restriction in developing new technologies may deprive future people of substantial benefits. For example, Savulescu's concept of *procreative beneficence* frames heritable genome editing not merely as permissible but as a moral obligation – to improve the well-being of future persons (Savulescu, 2001, 2007).

Both lines of argument reflect a broader danger: the risk of taking an overly narrow view of possible futures, including the evolution of values and the role technology plays in shaping them (Danaher, 2021). Focusing solely on hypothetical harms – or, conversely, on speculative benefits – can lead to ethically unjustified constraints. Instead, many agree that there exists a general moral obligation to ensure that future persons have access to the basic conditions necessary for a flourishing life.

A third moral concern involves the *unnoticed steering effect* of ethical discourse itself. Ethical evaluations of emerging technologies influence how society understands and debates those technologies. Considering the potential for reprogenetic enhancements to disrupt foundational values – such as justice, equality, and reproductive autonomy – Rueda et al. (2022) stress the importance of public deliberation about the kinds of biotechnology-driven moral changes we are willing to embrace. Ethical discourse, however, does not merely describe potential futures; it actively shapes them, and this shaping role must be critically examined considering its long-term impact.

While the intersection of technological innovation and value change is not new to bioethics, the long-term implications of emerging biotechnologies – such as heritable human genome editing – are increasingly significant. Given the accelerating pace of profound technological transformation, there is a pressing need to reflect on whether current bioethical frameworks are adequately equipped to address the challenges ahead.

## Four Bioethical Responses to Emerging Technologies and Value Change

I outline four areas of bioethics research that may be understood as responses to the phenomenon of future value change and its implications for assessing emerging technologies.

A first approach is what has been termed "informed speculation" (cf., e.g. Danaher, 2021, p. 6; Segers, 2023). Danaher (2021), for instance, develops the notion of *axiological futurism*, emphasising the need to engage in speculative inquiry with the goal of mapping plausible future scenarios. He explains:

> The job of the axiological futurist is to map the axiological possibility space and consider how civilisations might shift and change location within that possibility space in the future. The goal is not precise prediction but, rather, scenario planning. (Danaher, 2021)

This approach entails a systematic investigation into how values may evolve alongside technological developments (cf., e.g. Danaher & Sætra, 2023; Rueda, 2025), often through identifying and planning for the most likely scenarios (Danaher, 2021; Hopster, 2022). It is both broad – eschewing commitment to particular moral values – and pragmatic, focusing on probable outcomes. The rationale is twofold: first, that public engagement should accompany technological innovation, and second, that future persons, as stakeholders affected by the long-term consequences, can only be included through openness to the evolving moral frameworks that may shape future evaluations.

A second, complementary approach focuses on incorporating future value change into the design and development of technologies. This is exemplified by van de Poel's (2018) proposal. Recognising that technology is not morally neutral, he argues for designing technologies to be flexible, robust, and adaptable, thereby ensuring they remain responsive to value shifts in future stages of deployment and use.

This design ethics also responds to the threat of *technological lock-in* – a scenario in which early design decisions constrain future moral choices. Addressing technological lock-ins is motivated by the attempt to ensure that future generations retain access to alternative courses of action, especially if dominant technologies later conflict with prevailing moral values (Rueda et al., 2025). In this view, the task of applied ethics – including bioethics and the ethics of technology – is not just about anticipating moral attitudes, but about embedding structural options for adjustment or reversal into the technologies themselves. Beyond this focus on future value shifts in the assessment of technologies, the openness to alternative options resonates with the "right to an open future" of children (Feinberg, 2015) and the controversy on how it can be used within bioethics (cf., e.g. Millum, 2025).

Rather than adapting to or anticipating value change, a third approach looks for ethical constants. Beauchamp and Childress, in their *Principles of Biomedical Ethics*, draw on the notion of a *common morality* – a "set of universal norms shared by all persons committed to morality" (Beauchamp & Childress, 2019, p. 3). In view of its universality, the common morality provides a promising starting point for elements of morality more or less "resistant" to significant shifts over time. Beauchamp and Childress derive four core bioethical principles from the common morality: respect for autonomy, nonmaleficence, beneficence, and justice.

While these principles enjoy broad theoretical support, they offer only limited moral guidance due to their generality. As Beauchamp and Childress outline, the principles must be specified and weighed in context – a process shaped by cultural, temporal, and situational factors (Beauchamp & Childress, 2019, p. 448; Childress & Beauchamp, 2022). Consequently, while the appeal to universal norms can provide partial grounding for reflection on future values, it remains insufficient to fully resolve the challenges posed by future value change.

A fourth approach adopts a more proactive stance, arguing that bioethics should not merely respond to value change, but play a role in shaping it. Baker (2002) criticises the dominant focus in bioethics on "argumentation" and calls for increased emphasis on teaching and practicing *moral closure* – resolving ethical conflicts through negotiation and compromise. According to Baker, the negotiation of moral change involves seeking a compromise based on shared goals. This focus acknowledges that values and assumptions are increasingly no longer shared, shifting from argumentative consensus to societal compromise. He contends that bioethicists should play a more active role in shaping and advancing these societal compromises.

In *The Structure of Moral Revolutions* (2019), Baker refines this idea by distinguishing between *moral revolution*, which challenges foundational ethical paradigms, and *moral reform*, which promotes incremental adaptation of existing norms. Within "moral reforms", bioethics serves as a bridge between academic ethical analysis and social activism, contributing to governance processes without necessarily endorsing radical change. Other scholars (cf. e. g.

Löhr, 2024) support this view by positioning ethics as a connective discipline, facilitating dialogue between ethics and "activists".

## Bioethics' Role: Advisor, Activist, or Something Else?

Given the four approaches to addressing future value change, bioethics may assume different roles in responding to the moral challenges posed by emerging technologies.

In the first approach – informed speculation – bioethics takes on the role of analyst and planner, seeking to understand how values might shift in response to emerging biotechnologies and how society can best prepare for these potential futures. The task here is anticipatory: mapping the likely trajectories of value change and developing frameworks for ethical evaluation under future conditions.

The second and third approaches – designing for value change and appealing to universal values – position bioethics more as a reactive facilitator. In these perspectives, bioethics embraces change by ensuring both technologies and moral principles remain adaptable to evolving value patterns. Here, the discipline functions less as a predictive force and more as a responsive one, helping systems and norms adjust as new contexts emerge.

The fourth approach, by contrast, casts bioethics in a more activist role. It calls on bioethicists to go beyond observing moral change, to critically evaluate which shifts are desirable, and then actively shape future developments in line with these judgments. This includes not only contributing to public discourse but also influencing institutional practices and policy frameworks.

These roles are not mutually exclusive. In fact, the boundaries between them are often fluid. For example, one might plan for various value scenarios (advisor role) while also promoting certain trajectories deemed more desirable (activist role). What is more, embracing value change might be limited to those shifts identified as ethically desirable (Rueda, 2025).

This leads to a broader, underlying question: what should the role of bioethics be in the face of emerging biotechnologies and their tendency to provoke future value change? Should it remain an "advisor" – analysing trends, offering anticipatory ethical insights, and outlining various moral possibilities? Or should it promote a more "activist" stance – deliberately steering moral developments through advocacy, public engagement, and governance involvement?

Determining the most appropriate role for bioethics may depend, in part, on how well each position addresses the moral concerns raised by future value change.

## Four Bioethical Responses and Their Aptness to Address the Moral Issues Involved

As previously outlined, three major issues arise: first, shifting higher burdens to future generations – for example, underestimating long-term harms in emerging biotechnology. Second, foreclosing future benefits – such as by unduly restricting the development of technologies. And third, the unacknowledged steering effects – where ethical debate unintentionally shapes public attitudes and policy in a way that limits future moral diversity.

The advisory role addresses these issues by making potential harms and benefits visible, clarifying trade-offs, and offering ethical reasoning that can temper both overly liberal and overly restrictive policies. However, approaches like informed speculation, value-adaptive design, and the recourse to common morality tend to position bioethics as a passive observer. This passivity risks overlooking the field's own influence on value formation and decision-making.

In contrast, other have reimagined bioethics as an engaged discipline that not only evaluates but also participates in shaping societal paths. This role may be more appropriate in view of the third moral concern: the inadvertent and potentially unreflective shaping of values by ethical debates. By integrating the steering effect into the very practice of bioethics itself transparency may be achieved, as well as the purpose of an ethically guiding public discourse. However, if this practice of "negotiation", as Baker frames it, "does not require agreement on premises, or even conclusions" but rather "common constructions to serve shared goals" (2002, p. 452), this disciplinary shift may be disruptive for philosophical bioethics. This is because analytical investigations into the premises and conclusions underlying ethical assessments of bioethical issues are often regarded as core competency of the discipline.

## Bioethics: Which Competence and Insights Can it Contribute?

Beyond defining its general role, bioethics must also clarify what competences and insights it brings to society's broader effort to navigate value change. Focusing on the governance of human heritable genome editing, Rueda et al.,

(2025) offer four recommendations: first, update moral evaluations periodically to remain responsive to evolving values. Second, incorporate expert foresight and public engagement to anticipate developments and involve society in value reflection. Third, ensure representation of affected stakeholders, including representatives for the yet unborn. Fourth, guard against technological lock-in by preserving alternatives that future persons can choose from, should their moral outlook differ. These recommendations imply a broader vision of bioethics: one that supports democratic deliberation, long-term inclusivity, and value-sensitive governance.

To further moderate the steering effects of ethical discourse, additional insights come from investigations of the history of bioethics. Baker's concept of moral revolutions – inspired by Kuhn's theory of paradigm shifts – explores historical cases of technology-induced value change in medical ethics (e.g. regarding life-sustaining treatment after the invention of ventilators) and thereby illustrates how technologies catalyse moral change.

Danaher additionally emphasises methodological breadth in his account of axiological futurism. He envisions bioethics working alongside disciplines such as policy analysis, scenario planning, and systems design. Van de Poel, through his concept of value-sensitive design, calls in turn on bioethicists to engage directly in technology development and engineering discourse. Thus, the ability of bioethics to anticipate, assess, and potentially guide future value changes as long-term consequences of emerging technologies can only be realised through interdisciplinary collaboration.

## Outlook

These diverse approaches and roles highlight the manifold demands placed on bioethics. But they also reveal tensions. For instance, Baker's push for moral closure through compromise appears to conflict with the recommendation of Rueda et al. (2025) for continuous ethical iteration in response to value change. One seeks to stabilise societal compromises; the other prioritises openness to revision.

Despite these differences, a shared conviction unites the authors: in its assessment of emerging biotechnologies, bioethics must address future value change. To achieve this, the discipline must evolve on methodological, normative, and societal levels, integrating foresight, ethical analysis, and active engagement into a cohesive response to the moral challenges posed by emerging technologies and the potential shifts in values they bring.

## References


Baker, R. (2002). Bioethics and history. *The Journal of medicine and philosophy*, *27*(4), 447–474.

Baker, R. (2019). *The Structure of Moral Revolutions: Studies of Changes in the Morality of Abortion, Death, and the Bioethics Revolution*. Mit Press.

Beauchamp, T. L., & Childress, J. F. (2019). *Principles of biomedical ethics* (8th ed.). Oxford University Press.

Childress, J. F., & Beauchamp, T. L. (2022). Common Morality Principles in Biomedical Ethics: Responses to Critics. *Camb Q Healthc Ethics*, *31*(2), 164–176. https://doi.org/10.1017/S0963180121000566

Danaher, J. (2021). Axiological futurism: The systematic study of the future of values. *Futures*, *132*. https://doi.org/10.1016/j.futures.2021.102780

Danaher, J., & Sætra, H. S. (2023). Mechanisms of techno-moral change: A taxonomy and overview. *Ethical Theory and Moral Practice*, *26*(5), 763–784.

Davidson, M. D. (2015). Climate change and the ethics of discounting. *WIREs Climate Change*, *6*(4), 401–412. https://doi.org/https://doi.org/10.1002/wcc.347

de Melo-Martín, I. (2017). *Rethinking reprogenetics: Enhancing ethical analyses of reprogenetic technologies*. Oxford University Press.

De Proost, M., & Segers, S. (2022). We need to talk about disruption in bioethics: a commentary on Rueda, Pugh and Savulescu. *Trends Biotechnol*, *41*(6), 741–742. https://doi.org/10.1016/j.tibtech.2022.12.001

Feinberg, J. (2015). The child's right to an open future. In *Justice, politics, and the family* (pp. 145–158). Routledge.

Gardiner, S. M. (2010). A Perfect Moral Storm: Climate Change, Intergenerational Ethics, and the Problem of Moral Corruption. In S. M. Gardiner, S. Caney, D. Jamieson, & H. Shue (Eds.), *Climate Ethics: Essential Readings* (pp. 87–98). Oxford University Press. https://doi.org/10.1093/oso/9780195399622.003.0012

Greely, H. T. (2016). *The end of sex and the future of human reproduction*. Harvard University Press.

Halsband, A. (2025). Embryo selection, AI and reproductive choice. *AI and Ethics*, *5*(3), 3115–3127. https://doi.org/10.1007/s43681-024-00651-y

Löhr, G. (2024). If conceptual engineering is a new method in the ethics of AI, what method is it exactly? *AI and Ethics*, *4*(2), 575–585. https://doi.org/10.1007/s43681-023-00295-4

Millum, J. (2025). No right to an open future. *Journal of Applied Philosophy*. https://doi.org/10.1111/japp.12790

Rueda, J. (2025). Value change, reprogenetic technologies, and the axiological underpinnings of reproductive choice. *Bioethics*, *39*(5), 425–434. https://doi.org/10.1111/bioe.13287

Rueda, J., Pugh, J., & Savulescu, J. (2022). The morally disruptive future of reprogenetic enhancement technologies. *Trends Biotechnol*, *41*(5), 598–592. https://doi.org/10.1016/j.tibtech.2022.10.007

Rueda, J., Pugh, J., & Savulescu, J. (2023). Rethinking techno-moral disruption in bioethics, society, and justice. *Trends Biotechnol*, *41*(6), 743–744. https://doi.org/DOI:https://doi.org/10.1016/j.tibtech.2023.01.008

Rueda, J., Segers, S., Hopster, J., Kudlek, K., Liedo, B., Marchiori, S., & Danaher, J. (2025). Anticipatory gaps challenge the public governance of heritable human genome editing. *J Med Ethics*, *51*(5). https://doi.org/10.1136/jme-2023-109801

Savulescu, J. (2001). Procreative beneficence: why we should select the best children. *Bioethics*, *15*(5-6), 413–426.

Savulescu, J. (2007). In defence of procreative beneficence. *Journal of Medical Ethics*, *33*(5), 284–288.

Schroeder, M. (2024). Value Theory. In E. N. Zalta & U. Nodelman (Eds.), *The Stanford Encyclopedia of Philosophy*.

Segers, S. (2023). The IVG 'relatedness paradox': researchers should mind speculation. *Trends in Biotechnology*, *41*(10), 1220–1222.

Tamir, S. (2022). Artificial intelligence in human reproduction: charting the ethical debate over AI in IVF. *AI and Ethics*, *3*, 947–961. https://doi.org/10.1007/s43681-022-00216-x

van de Poel, I. (2018). Design for value change. *Ethics and Information Technology*, *23*(1), 27–31. https://doi.org/10.1007/s10676-018-9461-9

# Bioethics in the Anthropocene[1]

## Physicians' Duties, Patient Welfare, and Climate Protection

*Marius Bartmann*

### Introduction

Human health is connected to environmental factors in myriad ways (Romanello et al., 2024). Increase in heat stress, respiratory problems due to air pollution, and injuries and fatalities because of extreme weather events, such as storms, fires, and droughts are among the most palpable threats to human health in connection with climate change. Perhaps less obvious but no less severe climate change-induced threats to human health are pattern changes of vector-borne diseases, rising antimicrobial resistance, and mental health problems, where the latter are directly related to the experience of a deteriorating environment, a comparatively recent phenomenon called "eco-anxiety" (Bourban, 2024; Coffey et al., 2021). The *World Health Organization* thus considers climate change a "threat multiplier" exacerbating multifarious existing harms, conditions, and conflicts and therefore deems climate change a "fundamental threat to human health" (WHO, 2023).

Dealing with an increasing threat level to human health is not the only challenge climate change poses for the health sector, however. The health sector itself contributes to climate change: it is estimated that the environmental footprint of the health sector accounts for an equivalent of up to 5% of global greenhouse gas emissions (Karliner & Slotterback, 2019; Lenzen et al., 2020). And this figure does not even include the environmental impact of medical waste,

1 This publication emerged from the research project "PRACC – Practical Challenges of Climate Change: Intergenerational Justice and Freedom. Ethical, Legal, and Biodiversity Analyses", funded by the German Federal Ministry of Research, Technology and Space (grant number: 01GP2206A).

such as improperly disposed syringes from the estimated 16 billion injections administered globally each year (WHO, 2024).

Against the backdrop of these complex relations between climate change, human health and the health sector, there has been a surge in recent years in academic and policy approaches attempting to broaden the focus and integrate aspects of human health that go beyond an individual's welfare. Holistic approaches regarding the determinants of human health are gaining momentum. Planetary Health, for example, is a framework taking up a comprehensive perspective on the interrelation between human health, animals and ecosystems, a perspective that also has led to a stronger integration of ecological aspects into bioethics (Lanzerath, 2025). Furthermore, frameworks are emerging how the health sector can become sustainable. These include, for example, proposals for how to build "Green Hospitals" by increasing water and energy efficiency, use of environmentally friendly building materials, and a general reduction of resources (Lattanzio et al., 2022; Litke et al., 2020).

As adumbrated, these shifts in focus, perspective, and attitudes are also reflected in the theory and methodology of bioethics over the past few decades. For example, there is growing awareness that many bioethical issues are connected to broader structural problems, which must be dealt with "at the systemic level, not at the bedside" (Ravitsky, 2025, p. 90), thereby expanding the focus of bioethics and medical ethics. That is why Richie (2019), for example, has proposed principles for a "green bioethics", a novel bioethical framework attempting to accommodate the above-mentioned complex relations between environmental factors, human health and the health sector by putting the principle of justice centre stage.

A substantive part of these developments can be understood as a response to the fact that we have entered the "Anthropocene" (Crutzen & Stoermer, 2000), an epoch in which humans' long-term and profound impact on their environment has turned them into a kind of "geological force". Very recently, for example, a hotly debated issue has emerged that epitomizes the shifts and tensions bioethical thought is currently undergoing, particularly regarding the relation between autonomy and justice, the individual and the collective. This debate is about whether physicians' moral obligations also extend to climate protection.[2] Should collective matters of justice be incorporated into a physician's professional DNA or are we overburdening the individual

2 Cf. the recent issues of the *Journal of Medical Ethics* (50/6, 2024) and *Ethik in der Medizin* (37, 2025).

physician-patient-relationship, which should be primarily oriented towards patient autonomy?

In this contribution, I will attempt to sketch an answer to this question. In a first step, I will review the arguments of the debate put forth so far. In a second step, I will then outline an approach that may allow for bypassing the dichotomy between autonomy and justice, the individual and the collective, by which the debate seems to be characterized.

## Patient Welfare and Climate Protection

In a feature article published alongside several critical commentaries, van Gils-Schmidt and Salloch (2024b) employ the concept of practical identity developed by Korsgaard (1996) and apply it to the physician's professional ethos to ground duties for climate protection. In the following, I will briefly sketch their account and then turn to the commentaries.

According to Korsgaard (1996, p. 101), a practical identity is "a description under which you value yourself, a description under which you find your life to be worth living and your actions to be worth undertaking." The most important aspect to note about persons' practical identities for the purposes of the debate is that it generates reasons for action since it is an expression of their innermost values forming a substantive part of their self-image. The kind of reasons people possess for performing actions thus depend in large part on what kind of person they take themselves to be, i.e. their practical identity.

The concept of practical identity can be used to explain the conflicting moral obligations a physician might experience when confronted with the need to balance patient welfare against environmental protection. According to van Gils-Schmidt and Salloch (2024b, p. 370), this tension can be traced back to the fact that people usually possess multiple practical identities (e.g. they may value their identity as parents, spouses, or citizens) providing them with different sources of reasons for action. And in some circumstances, these practical identities (and the reasons they generate) may pull in different directions. As a physician, for example, patient welfare may be assigned the utmost priority. But the physician may just as well be heavily invested in environmental causes, participating in marches to promote climate action on weekends. Confronted with the decision for or against a particular medical procedure with a high carbon footprint, a person's practical identities – being a physician and an environmentalist – may generate reasons for action that seem irreconcilable with each other. How can this conflict be resolved?

The argument seems to run as follows (van Gils-Schmidt & Salloch, 2024b, p. 371f.). The starting point is the rather uncontroversial consensus that people's autonomy and their right to express their practical identities should be *pro tanto* respected. The next step consists in the insight that expressing one's practical identity presupposes that basic needs are met, such as food, water, and shelter, as well as access to elementary social institutions and services (schools, healthcare etc.). Now, a large part of what constitutes basic needs can also be subsumed under the heading (physical and mental) "human health". Since physicians can naturally be considered "advocates of health" (van Gils-Schmidt & Salloch, 2024b, p. 371), and climate change, as we have seen, plays a huge role in the determinants of human health, it seems to follow that physicians thereby also need to take on climate protection duties.[3]

This changed perspective allows physicians to incorporate considerations for climate protection into their practical identity as physicians. As conflicts between obligations towards patient welfare and climate protection may still arise within the practical identity of being a physician, van Gils-Schmidt and Salloch suggest that physicians view their advocacy for health not as applying only to the actual individuals they are treating but also as applying to patients they will treat in the future. This wider scope seems then to entail that to ensure the health not only of current but also of future patients, physicians should also take on climate protection duties by contributing to a sustainably operated workplace (e.g. in practices, clinics, and hospitals).

Unsurprisingly, van Gils-Schmidt and Salloch's account has been met with strong criticism given that it entails profound changes of physicians' professional ethos. For example, Ghinea (2024) argues that putting physicians in a position in which they balance patient welfare and climate protection would seriously compromise the physician-patient relationship.[4] The reason is that a physician with a very strong commitment to climate protection may devote

---

3 For a similar argument (albeit without the Korsgaardian background), cf. Wild (2025). She also maintains that a physician's responsibility for health together with the fact that climate change figures among the determinants of health yields the conclusion that physicians are also responsible for addressing climate change (Wild, 2025, p. 192).

4 Bozzaro and Koesling (2025, p. 201f.) similarly argue that a radical environmental commitment may even lead to questioning the rationale of certain medical procedures such as intensive care, which would amount to a *reductio* of healthcare professionals' ethos.

fewer medical resources to a patient to pursue this objective. But if patients must reckon with the possibility of physicians' providing them with less adequate healthcare because of their environmental beliefs, then how can the physician-patient-relationship remain intact? If personal and political views become relevant in the doctor's office, then patients would always have to be suspicious of their physicians' motives for treatment decisions, which will inevitably destroy the trust between them. As a consequence, Ghinea (2024, p. 375) is highly doubtful that physicians' professional ethos can accommodate climate protection duties "without undermining the very core of what it means to be a physician".

In their critical commentary, Lignou and Hart (2024) focus on problems that raise specifically practical issues. One of the suggestions by van Gils-Schmidt and Salloch to reconcile conflicting moral obligations was that physicians should take the long view, so to speak, and consider not only actual but also future patients in their decision-making. But how, Lignou and Hart wonder, can such a deliberation be carried out? To make an informed decision, physicians would have to perform massive calculations, evaluating the trade-offs of the environmental impact of numerous medical decisions for a timeframe spanning several decades, which would require a lot of scientific data. Furthermore, these trade-offs are connected to macro-level resource allocations over which physicians have only limited control. Balancing patient welfare and climate protection thus poses a serious practical challenge for physicians. Lignou and Hart (2024, p. 376) also voice an ethical concern in connection with this practical challenge, namely that "healthcare professionals lack the relevant authority to make value judgements required for climate protection decisions". But without the proper authority it is up to physicians how much weight they assign to the environmental impact of various medical procedures and resources. This introduces a significant variance in the kind of care potentially provided to patients, which in turn threatens the trust between physician and patient.

Samuel et al. (2024) home in on an issue also briefly broached by Lignou and Hart. They are concerned that addressing the relation between health and climate change by focusing on the physician-patient-relationship carries two risks. One the one hand, it obscures the fact that climate change is a structural problem that must be dealt with at a systemic level and on the other hand it may create the false impression that the individual level is the proper place to address climate change (even though the individual level is not irrelevant for climate action). To illustrate their point, they present a short case study of the so-called "green inhaler".

The green inhaler is a medical device to treat asthma and other pulmonary diseases and has a lower carbon footprint than the prevailing metered-dose inhaler. The UK's *National Health Service* (NHS) thus made it part of their policy that switching inhalers be a topic of discussion in the physician-patient-relationship. However, Samuel et al. (2024) argue that this policy is a distraction from the real issues. For one thing, ensuring that the production and distribution of medical resources is subject to environmental standards is the task of proper governmental regulation at a systemic level and would be much more efficient than convincing individuals on a case-by-case basis. For another, discussing the carbon footprint of certain medical devices prevents a necessary discussion about the "social and environmental factors associated with poor respiratory health, which have led to an increased need for inhalers in the first place" (Samuel et al., 2024, p. 380). Poor air quality due to continued fossil fuel combustion and precarious living conditions connected to economic inequality are the actual issues that should be at the top of the political agenda. That is also why Baeroe et al. (2024), in their commentary, rather than offering a direct critique of van Gils-Schmidt and Salloch propose a model and tasks for an environmentally sensitive healthcare ethics.

## Individual and Collective Responsibility

Where does that leave us? In a short commentary, van Gils-Schmidt and Salloch (2024a) have replied to their critics, in which they respond to objections and add clarifications. I will briefly review them because their proper analysis points to a solution.

First, they acknowledge that addressing the adverse consequences of climate change and promoting climate justice is a collective responsibility and therefore requires collective action at a societal level. Nevertheless, they argue that this fact does not and should not preclude our asking whether the need for climate protection also has implications for individual responsibility and thus for action at an individual level. The connection between the individual and the collective level is said to be twofold. For one thing, climate change figures prominently among the determinants of health, and for another, the health sector itself contributes significantly to climate change by way of greenhouse gas emissions and medical waste. Since physicians are "advocates of health" and important agents in the health sector, the strong link between climate change and the health sector cannot but affect health professionals' ethos.

One of critics' deepest concerns was that physicians may provide lesser care to patients because of environmental considerations. Van Gils-Schmidt and Salloch attempt to alleviate these concerns by emphasizing joint decision-making in the physician-patient-relationship. Here van Gils-Schmidt and Salloch build on approaches developed in the literature, such as "green informed consent" (Richie, 2023), according to which discussions of healthcare options with a lower carbon footprint should factor in the decision-making jointly exercised by physician and patient. This way, the fear of medical decisions negatively affecting patient welfare due to environmental considerations can be averted.

A third point pertains to the core of the debate about physicians' climate protection duties and will become significant for a possible solution to the conflict: the determination of the physician's professional ethos. In this context, van Gils-Schmidt and Salloch (2024a, p. 379) also correct a possible misunderstanding. Their Korsgaardian model of practical identities was not intended to analyse the conflict as one between two identities – physician and environmentalist – where the worry is that the latter may win out with negative consequences for patient welfare. Rather, their goal was to argue for incorporating climate protection considerations into the physician's practical identity given the undeniable connection between climate change and health.

The significance of this change in perspective has to do with circumventing a problem also raised by critics. If physicians need to balance two competing practical identities, then medical decisions become subjective insofar as it depends on a physician's personal preferences how much weight each identity is assigned and therefore which reasons for action will be decisive. This is not the case, or so van Gils-Schmidt and Salloch argue, with the view that the practical identity of being a physician comes with the moral obligation to be sensitive regarding issues of climate change. The difference is supposed to be that the practical identity of being a physician is connected to a professional ethos whose content is determined not by single individuals but (ideally) by the entire collective of physicians. It follows that an individual subscribing to the practical identity of being a physician automatically becomes subject to its collectively determined standards, and hence it is not entirely up to an individual what it means to be a physician (and hence what medical decisions can legitimately be made).

However, it is not entirely clear if this change in perspective resolves the issues raised by critics. It seems the conflicting moral obligations now arise as a conflict not between two identities but within one and the same identity. This identity – the practical identity of being a physician – may be governed by collectively determined standards of the profession. But, on the one hand, the question whether the medical ethos should be sensitive to climate change seems to reoccur for the collective of physicians – and here critics could reiterate their scepticism and advocate for climate protection to be a matter for politics only. On the other hand, these standards seem to be too broad to be action-guiding in the particular case. What does the abstract goal of jointly promoting climate protection and patient welfare actually require of physicians in different circumstances? This abstract goal is rather vague and allows for it to be realized in very different ways.

At this point, van Gils-Schmidt and Salloch (2024a, p. 378) specify that although climate protection is part of a physician's DNA, "the primacy must be in the individual patient's well-being and autonomy". However, they do not seem to offer a reason why the balance between individual and societal concerns should always be in favour of autonomy. Imagine a physician with a radical commitment to climate protection – why should she not deny a patient a certain medical procedure if she believes it to be harmful to the environment?

I want to offer a distinction that may be helpful in analysing the conflict between patient welfare and environmental considerations, between individual and collective responsibility. The debate often appears as if the fundamental principles of patient autonomy and social justice are directly opposed in a single instance (a concrete physician-patient-relationship), which is why different weights to each principle must be assigned to reach a decision. But this head-on collision between fundamental principles may be avoided or at least alleviated if we distinguish between the *context of acquiring moral responsibility* and the *context of discharging corresponding moral obligations*, and acknowledge that both contexts do not necessarily coincide.

For example, there are several ways in which physicians can be attributed moral responsibility for climate protection. One way would be by pointing out that their actions are involved in producing greenhouse gas emissions and medical waste, just as other people's actions are contributing to climate change by driving a car, eating meat, or taking the plane. This is a complex issue I cannot address here and belongs to the larger question whether individuals can be attributed moral responsibility for climate change at all (Bartmann, 2024). Another way could be – as Wild (2025, p. 193) does – to draw on the *social connection model* by Young (2011) and argue that physicians possess specific collective abilities, enjoy certain privileges, and are in a particular position of power, which makes them morally responsible not because of their individual actions but rather on account of their social status. Whichever way one may construe physicians' moral responsibility for climate action, my point is that physicians do not have to discharge corresponding moral obligations in the same context in which they were acquired.

For example, even if it is (correctly) claimed that a certain medical procedure may contribute (if minimally) to climate change, it does not have to follow that a physician's ethos sensitive to climate protection speaks against performing the medical procedure. Physicians operate within a healthcare infrastructure that is not entirely in their control, and they must make use of the resources at their disposal to provide their patients with the best possible care. If there are options with a lower carbon footprint available, then these options could be discussed using the approach of a "green informed consent" (see the green inhaler example). But if there are no such options, then not performing the medical procedure for environmental reasons does not follow. The moral obligation for climate protection can and should be discharged in contexts in which influence on structural matters can be exerted, i.e. where the range of options for certain medical procedures is set. For example, physicians can discharge their climate protection duties by expressing their opinions through papers, conference participation, voting behaviour in board meetings and other forms of professional and public engagement. This way, the integrity of the physician-patient-relationship remains intact and patient trust will not be eroded because patients do not have to fear that physicians balance their welfare against climate protection, individual against collective responsibility in the doctor's office. Climate change is fundamentally a structural issue that also manifests in the physician-patient-relationship and plays a role in the doctor's office. But that does not mean climate change must be solved there as well.

## References

Baeroe, K., Bhopal, A. S., & Gundersen, T. (2024). Towards an environmentally sensitive healthcare ethics: ten tasks and one model. *J Med Ethics*, *50*(6), 382–383. https://doi.org/10.1136/jme-2024-109875

Bartmann, M. (2024). Brauchen wir eine neue Ethik für das Anthropozän? Individuelle Verantwortung für kollektive Schäden im Kontext des Klimawandels. *Zeitschrift für Praktische Philosophie*, *11*(2), 119–146. https://doi.org/10.22613/zfpp/11.2.6

Bourban, M. (2024). Eco-Anxiety: A Philosophical Approach. In K. Struve, M. I. Schapira, U. Hoinkes, & J. P. Allegrante (Eds.), *Anxiety Culture* (pp. 55–69). Johns Hopkins University Press.

Bozzaro, C., & Koesling, D. (2025). Tragen Mitarbeitende im Gesundheitswesen eine besondere Verantwortung für ökologische Nachhaltigkeit? – Contra. *Ethik in der Medizin*, *37*(2), 199–204. https://doi.org/10.1007/s00481-025-00862-9

Coffey, Y., Bhullar, N., Durkin, J., Islam, M. S., & Usher, K. (2021). Understanding Eco-anxiety: A Systematic Scoping Review of Current Literature and Identified Knowledge Gaps. *The Journal of Climate Change and Health*, *3*. https://doi.org/10.1016/j.joclim.2021.100047

Crutzen, P. J., & Stoermer, E. F. (2000). The "Anthropocene". *The International Geosphere-Biosphere Programme (IGBP)*, (41), 17–18.

Ghinea, N. (2024). A physician's identity can never be reconfigured to put climate protection on par with an individual patient's best interests. *J Med Ethics*, *50*(6), 375. https://doi.org/10.1136/jme-2023-109823

Karliner, J., & Slotterback, S. (2019). *Health Care's Climate Footprint. How the Health Sector contributes to the Global Climate Crisis and Opportunities for Action*. HCWH / ARUP.

Korsgaard, C. M. (1996). *Sources of Normativity*. Cambridge University Press.

Lanzerath, D. (2025). Planetary Health und Bioethik. *Zeitschrift für medizinische Ethik*, *71*(1), 102–108. https://doi.org/10.30965/29498570-20250110

Lattanzio, S., Stefanizzi, P., D'Ambrosio, M., Cuscianna, E., Riformato, G., Migliore, G., Tafuri, S., & Bianchi, F. P. (2022). Waste Management and the Perspective of a Green Hospital – A Systematic Narrative Review. *Int J Environ Res Public Health*, *19*(23). https://doi.org/10.3390/ijerph192315812

Lenzen, M., Malik, A., Li, M., Fry, J., Weisz, H., Pichler, P. P., Chaves, L. S. M., Capon, A., & Pencheon, D. (2020). The environmental footprint of health care: a global assessment. *Lancet Planet Health*, *4*(7), e271–e279. https://doi.org/10.1016/S2542-5196(20)30121-2

Lignou, S., & Hart, J. (2024). Navigating climate responsibility: a critical examination of healthcare professionals' moral duties. *J Med Ethics*, *50*(6), 376–377. https://doi.org/10.1136/jme-2024-109883

Litke, N., Szecsenyi, J., Wensing, M., & Weis, A. (2020). Green Hospitals: Klimaschutz im Krankenhaus. *Deutsches Ärzteblatt*, *117*(11), A 544–A 547.

Ravitsky, V. (2025), in this volume. (Reprinted from "A Path Forward – and outward: repositioning bioethics to face future challenges", 2023. *Hastings Center Report*, *53*(5), 7–10. https://doi.org/10.1002/hast.1510)

Richie, C. (2019). *Principles of Green Bioethics: Sustainability in Health Care*. Michigan State University Press. https://doi.org/10.14321/j.ctvhrd1wq

Richie, C. (2023). "Green informed consent" in the classroom, clinic, and consultation room. *Med Health Care Philos*, *26*(4), 507–515. https://doi.org/10.1007/s11019-023-10163-x

Romanello, M., Walawender, M., Hsu, S. C., Moskeland, A., Palmeiro-Silva, Y., Scamman, D., Ali, Z., Ameli, N., Angelova, D., Ayeb-Karlsson, S., Basart, S., Beagley, J., Beggs, P. J., Blanco-Villafuerte, L., Cai, W., Callaghan, M., Campbell-Lendrum, D., Chambers, J. D., Chicmana-Zapata, V., ...Costello, A. (2024). The 2024 report of the Lancet Countdown on health and climate change: facing record-breaking threats from delayed action. *Lancet*, 404(10465), 1847–1896. https://doi.org/10.1016/S0140-6736(24)01822-1

Samuel, G., Briggs, S., Hardcastle, F., Lyle, K., Parker, E., & Lucassen, A. M. (2024). Focusing attention on physicians' climate-related duties may risk missing the bigger picture: towards a systems approach to health and climate. *J Med Ethics*, *50*(6), 380–381. https://doi.org/10.1136/jme-2024-109953

van Gils-Schmidt, H. J., & Salloch, S. (2024a). The micro-level of climate protection in healthcare and physicians' professional ethos: a reply to the commentaries. *J Med Ethics*, *50*(6), 378–379. https://doi.org/10.1136/jme-2024-110005

van Gils-Schmidt, H. J., & Salloch, S. (2024b). Physicians' duty to climate protection as an expression of their professional identity: a defence from Korsgaard's neo-Kantian moral framework. *J Med Ethics*, *50*(6), 368–374. https://doi.org/10.1136/jme-2023-109203

WHO. (2023). *Climate change*. Retrieved 31.07.2025 from https://www.who.int/news-room/fact-sheets/detail/climate-change-and-health

WHO. (2024). *Health-care waste*. Retrieved 31.07.2025 from https://www.who.int/news-room/fact-sheets/detail/health-care-waste

Wild, V. (2025). Tragen Mitarbeitende im Gesundheitswesen eine besondere Verantwortung für ökologische Nachhaltigkeit? – Pro. *Ethik in der Medizin*, *37*(2), 189–198. https://doi.org/10.1007/s00481-025-00861-w

Young, I. M. (2011). *Responsibility for Justice*. Oxford University Press.

# Appendix

# Notes on Contributors

**David Archard** is Emeritus Professor of Philosophy at Queen's University Belfast, having previously taught at the Universities of Ulster, St. Andrews and Lancaster. He has published extensively in applied ethics, political philosophy, and philosophy of law, especially on the topics of children, the family, sexual consent and the public role of philosophy. Until 2023 he was Chair of the Nuffield Council on Bioethics, the United Kingdom's national ethics committee, and is a Member of the Clinical Ethics Committee of Great Ormond Street Hospital in London.

**Caesar A. Atuire** is Professor of Global Health Ethics at the University of Oxford and Adjunct Professor of Philosophy at the University of Ghana. He is President of the International Association of Bioethics (2024–2026). Prof. Atuire is a member of the WHO Ethics & Governance of Infectious Disease Outbreaks Working Group and the Steering Committee of the Global Forum for Bioethics in Research. He is currently leading a global research project on unearthing different meanings of solidarity and its real applications in global health. His research areas are in moral philosophy, bioethics, African philosophy, ancient and medieval philosophy, global health, with particular interest in global justice, ethics in low resource settings, international research ethics, and mental health ethics.

**Marius Bartmann** is a Postdoctoral Research Fellow at the DRZE and the ethics project leader in the interdisciplinary project "Practical Challenges of Climate Change" (funded by the German Federal Ministry of Research, Technology and Space). He holds a PhD in Philosophy from the University of Bonn. His current research focuses on the ethics of climate change, the ethics of artificial intelligence, and also metaethics. In particular, he writes on ethical questions of intergenerational justice and collective responsibility in the context of climate change, as well as on questions of practical deliberation and personal autonomy, particularly regarding digital spaces.

**James Childress** is Professor Emeritus at the University of Virginia, where he was the John Allen Hollingsworth Professor of Ethics, Professor of Religious Studies, Professor of Public Policy, and Professor of Research in Medical Education in the School of Medicine. He is currently a Member of the Core Faculty of the Center for Health Humanities and Ethics at the School of Medicine. James Childress was the Founding Director of the Institute for Practical Ethics and Public Life and is the author of numerous articles and several books. His well-known books include Principles of Biomedical Ethics (with Tom L. Beauchamp), now in its 8th edition and translated into several languages.

**Hervé Chneiweiss** is Emeritus Research Director at CNRS. He is studying molecular mechanisms involved in glial plasticity and underlying brain tumor development. First trained as a neurologist, he was involved in the neurogenetics of human diseases such as cerebellar ataxias. He is also deeply involved in bioethics, Former Chair of the UNESCO International Bioethics Committee, and presently chairs the INSERM Ethics Committee, EBRAINS Science and Society Committee and EMBL Ethics Board.

**Sarah Cunningham-Burley** is Chair of the Nuffield Council on Bioethics (NCOB). The NCOB is the UK's foremost bioethics body and a leading independent policy and research centre. The NCOB works to put ethics at the centre of decisions regarding biomedicine and health, so we all benefit. She is also Professor of Medical and Family Sociology and Co-Head of the Centre for Biomedicine, Self and Society, Usher Institute, School of Population Health Sciences, University of Edinburgh. This is an interdisciplinary social science and humanities research centre, focusing on developments in health-related science and care. Her own research interests include the social and ethical issues in genomics, personalized medicine, AI and data science. She is also active in public engagement and the integration of patient and public perspectives in research and policy.

**Aurélie Halsband** is Head of the Scientific Department of the German Reference Centre for Ethics in the Life Sciences (DRZE) at the University of Bonn. The bioethicist received her doctorate in philosophy from the University of Göttingen in 2016. In the winter term of 2022/2023, she held a visiting professorship in applied ethics at the University of Vienna. Her research addresses ethical implications of emerging biotechnologies and artificial intelligence, as well as the normative foundations of intergenerational justice and sustainability.

**Ludger Honnefelder** is Professor emeritus at the University of Bonn and the founding director of the DRZE. After studying philosophy and Catholic theology, he taught as a professor at the University of Trier and the Freie Universität Berlin. From 1988 to 2001, he held a chair in philosophy at the University of Bonn. From 1993 to 2007 he was Managing Director of the Institute for Science and Ethics (IWE) at the University of Bonn, which he co-founded, and from 1999 to 2007 he was Managing Director of the newly founded German Reference Centre for Ethics in the Life Sciences (DRZE) at the University of Bonn. From 2005 to 2007 he held the Guardini Professorship and from 2009 to 2012 an Otto Warburg Senior Research Professorship at the Humboldt University in Berlin. He is a member of the North Rhine-Westphalian Academy of Sciences, Humanities and the Arts. From 1998 to 2013, he was a member of the Permanent Working Group on Science and Ethics of the All European Academies (ALLEA). From 1993 to 2012, he was a member of the German delegation to the Steering Committee on Bioethics (CDBI) of the Council of Europe and from 2000 to 2005 a member of the German Bundestag's Enquete Commission on Law and Ethics of Modern Medicine. His teaching and research focuses on metaphysics, ethics and applied ethics as well as the history of medieval and early modern philosophy.

**Nancy S. Jecker** is Professor of Bioethics & Humanities at the University of Washington School of Medicine. She holds Adjunct Professorships at the university's Department of Philosophy, School of Law, and Department of Global Health. Nancy Jecker is a Distinguished Visiting Professor at the University of Johannesburg, African Centre for Epistemology and Philosophy of Science and Department of Philosophy and Honorary Visiting Professor at the Chinese University of Hong Kong Centre for Bioethics. Dr. Jecker was elected President of the International Association of Bioethics (2022–2024) and serves on its Board of Directors (2019-present). Her research explores global bioethics, justice, and moral philosophy. It spans a range of topics, most notably justice within and between nations; capabilities and human dignity; sub-Saharan African Philosophy; individual and social aging; ethics of AI; and moral personhood. Dr. Jecker has published over 200 articles and five books.

**Dirk Lanzerath** is Professor of Philosophy at the University of Bonn and Director of the German Reference Centre for Ethics in the Life Sciences (DRZE) in Bonn and has served as its Managing Director since 2002. From 1999 to 2002, he ran the Scientific Department of the DRZE. Since 2018, he has been Honorary Professor for Ethics and Research Ethics at the Hochschule Bonn-Rhein-Sieg University of Applied Sciences. In 2024, he was elected Chairman of the Ethics Committee of the Johannes Rau Research Foundation (JRF) and Deputy Chairman of the Central Ethics Committee of the German Medical Association (ZEKO) for the 2023–25 term of office, where he's been a Member since 2009. He has been a Board Member and Secretary General of the European Network of Research Ethics Committees (EUREC) since 2012. Dirk Lanzerath studied biology, philosophy, catholic theology and educational science and completed his state exam in philosophy and biology in Bonn in 1993. He received his doctorate from the Faculty of Philosophy there in 1999, was thereafter (2003) a Visiting Scholar at the Kennedy Institute of Ethics at Georgetown University, Washington DC, and completed his habilitation in philosophy in Bonn in 2013. His research areas are in applied ethics, particularly in the fields of bioethics and environmental ethics as well as research ethics and techno-ethics.

**Laura Palazzani** is a Professor of Philosophy of Law at LUMSA University in Rome. She earned her doctorate in Bioethics at the Catholic University of the Sacred Heart, Rome, Italy. Her teaching focuses mainly on philosophy of law, bioethics, biolaw and ethics of emerging technologies. She extends her service as an Official Member and Vice Chair for many national and international bioethical committees such as the European Group on Ethics (EGE) and is also part of many research programs. Laura Palazzani has coordinated many national and international research units.

**Vardit Ravitsky** is President and CEO of The Hastings Center for Bioethics, an independent, nonpartisan bioethics research institute that is among the most prestigious bioethics and health policy institutes in the world. She is past Full Professor at the Bioethics Program, School of Public Health, University of Montreal and currently a Senior Lecturer on Global Health and Social Medicine at Harvard Medical School. She is Past President of the International Association of Bioethics and a Fellow of the Canadian Academy of Health Sciences. Her research focuses on the ethics of genomics and reproduction, as well as the use of AI in biomedical research, and is funded by Canada's leading funding agencies and the NIH. She published over 250 articles and commentaries on bioethical issues and an award-winning book. She has given over 300 talks world-wide and over 400 media interviews.

**Dieter Sturma** is Professor Emeritus at the University of Bonn. Until his retirement, he held the chair for Philosophy with a special focus on Ethics in the Life Sciences at the University of Bonn, and served as Director of the Institute for Science and Ethics (IWE), as Director of the German Reference Centre for Ethics in the Life Sciences (DRZE), as Head of the working group "Foundations, Norms and Criteria of Ethical Judgement in the Life Sciences" at the North Rhine-Westphalian Academy of Sciences, Humanities and the Arts, and as Director of the Institute for Ethics in the Neurosciences (INM-8) at the Research Centre Jülich. He has published numerous books and essays on philosophy of mind, ethics, applied ethics, philosophical anthropology, and German and French philosophy of the 18th century.

**Roman Wagner** is a Postdoctoral Research Fellow at the DRZE and part of the ethics project in the interdisciplinary project "FRAIM". He studied philosophy and English and American studies at the Rheinische Friedrich-Wilhelms-Universität Bonn. During his studies, he worked as a Student and Research Assistant and as a Research Associate at the DRZE and the Institute for Science and Ethics (IWE). Following his studies, he completed his doctorate, titled "The Standard of Autonomy". Since 2021, he has been involved in various fields as a Research Assistant at the DRZE and primarily researches the ethics of the use of AI in medicine as well as fundamental metaethical and metaphysical issues.

**Wei Zhu** is a Scholar and Professor of Bioethics at Fudan University in Shanghai. Her research interest covers areas ranging from informed consent, social justice and human rights to genetic ethics. She is a Fellow of The Hastings Center and served as a Fellow in Research Ethics at Harvard School of Public Health from 2002 to 2004. She also acts as Member and Chairperson of several Ethics Committees, such as the Shanghai Ethics Committee for Clinical Research.